# The Original Thai Cookbook

A GD/PERIGEE BOOK

*To my son, Jonathan,*
*who loved Thailand*

Perigee Books
are published by
The Putnam Publishing Group
200 Madison Avenue
New York, New York 10016


Published simultaneously in Canada by
General Publishing Co. Limited, Toronto.

Library of Congress Cataloging in Publication Data

Brennan, Jennifer.
The original Thai cookbook.

Reprint. Originally published: New York : Coward,
McCann & Geoghegan, 1981.
"A GD/Perigee book."
Includes index.
1. Cookery, Thai. I. Title.
[TX724.5.T5B73 1984] 641.59593 83-27068
ISBN 0-399-51033-8 (pbk.)

Illustrations by the author
Design by Lynn Braswell
First Perigee printing, 1984
Printed in the United States of America
5 6 7 8 9

# ACKNOWLEDGMENTS

It is difficult to say when this book actually began, but my gratitude extends back over many years and across many oceans to Thailand and to the first people who introduced me to and enhanced my awareness of that colorful and fascinating country: to Prince Piya Rangsit and his late wife, for my introduction to Thai culture and customs; to Prince Prem Purachatr, my Thai sponsor and culinary guide, with an infectious enthusiasm for good food, with whom I first explored the finest restaurants in Bangkok. My thanks go also to Princess Chumbhot of Nagara Svarga, for assisting my research and for producing for me the most perfect examples of Thai carved ginger. To my mother, my loving thanks. While continuing to live in Thailand after I had left, she spent innumerable hours locating research materials and battling the international postal system to send them to me with the utmost speed.

I am profoundly grateful to Kit Snedaker, for putting my feet in the right paths; to Bob Cornfield, for his faith and enthusiasm; to Frances McCullough, for her warmth and encouragement. Also to my editor, Joyce Engelson, my deep appreciation for the care and concern with which she steered me through the multiple steps toward publication.

My thanks to Dr. A. B. Graf, whose book, *Tropica*, Roehrs Company, Publishers, East Rutherford, New Jersey, has been my bible, and who personally gave me instant answers to difficult questions; to his assistant, Ellen Ritchie, who carefully proofed and updated the Glossary; to Dr. W. P. Bitters of the Citrus Research Center and Agricultural Experimental Station, University of California, Riverside, for his help and interest and for the rare tropical citrus fruit he sent. My thanks also to Donald W. Wilkie, Director of the Scripps Aquarium-Museum of the Scripps Institution of Oceanography, for his definitive pronouncements on the varieties of fish to be found in tropical waters, and to Dr. Stanley Rosen of the School of International Relations, University of Southern California in Los Angeles, for his generous help with my historical research.

Here in Los Angeles, also, I would particularly like to thank Piya Sawatdee for cheerfully answering my million questions at any time during his busy day; Chomsri Lewinter and Peter Boonyapitak, for carefully checking the Thai phonetic spelling, and Opaso, for his own creative cooking and insistence on the individuality of interpretation of Thai dishes.

My warmest and deepest appreciation to my devoted students, who cooked and cooked and cooked, and whose faith and eagerness never wavered.

Finally, a loving tribute to those who have chosen to remain anonymous but who have given so freely and generously of their time, wisdom and support.

# PREFACE

Thai or Siamese cuisine was largely unknown outside Thailand until the middle of this century. In the 1950's and 1960's, the world political spotlight fell on Indochina specifically and, then, later broadened to include all of Southeast Asia, as first France and, then, America became embroiled in the Vietnamese conflict.

At the beginning of the 1960's when I first came to Thailand, Bangkok was a small, charming city, criss-crossed with canals and tree-lined roads. The pace of life was leisurely, the motorized traffic sparse and the foreign community evenly divided in its mixture of nationalities. By 1965, the American presence had expanded enormously. Bangkok became a designated venue for rest and recreation—the lusty "R & R" for primarily American military—and American dependents moved to the city to be near their husbands. Trade with the United States considerably expanded, and American companies opened offices requiring wholesale personnel transfers.

Because of this influx, construction boomed and the peace of the days was rent with the noise of pile drivers and pneumatic drills as new hotels, office buildings, department stores and apartment houses mushroomed. The low city skyline changed rapidly. In 1963, the Rama Hotel, on Silom Road in the Western section of Bangkok, alone boasted the dizzy height of ten stories. I could stand on the terrace of the penthouse and look, without visual interruption, west across to the Chao Phya River, where the only other tall building was the modest tower of the renowned Oriental Hotel. In the other direction, to the north, I could look over four miles of low wooden roofed houses to the hill, topped by the temple of the Golden Mount. Today the city bears a strong resemblance to Los Angeles in size and skyline, although Bangkok has no freeways.

As tours of duty or company overseas postings ended, Americans returned home with fond memories of the friendly Thai, their picturesque customs and fascinating food. Thailand, in particular Bangkok, became a major tourist destination.

The Thai themselves ventured to America to experience the good life and opportunity they had heard so much about, settling in large communities in major cities. They quickly adapted to all things American except our food. The expatriate Thai soon misses the spiciness and unique blend of flavors of his own cuisine. Thai restaurants opened all over America in increasing numbers, and adventuresome Americans soon began to frequent them, finding a cuisine that appeals to *all* the senses: elaborate preparation and decoration of each dish; unusual aromas, fragrant jasmine to pungent shrimp paste; a variety of textures and combinations of finger foods; percussive musical sounds of fresh, juicy vegetables first contacting hot oil in a wok; and the rhythmic beat of a cleaver rapidly chopping on a board, counterpointed by the cadence of the "thunk, thunk" of a mortar hammering in a pestle—all climaxed by the incomparable, savory taste delight that is Thai. Obviously, the popularity of this culinary experience soon spread among Westerners.

Not too many years ago, it was difficult to reproduce Thai dishes in a Western kitchen because many esoteric ingredients were unavailable. Now, Oriental and Thai markets have opened in nearly every town, stocking a dazzling and, sometimes, baffling array of foodstuffs: native herbs and spices, dried and fresh; unusual species of fish (mostly dried); unlabeled cuts of meat; vegetables you might consider weeding from your garden; assortments of strange canned foods and sauces—all with exotic names, sometimes foreign language labels—all purveyed by shopkeepers unfamiliar with English.

If you considered overcoming these obstacles, there remained a singular barrier—a paucity of cookbooks for Thai. Usually Thai cooking was relegated to sparse references in Asian cookbooks, if at all. For the Thai, like many other races, pass their recipes verbally down through generations, seldom committing their accumulated knowledge to paper. Even when pressed for a particular recipe, the Thai have some considerable difficulty translating their knowledge to English; language, procedures and ingredients.

After nine exhilarating years in Thailand and because of an abiding love affair with Thai food, I came to America with a clutch of treasured Thai recipes—recipes developed over many hours in Thai markets and my Bangkok kitchen, abetted by a changing parade of patient Thai household cooks, while I discovered and explored the intricacies of this fascinating cuisine.

This book is an expansion and amplification of those recipes with the help, input and loyal support of my students, who insisted we cook Thai at every opportunity. It represents countless hours of rigorous testing and research during, and for, my cooking classes conducted over the past three years since my return from Bangkok. I have attempted to bridge the gap that occurs when one tries to reproduce the cuisine of a distant, unfamiliar country in a Western kitchen. Whenever possible, I have tried to share my knowledge of the customs and culture of Thailand so, armed with this background, you will be able to travel

*This Sukhothai is good.*
*In the water, there is fish;*
*in the fields, there is rice.*
*The King takes no advantage*
*of the people. Whoever wants*
*to trade, trades. The faces of*
*the people shine bright with*
*happiness.*

INSCRIPTION ON A STONE TABLET IN SUKHOTHAI, THE ANCIENT KINGDOM OF SIAM IN THE TWELFTH AND THIRTEENTH CENTURIES.

# Contents

# The Original Thai Cookbook

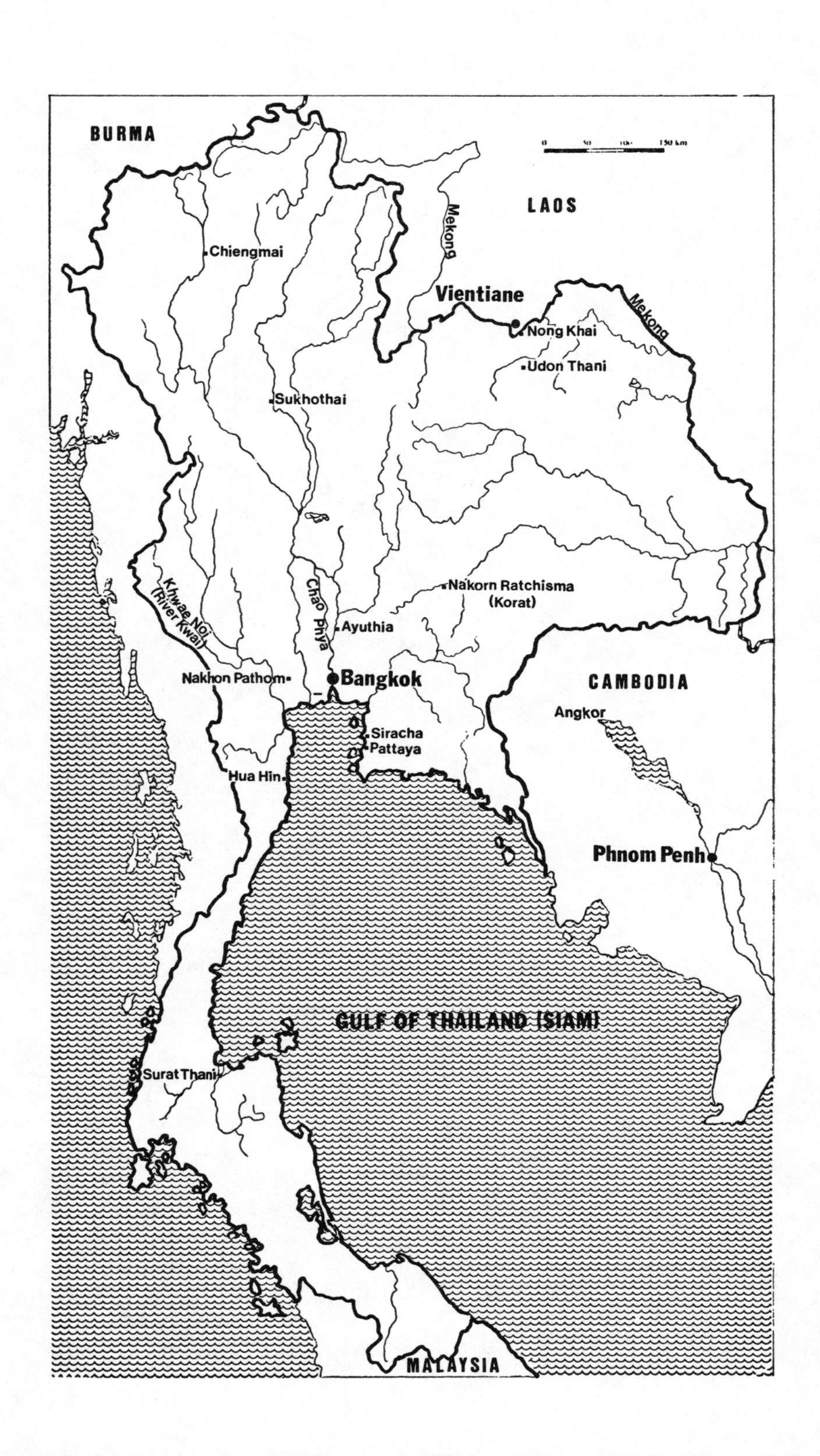
BURMA
LAOS
Mekong
Chiengmai
Vientiane
Mekong
Nong Khai
Udon Thani
Sukhothai
Nakorn Ratchisma
(Korat)
Chao Phya
Khwae Noi
(River Kwai)
Ayuthia
Nakhon Pathom
Bangkok
CAMBODIA
Angkor
Siracha
Pattaya
Hua Hin
Phnom Penh
GULF OF THAILAND (SIAM)
Surat Thani
MALAYSIA

# Introduction

## DINING IN THAILAND

It is dusk in Bangkok and you are going out to dinner. The chauffeured Mercedes 280 sweeps you from your luxury hotel through streets lined with large, spreading trees and picturesque tile-roofed wooden shops and houses. The light of the sweltering day is fading and the street lamps are already glowing. Private cars, predominantly Japanese imports, overflow the streets in a chaotic mass of traffic, studded here and there by noisy buses with large Thai characters painted on their sides and little, three-wheeled motorized pedicabs called *samlors*. Jostling crowds of young men bent on an evening's pleasure and women in colorful blouses and vivid *Pasins* thread their way past street pedlars setting up their bicycle-wheeled carts filled with fruits and dried fish. Street urchins, hawking fragrant garlands of jasmine, dart into the street of adults and tug at sleeves and hems, stridently demanding a few *baht* for their merchandise: "Hey, you, YOU! Gimme fi baht!"

Delicious smells of spiced, barbecued chicken and pungent curries assail your nostrils and sharpen your appetite as your car passes little street-front restaurants already packed with diners seated on wooden chairs at Formica topped tables, every square inch of which is covered with bowls of food.

Your limousine enters a quieter, more elegant area: the streets are wider, more tranquil, lined with feathery Flame-of-the-Forest trees ablaze with orange flowers, through which can be seen well-trimmed hedges and the wrought-iron gates of large houses and foreign embassies. On your left, gilded spires and the steep orange and green roof of a Thai temple pierce the sky—the body of the temple is veiled behind a high, crenellated and stuccoed wall.

The crunch of tires on gravel announces that you have arrived at your destination as your car winds round a drive lined with cannas and hibiscus. You pull up before a traditional teakwood Thai house, heavily decorated with intricate carving. You are greeted by an exquisite, delicately boned Thai woman, youthful but of indeterminate age. The blossoms in her hair catch the lamplight as she bows her head to her fingertips, placed together in the formal Thai greeting, *wai*. She walks before you up the ornate exterior wood staircase, her slippered feet slapping softly on the steps underneath her long, gold-brocaded dress.

Following the example of your hostess, you leave your shoes at the door. Barefoot, you enter a paneled foyer with a formal arrangement of mother-of-pearl-decorated ebony chairs and tables. Seated in these ornate chairs, you are aware of a soft voice at your elbow as another slender girl in traditional Thai dress offers drinks and places a bronze tray filled with an assortment of tiny *hors d'oeuvres* before you. These appetizers or *kong Tan Lin* are a stimulating kaleidoscope of colors and skillfully carved shapes. There is a scent of jasmine and magnolia in the air and, from somewhere, comes the soft atonal melody of Thai music—flute accompanied by finger cymbals.

Finishing your drink, you rise at the behest of your hostess and are escorted into a steeply beamed, large room; softly lighted with bronze fixtures that are decoratively perforated. Low carved tables graced with vivid flower arrangements direct your attention to the center of the room; each table bordered with jewel-colored Thai silk floor cushions and firm, peaked, triangular reclining support pillows. You try to sit down as gracefully as your tall, angular Western frame will allow, and finger bowls with floating jasmine petals and cologne-iced towels are presented for your refreshment before the meal commences.

A parade of unfamiliar and exotic dishes is brought to your table and arranged in serried ranks before you. Lidded bowls of blue and white porcelain open to disclose mounds of snowy-white, steamed rice. A clear, sour and spicy soup, *Dom Yam Gung*, is ornamented with pink shrimp floating amid the green of lemon grass and coriander leaves. Sizzling sticks of *Satay* are flanked by bowls of aromatic curries, such as Green Curry of Duck. A delicate *Gai Sawan*, Heavenly Chicken, is counterbalanced by the robust flavor of *Gaeng Mussaman* or Thai Muslim Curry. The Siamese Fried Chicken, *Gai Tord*, is accompanied by a pungent and spicy *Nam Prik* dipping sauce. A mound of raw, minced beef spiced with lemon grass and chillies is physically and gastronomically supported by mint leaves and lime slices. A lordly, whole, cooked snapper appears, resplendent in a glistening sauce of ginger and garlic ornamented with flowers cut from chillies and tomatoes, *Pla Brio Wan*. With scarcely a pause, side dishes of fat omelets stuffed with pork and stir-fried leafy greens join in the seemingly endless procession. Now appears the Thai masterpiece of *Mee Krob*, a golden mount of crisp-fried noodles, tumbled with tiny nuggets of chicken and shrimp, sauced with a sweet/sour/salt dressing and crowned with red chilli flowers and tassels of green onion. Finally, to clear the palate, a tray of magnificent fruit arrives, carefully carved and lavishly presented. With this, a dish of candied bananas, speckled with sesame seeds and a bowl of chilled lichees in custard. The sensuous experience of this delectable panorama has you totally absorbed. You have just experienced your first Thai meal!

## EMIGRATION, CONFRONTATION AND ACCOMMODATION

After the first few mouthfuls of a Thai meal, whether it be a splendid feast enjoyed in a formal setting, as the previous idealized banquet, or a simple assortment of dishes at the house of a friend, it becomes evident that this is a unique cuisine and not, merely, a regional adaptation of Chinese food. To understand how this cuisine evolved, one must first know something of the Thai people and their history.

One of their main characteristics is the ability to absorb foreign influences and translate them into something uniquely Thai. As a race, their origins are far from their present homeland. Their religion is an adaptation of Indian Buddhism. Their language is a synthesis of several tongues. Their culture is an amalgam of those of their neighbors—yet they possess an ethnic cohesiveness lacking in other Southeast Asian countries. They are an independent people with a deep, emotional bond to their country. In order to survive, or perhaps because of their continuing survival, they have the capacity to bend with prevailing winds, whether political, martial, religious or cultural, and spring back to original positions. The exercise of this trait has ensured their historic continuity with independence and sovereignty. In the winds of colonial wars, the European oak could crack while the Thai bamboo would bend but, invariably, whip back to its firmly rooted, original posture.

At the time of the Han Dynasty in China and just after the birth of Christ, T'ai tribes occupied a vast area of steep mountain valley territories along the South China border in Yunnan. They settled between the headwaters of the Red River, the upper Mekong River and the Yangtze.

This tribal area lay astride the important overland trade route between China and India and, before long, the tribal chiefs flexed their muscles and closed the ancient route, denying China, during the Tang Dynasty, access to the West.

The most important of six, petty tribal states in the region was Nan Chao which lay in the Tali Lake plain, east of the Mekong Gorge and about two hundred miles west of present-day Kunming. The chiefs of Nan Chao, however, were not T'ai but Lolo.

About the time of the fall of the Roman Empire, the leaders of Nan Chao began to extend control over neighboring states. Eventually China decided to subdue this warlike and expansionistic State and bring it under Chinese dominion, ensuring the protection of the western trade route. China attacked, but Nan Chao repelled three successive invasions. Finally Nan Chao and China united against the threat of Tibetan aggression from the west. The T'ai appetite for conquest was not sated, however, and in the next one hundred years, they conquered Halingyi, the capital of the North Burma state of Pyu. The overextended Nan Chao armies then withdrew, taking with them Pyu soldiers as vassals or slave troops. These troops accompanied them when they attacked and captured Hanoi in A.D. 863.

The close, although sometimes hostile, association of the T'ai with the Chinese resulted in similarities of dress, customs and craftsmanship. The T'ai shared common geographical origins with the peoples south of the middle Yangtze and their speech was a dialect of Southern Chinese. The sons of the chieftans of Nan Chao were sent to Chinese cities to be educated. However, probably because of its exposure to Indian traders and monks traveling the trade route and to a certain natural antipathy to the civilization of a dominant country bent on subjugation, Nan Chao repudiated the Chinese written character system, adopting instead the Sanskrit and Pali scripts.

No one knows the exact reason why the T'ai peoples started to emigrate south. It may have been the desire for freedom from the Chinese or, merely, a natural wish to follow the many rivers south. Their migration followed previous migrations of other races who had already settled and populated Southeast Asia. The facts are that, from as far back as the first century A.D., the T'ai began heading south and west settling in parts of present-day Burma, Laos, Assam, Vietnam and, of course, Thailand.

As the Mongols, the fierce warriors from the north, swept into China and conquered one province after another, the exodus of the T'ai accelerated from a trickle to a flood. In the middle of the thirteenth century, Nan Chao fell to the Mongols under the legendary Kublai Khan. The T'ai who remained in Southern China still retain their own cultural and ethnic identity to this day.

When the T'ai entered the area that is now Thailand, it was not a separate country but, rather, a large region, sparsely inhabited by small settlements of tribespeople. The two main and overlapping spheres of influence were the Mon (Burmese) and the Khmer (Cambodians). In the sixth and seventh centuries, the former had established a loose federation of small states including Dvaravati, centered in Lavo (now Lopburi), just north of present-day Bangkok and Haripunjaya around Lamphun in the north. The latter, Khmer, had pushed their authority west to the banks of the lower Menam Chao Phya River and north to the borders of Lao country.

Both the Mon and Khmer bore the imprint of India in religion, government, arts and language. One thousand years earlier, King Ashoka of India sent Buddhist missionary monks to Southeast Asia and, through the centuries, Indian traders and wealthy merchants settled in the seaports, bringing their priests and teachers with them. Buddhism and Hinduism existed side-by-side in harmony.

The star of the Mon began to dim. By the eleventh century, the Khmer pushed them out of the fertile Menam Chao Phya Basin in what is now central Thailand. The Khmer kingdom reached the zenith of its power. It stretched over present-day Cambodia, the South of Laos and Thailand. Centered in the capital cities of Angkor, it was a kingdom of fabled splendor. The plunder of war and the labor of captives was used to build the miles of ornate terraces and temples in the city. The ruins of the temple of Angkor Wat still remain one of the wonders of the world.

The T'ai tribes, meanwhile, had settled in the north of present-day Thailand and, augmented by the continuing flood of immigrants from Nan Chao, were spreading out into small settlements and, then, into principalities.

Through superior organizational ability and military prowess, the T'ai started to emerge politically and supplant the Khmer. After a long period of skirmishes and small battles, the Khmer lost control over the Thailand peninsula. In 1238, the independent Kingdom of Sukhothai Syam was established. The name Sukhothai means "Dawn of Happiness" and, indeed, it was the dawning of an independent T'(h)ai nation. The people that then formed this nation had absorbed many elements of the cultures of the races around them and, in fact, this "dawning" did not represent a dramatic ethnic change in the character of the area. There was no massive displacement of indigenous population but rather a seizure of power by a T'ai governing class.

Originally, they had spoken a dialect of Chinese; now they incorporated much of the Hindu dialects from the Mon and Khmer. They adopted the Mon form of Buddhism with some of the Burman animistic beliefs, and borrowed from both the Mon and Khmer alphabets. The T'ai admired the militaristic organization of the Mongols and modeled their own forces similarly. They also adopted the Mongol, three-fold division of society. Sukhothai was populated by warrior freemen who were T'ai, civilian commoners and serfs or slaves who were drawn from conquered races. Gradually the land they dominated became known as Siam and the people themselves Siamese.

Some years after the founding of Sukhothai, another kingdom state was established in Chiengmai. The center of the national culture and consciousness remained, however, Sukhothai. The Sukhothai people were described as pleasure loving, proud of themselves and their freedom—and very independent. Their kingdom represented the first flowering of their creative and artistic achievement. Their rulers boasted of the difference between Sukhothai social order and that of their Khmer predecessors and adversaries. Emphasis was placed on their human and humane king as opposed to the god-king concept of the Khmer and the cruel punishments often meted out to misdemeanor offenders. The first Sukhothai king, Phra Ruang, while a warrior and not considered divine, was in fact endowed with supernatural powers and the subject of many legends. It is said that, at his command, a fish skeleton thrown into the water came to life and swam away. In Thailand, today, a popular saying is "he has Pra Ruang's tongue," meaning that the person can affect physical miracles with mere words.

By all accounts and from examination of the ruins that remain, Sukhothai was a beautiful city. Set against a backdrop of a mountain range to the west, it was supplied with water by two canals. The city layout was spacious with broad avenues shaded by rain trees. Spired temples, set like jewels in the middle of ornamental lakes, were lined with rows of gracefully carved stone Buddha images. The fortifications of the city were quite impressive. Three rings of earth ramparts circled the city with a moat between each ring. The rectangular plan included gateways at the cardinal points with a small fort guarding each.

The third King, Ram Khamhaeng, is reputed to have visited Peking to enlist Mongol support for the expansion of his kingdom. He had a stone stele carved with an account of the kingdom, its life and people. The inscription is the first written record of the Thai people. Following is an excerpt of the inscription; a charming description of the celebration of the Kathin Festival when new robes are presented to the monks:

"On their return to the city, they line up from Aranyik [a forest monastery] yonder to the border of the open ground, joining together in striking up the sound of musical instruments and lutes, carolling and singing. Whoever wants to play, plays.

Whoever wants to laugh, laughs. Whoever wants to sing, sings. This Muang Sukhothai has four main gateways. People would flock in to see the King light the candles and play with fireworks. This Muang Sukhothai is noisy as if it would burst."

The kingdom lasted for two hundred years. In 1350, an ambitious prince, Ramatibodi, a Dvaravati Mon leader, split away and founded the kingdom of Ayuthia, further to the south. Ayuthia grew enormously powerful and finally conquered the Khmer capital, Angkor. The capital was sacked and the entire court carried back to Siam, complete with dancing girls, poets, cooks, actors and musicians. The Siamese were now riding high on a wave of military power and conquest. They pushed back the borders of the kingdom to include much of present-day Laos and Cambodia.

The unfortunate minority tribes of the area again saw the tug-of-war pass through their villages. Men were impressed to fight and to build new temples and palaces for the victors. Villagers were taxed to provide funds for the military machine. From the north, in what is now Laos, rose a saying: "When the elephants make war, the grass is trampled."

By mid-fifteenth century, the Siamese had complete control over the fertile Menam Chao Phya River basin and it became the greatest rice-producing area in the world. Their capital, Ayuthia, became the finest city that skill, imagination and money could provide. Now the wealthiest city in Southeast Asia, it lay mainly on an island and on the banks of the Menam Chao Phya River in the middle of a large, fertile plain. It was bounded by stone walls and contained magnificent temples and elaborate, gilded palaces. The Siamese adopted the Brahmin traditions of conquered Angkor and the king became a god-king. A formal hierarchy of nobles and high officials was established. By the early 1500's, just at the time Henry VIII became King of England, Ayuthia was a vast city of one million inhabitants and the center of trade between India and China. For traders, the journey around the Strait of Malacca, between Malaysia and Indonesia, was long and dangerous—attacks by Malay pirates were frequent and ferocious. Merchants from India landed at Mergui on the West coast of Siam and journeyed overland to Ayuthia where they were met by Chinese traders who sailed to the south-eastern coastal ports and up the rivers. Chinese and Japanese silks, ceramics, copper and teas all were brought to the City to be traded for pepper, rare woods and animal skins.

Vasco da Gama, the Portuguese navigator, having recently completed his epic voyage around the world, opened the way to Southeast Asia for the Europeans, and the Portuguese arrived in Siam in 1511, followed by the Dutch, English, Danes and French in rapid succession.

Reports of life in Ayuthia exist from the writings of Europeans. The Abbé de Choisy wrote of a visit to the capital in a journal published in 1687:

"We went for a walk outside the town. I stood frequently in admiration of the strong, great city, seated upon an island round which flowed a river three times the size of the Seine. There rode ships from France, England, Holland, China and Japan while innumerable boats and gilded barges rowed by sixty men plied to and fro. No less extraordinary were the camps or villages outside the walls inhabited by the different nations who come trading there, with all the wooden houses standing on posts over the water; the bulls, cows and pigs are on dry land. The streets, stretching out of sight, are alleys of clear running water. Under the great green trees and in the little houses crowd the people. Beyond these camps of the nations are the wide rice fields. The horizon is tall trees, above which are visible the sparkling towers and pyramids of the pagodas."

Unfortunately, the Europeans became rapacious in their trading demands and increasingly truculent with their treaty requirements; greedy in their ambitions toward the new country. The Siamese played them off, one against the other. But after an episode in the late 1600's where a Greek adventurer named Phaulkon rose to be Foreign Minister and enlisted the support of the French, overtly and legitimately but aided, covertly, by a secret Franco-Siamese treaty, to stem the English and Dutch aggrandizement (Phaulkon's scheme backfired, almost leading to the

French overthrow of Siam), the Siamese became xenophobic, expelling all Westerners and sealing themselves off for one hundred and fifty years—incidentally, beheading Phaulkon.

The Siamese were not so fortunate in the outcome of their ongoing wars with the Burmese. The current quarrel started three hundred years previously when the King of Burma had asked the King of Siam to give him a sacred white elephant. He probably felt it was a reasonable request as the Siamese king owned seven large, white, sacred pachyderms. The Siamese king, however, refused, and hostilities escalated. In fact, after a successful campaign in the mid-sixteenth century, the Burmese overran most of Siam and it became a Burmese suzerainty. Ayuthia itself was ruled by Burmese for fifteen years. In 1585, King Naresuan restored the kingdom to Thai sovereignty after an arduous military struggle. However, in 1765, ten years before the start of the American Revolution, the Burmese began another siege of Ayuthia that lasted two years. The city fell and the Burmese pillaged and laid waste to the entire area. Golden Ayuthia was sacked and an entire civilization—documents, law books, scripture, art and literature—went up in flames. Of the city's million inhabitants, only about ten thousand remained. The king took refuge in a temple but was found and killed. One general escaped, Taksin. It is said that he left the city with five hundred followers in a fit of pique because the king would not let him fire on the invading Burmese without prior permission.

Taksin fled south about forty miles to the village of Dhonburi, on the banks of the Menam Chao Phya River (now, merely referred to as the Chao Phya), just opposite from Bangkok, at the yawn of the River to the Gulf of Siam (Thailand). Here he rallied the Siamese.

The Burmese, having destroyed Ayuthia, had no intention of remaining in Siam. The small occupational forces they left behind were easily defeated and Taksin proclaimed himself King, with Dhonburi his capital.

His reign only lasted for fifteen years because he became

paranoid with delusions of grandeur and, gradually, insane. For instance, he thought himself to be a reincarnation of Buddha and believed he could fly. A bloodless revolt by his former fellow officers led to another general, Chakri, being offered the Throne. He became King Rama I, the inception of the present royal dynasty. He founded his capital on the opposite bank of the river and called it Krung Thep or Bangkok. This signals the birth of the present capital city and the beginning of the "Bangkok Period" on the site of a fort and a small village of Chinese merchants.

The city was built as a replica of Ayuthia, even incorporating some of the original stones from the former, ruined capital. Because Ayuthia had stood on an island, surrounded on the four sides of a rectangle by rivers, Rama I had canals (*klongs*) cut around his city to join the Chao Phya and make it, also, an island. He built the elaborate Grand Palace complex, covering one square mile. Rama I also initiated the Royal Barge Procession, commissioning elaborate, gilded boats, which can still be seen today.

During and just after the incline from the eighteenth to the nineteenth centuries on our Gregorian Calendar, the City and Nation of Bangkok flourished. Again, the Europeans cast covetous eyes at Siam and many attempts were made to open missions and establish footholds in the country. From a British envoy, John Crawfurd, we get a vivid description of Bangkok during the reign of Rama II.

"Numerous temples of Buddha with tall spires attached to them, frequently glittering with gilding, were conspicuous among the mean huts and hovels of the natives, throughout which were interspersed a profusion of palms, ordinary fruit and the sacred fig. . . . The face of the river presented a busy scene, from the number of boats and canoes of every size and description that were passing to and fro. The number of these struck us as very great at the time, for we were not aware that there are no or few roads in Bangkok and that the river and canals form the common highways, not only for goods but for passengers of every description."

During this time, the early Bangkok Period, the kings

were mostly engaged in restoration, both of the country and of its laws; most of which had been destroyed in the rape of Ayuthia. In 1826, the Siamese defeated Burma and ended the rivalry between the two countries.

Trade with China began to grow rapidly. Chinese entrepreneurs in Bangkok started a sugar industry, which soon became the most important commodity in commerce between China and Siam. Sugar was responsible for a massive influx of Chinese who settled to work in the new trade. By the middle of the nineteenth century, one-half of Bangkok's estimated population of four hundred thousand was Chinese. The Muslim population in Siam had also increased. In the Sukhothai Period, trade with Arab and Indian merchants began and increased through Ayuthian times. Arab traders settled in Siam and, by the middle of the eighteenth century, there were Muslim enclaves in and around Bangkok. Later, in a slow but continuing procession, further groups of Muslims arrived in Bangkok from the South where they, historically, comprise the overwhelming spiritual majority.

Rama III fought several campaigns against the Vietnamese, who were extending their power into Cambodia. The hostilities ended in Cambodia becoming a tributary state to both Thailand and Vietnam—a state of affairs which continued until the French domination of Indochina.

The fourth Rama, King Mongkut, famous to the West through his amusing but inaccurate portrait (caricature) in "The King and I," brought Siam safely through threats of Western colonization and established strong ties of trade and culture with the rest of the world. He was forced to grant trade treaties with the West as a means of balancing the growing British presence in Burma and Malaysia and the opening of China to the Western powers. In 1855, treaties were established with England; the next year with the United States under President Franklin Pierce, and also in 1856, with France. King Mongkut realized that the West had the power to colonize his country and yielded to Western pressure, thus opening the country up to full trade and modernization. He encouraged Christian missionaries to introduce Western medicine and education to his people. The chief result of the increased trade was that rice from the Menam Delta could now be exported; a very favorable arrangement for all concerned. Demand for it increased and Mongkut ordered that vast, flat Delta be irrigated for increased rice cultivation. The burgeoning rice trade brought a new wealth to the upper classes, and European imports began to appear in the central shops and marketplaces.

Trade concessions were followed by territorial capitulation and, in 1867, Siam relinquished its Cambodian territories to the French.

King Chulalongkorn, the fifteen-year-old son of Mongkut, succeeded his father as Rama V. Aided by far-sighted advisers, he continued the modernization of Siam. The administration of the country was centralized; railway and telegraph systems installed. He also abolished the feudalistic remnants of slavery and conscript labor about a decade after Lincoln's Emancipation Proclamation.

Siam was fortunate enough to continue into the twentieth century with wise rulers guiding its affairs. In 1917, Rama VI took the country into World War I on the side of the Allies and, in 1918, sent a small, volunteer force to France.

Until 1932, the country was under the reign of an absolute monarchy but, after a revolt of the new, emerging middle class, became a constitutional monarchy. In 1939, the country changed its name from Siam to Thailand, a change formalized in 1949.

In 1942, under the threat of Japanese occupation and domination, Thailand once again exercised its "bamboo diplomacy" and declared war on the United States—a declaration not recognized by the Allies partially because of the circumstances (Japanese invasion) under which it was made but, mainly, because the formal, declaratory document was deliberately misplaced by the Thai ambassador in Washington and, therefore, reply impossible.

After World War II, Thailand opted to join the Western

sphere of influence with eager participation from the United States and Great Britain.

The present King, Bhumibol Aduldej, Rama IX, ascended to the Throne in 1946.

## COOK'S TOUR

The visitor to Thailand, arriving by air, immediately realizes that the wealth of the country is gathered in the vast rice bowl of the Central Plain. As your plane leaves the realm of clouds and descends toward Bangkok, the fertile earth draws closer beneath your windows. You fly over an endless checkerboard of rice paddies, sharply outlined by low dikes. The sunlight moves in dazzling flashes over the flooded paddies, speckled with the green fuzz of the young rice. An arrow-straight canal becomes a boundary; its surface dotted with minuscule boats and its banks lined with small puffs of green trees and toy-sized, wooden houses. A tiny temple complex interrupts the pattern of rice fields and canals.

There is no warning that you are approaching the airport, merely that the landscape is growing larger and closer. Suddenly the wheels of your plane are seeking contact with the earth. You are startled to see the perfectly-manicured greens of a golf course roll by at the edge of the runway. You have landed at Don Muang Airport and are about to be driven into Bangkok.

Central Thailand, together with the higher plateaus of the Northeast, is one of three, main geographical regions into which the country is divided. The Thai call the central region Issan. Northern Thailand, Lana Thai, is mostly highlands and mountain ranges. These mountains give birth to the many rivers which flow through the central plain on their way to the Gulf of Thailand (Siam). To the west, the mountain ranges, an eastward extension of the Himalayas, form the boundary with Burma and then run like a jagged spine southward. This backbone of mountains continues along the elongated neck of land which divides the Andaman Sea from the Gulf of Thailand and joins Thailand to Malaysia. This southern and western region is known as Pak Thai.

Thailand has a monsoon climate influenced by the variable winds which blow in opposing directions according to the time of year. This climate divides into three seasons: a relatively cool season from December to February when the humidity and temperature stay at reasonable levels and there is no rain; a hot season from February to May when the heat is enervating to both visitor and native alike and the pace of life moves sluggishly; the rainy season, May to October, heralded by thunderstorms. The tropical rains start with great pattering drops which hiss when they hit the parched earth. Then the heavens open and the monsoon rain pours down in sheets. The rivers overflow, the streets become rivers and everything and everybody is soaked. These rains change into a steady pattern of daily downpours. The clouds gather, empty their watery load and are then dispelled by the sun, which turns the atmosphere into a gigantic steambath.

This abundant rainfall is responsible for the lush vegetation and favorable agronomy of the alluvial plains, the rampant jungles of the south and the great, deciduous rain forests, which cover the mountains.

The wide rice bowl of the central plains was once forested by the trees which covered three-quarters of the country. As civilization expanded, the area was gradually cleared—forests were cut down, irrigation canals dug. During the rainy season, the flooding waters cover the land with rich, fecund mud. The planting and harvesting of the precious rice forms the main rhythm of Thai country life.

From the plains, the ground rises in plateaus. The vegetation is sparse because abundant rainfall leaches the nutrients from the topsoil. Agriculture is more varied and livestock is raised. In the great mountain forests beyond these high plains, teak and other valuable woods are felled and dragged from these forests by work elephants; the logs then float down river to the sawmills. The nomadic hill tribes move through the forests, clearing small patches of land for farming, then move on when the topsoil is exhausted.

In the south, the jungles fight to take over the narrow strips of rice fields. Coconut palms, the source of another thriving industry, line beaches of white sand and the warm, placid waters of the Gulf of Thailand teem with all kinds of fish. Further south, where the Kra Isthmus joins Thailand and Malaysia—where the rocky, west-facing coast on the Andaman Sea and Strait of Malacca is no longer Burmese but Thai—seafood is paramount and large, luscious lobsters are hauled from the water.

This is the hospitable country that has given birth to such a wide range of food—floral and faunal. In the remote forests of the north, fierce wild buffalo crash through the undergrowth; cousins to the domestic beasts of burden which pull the ploughs and occasionally provide meat for the table. Small, timid mouse deer and their larger cousins furnish treats of venison for the hill tribes. The "whirr" of pheasant wings is heard through the forests. Here, too, peacocks used to strut and flourish until the culinary and ornamental demands of the kings' palaces made them almost extinct.

When the T'ai tribes came south to this fertile country, they brought many of their eating habits and customary dishes with them. They were already rice eaters, probably of the short grain, glutinous variety. Their descendants today in Laos and northeastern Thailand still prefer the same rice. Their food is dry, eaten with the fingers, and the sticky rice is pressed into balls and used to scoop up the food.

One of their dishes, eaten in Nan Chao, was a mixture of raw, chopped beef, mixed with ground rice, herbs and spices. Called *Laap*, it exists in northeast Thailand today in the same form. Marco Polo, journeying through Yunnan in the thirteenth century, after it had been conquered by the Mongols, observed that the people ate their meat raw:

"The poorer sort go to the shambles and take the raw liver as soon as it is drawn from the beasts; then they chop it up small, put it in garlic sauce and eat it there and then. And then they do likewise with every other kind of flesh. The gentry also eat their meat raw."

Our "Steak Tartare" may well have originated with those distant ancestors of the modern Thai, especially since Marco Polo was frequently apt to refer to the Mongols as Tartars.

The cultural intermingling of the T'ai and Chinese led to the adoption by the T'ai of many Chinese culinary practices. This Chinese influence was further strengthened in later centuries by the immigration of more Chinese down into Thailand.

The *Lun Yu*, an ancient collection of Confucius's precepts, recounts how a man should prepare himself in his diet before making sacrifice to the spirits:

"There is no objection to his rice being of the highest quality, nor to his meat being finely minced. Rice affected by the weather or turned he must not eat, nor fish that is not sound, nor meat that is high. . . . He must not eat what has been crookedly cut nor any dish that lacks its proper seasoning."

Anyone observing the care with which the present-day Thai market and prepare their food can see that they follow this sound, culinary common sense.

A third century B.C. Chinese poem, called *The Summons of the Soul*, refers to the concept of five flavors—bitter, salt, sour, hot, sweet—a balance established early in Chinese cuisine that certainly describes Thai food today. Part of the poem reads:

"Bitter, salt, sour, hot and sweet: there are dishes of all flavors.
Ribs of fatted ox cooked tender and succulent:
Sour and bitter blended in the soup of Wu;"

I do not know where Wu was but many Thai soups are either sour and bitter or sour and hot as seen in the premier Thai shrimp soup, *Dom Yam Gung*. Indeed, this rule of five flavors applies to the skillful balancing involved in preparing a Thai menu.

Stir-fry cooking is the dominant method that has shaped Thai cuisine. The durable wok, too, has historically survived intact owing to, in no small part, its amazing versatility and functionality.

Many dishes, now changed and incorporated in Thai cuisine, obviously have their origins in China. Fish, for instance, is a very central item in both Chinese and Thai diets. The Thai dish of whole fish sauced with soy and ginger, *Pla Brio Wan,* is almost identical to the Chinese *Ho Nan Jum Choa Yue,* but with its own subtle nuances. The delicious dessert of bananas dipped in caramel and sprinkled with sesame seeds seems to be an adaptation of the northern Chinese and Mongolian dish which uses apples as the fruit.

Other Thai dishes with almost certain Chinese origins include: pork-stuffed omelets, which the Thai love to eat for a light lunch; side dishes of various greens sautéed with garlic mixed with occasional bits of chicken or shrimp and, of course, their chef d'oeuvre, *Mee Krob,* the dish of crisp-fried rice noodles with various meats, seafood and bean sprouts—surely a first cousin to the Chinese chicken salad with crispy noodles.

The Thai fondness for duck almost certainly has Chinese roots and the place that noodles occupy in their diet is identical to Chinese noodle-eating habits. In sixteenth-century China, noodles were considered coarse and vulgar food and were not included in *haute cuisine.* In Thailand today, noodles are eaten for lunch and as snacks or "fast food," although *Mee Krob* is fast becoming elevated into the more refined culinary circles.

In turn, the ancient T'ai certainly left their culinary imprint on the regions they influenced. The present-day cuisines of both Szechwan and Yunnan tend to be hot and spicy; probably, at least, the godfather of today's Thai food.

The Indian influence on Thai food is more subtle and difficult to trace. Some dishes, such as *Gaeng Mussaman,* have come directly from the cuisine of Muslim immigrants and the ubiquitous *Satay,* which first appealed to the palates of the kingdoms south of ancient Siam, Malay and the Spice Islands, was surely introduced by Arab traders from the Middle East. The rest is conjecture, supposition and historically based logic.

When the Siamese defeated the Khmer and when they adopted Buddhism, I am sure that they assimilated the Brahmin and Buddhist proscription on the killing of animals. It is possible that the Thai reluctance to slaughter for food and the sparseness of meat in an average meal may well be linked to these religious traditions.

Fish are a slightly different matter. Although the Buddhist teachings caution against the taking of any creature's life, the Thai diet is very dependent on fish and would lack necessary nutrition without it. The Thai rationalization for their apparent transgression is charming. They say that the fish is stupid to enter their traps and die. They do not kill the fish, they merely take it from the water. If an animal dies, does it matter who eats it?

In Thailand today, the beef butchers are often Pathans from the Northwest Frontier Province of Pakistan; the pork and poultry butchers, Chinese. The Thai hold hunters in contempt. Historically, their kings forbade hunting and fishing on holy days. The wealthy Thai used to buy whole cargoes of fish and return them to the sea as an act of merit. I remember, in Bangkok, being offered a caged bird for sale in order that I may buy it and set it free.

The true Indian curry, a sauce designed to add relish to rice, is an antecedent to many Thai curries. "A little goes a long way," as it is meant to do. The use of coconut milk in Southern India as an agent to dilute the fierce attack of the ground spices in the curry paste is identical to its use in curries and meat dishes in Thailand. Other types of Indian curries were historically described as ". . . a spicy stew of vegetables, fish or meat." What better way to describe the curries of Thailand?

We know what the early Siamese ate during the period of their beloved Kingdom of Sukhothai. The stone stele engraved during the reign of Ram Khamhaeng tells us that the people had rice, fish and game. The rice was probably glutinous rice and was eaten with sauces of garlic, peppercorns and ginger—no chillies, those came later. The Siamese built large ponds in the city for freshwater fish. Vegetables, such as taro and yams, were cultivated and the king owned orchards of mangoes, coconuts, areca nut and betel. (The Indian influence of chewing betel was widespread and lasted in the country until World War II when a Thai premier, Pibul, ordered all betel trees cut down—the occupying Japanese did not like to see stained teeth!)

Sugarcane was also grown locally at the time of the Sukhothai but was not commercially exported for another seven hundred years. We know that they prepared their food in the same fashion as it is cooked today. Mortars and pestles, coconut shredders for the making of coconut milk and rice pots were all part of the domestic equipment of the early households.

In the later centuries, as trading expanded and the country was exposed to Indian and Arab merchants, certain other spices such as cardamom, coriander (known as Chinese parsley or cilantro) and cumin were introduced; cardamom from India and coriander and cumin from the Middle East. (Growing ginger was carried on boats between China and Southeast Asia and eaten to prevent scurvy hundreds of years before Europeans discovered that citrus fruits would perform the same miracle.)

The spices from the Spice Islands—nutmeg, cloves and mace—were traded directly to India and then to the West. They figure in Thai medicine, which is Chinese influenced, but not significantly in the cuisine.

The Indians and Arabs dominated the spice trade for centuries until Europeans discovered their secret for sailing with the monsoon winds and broke their monopoly. It was the search for the valued spices which finally led the Europeans to attempt to find the fabulous Indies. In Europe, in the late Middle Ages, one pound of saffron could be traded for a horse, a pound of ginger for a sheep, two pounds of mace for a cow and German records from 1393 show a pound of nutmeg going for seven fat oxen!

Like inflation today, it was getting too much to be borne. In 1271, Niceo and Maffeo Polo took Marco to China with them. The sequel is history.

In the year that every schoolchild knows, Martin Alonsa Pinzón, a Portuguese captain of one of Columbus's ships, the *Pinta*, found some elongated little fruits that were attractive red and green. I should like to have seen the face of the first, intrepid Portuguese who bit into one. They had discovered the chilli pepper or Capsicum. It traveled with them back to Europe and, later, to Thailand around 1511 when the first Portuguese discovered the fabled Kingdom of Ayuthia. For the spice-loving Siamese, the discovery of a new and hotter spice than their beloved black pepper must have been revolutionary. The plants thrived in the soil and climate and the fiery little fruits found their way into almost every part of the cuisine.

The Spanish introduced the chicle fruit or sapodilla to the Philippines. Sometime thereafter, it made its way to Thailand. Tomatoes were also introduced to the country by the Europeans. Tapioca, now a staple of the modern Thai diet and grown in great, waving, green fields in Central and Southern Thailand, was successfully transplanted from Central America.

In the nineteenth century, when Bangkok had become the capital of Thailand, a French Bishop, Monseigneur Pallegoix, who seems to have had the typical Frenchman's regard for his stomach, visited the capital. He wrote a detailed description of Siamese life at the time in his book, *Description du Royaume Thai ou Siam*, published in 1854, and outlined the eating habits of the Thai. He tells of the making of *Nam Prik* sauce, meticulously noting that red pepper was bruised in a mortar then shrimp paste was added, together with onions, black pepper and garlic. He observed that brine and lemon juice (I think he referred to lime juice because lemons were not indigenous), ginger, tamarinds and gourd seeds were added with fish in an early stage of putridity (his words, not mine!), mango sprouts and chillies.

The good Bishop appears to have spent some time in a

Siamese kitchen because he then details the way that rice was cooked, noting precisely that it was washed four times before being placed in a pot of water. His description tallies very much with the way in which rice is cooked today in households without electric rice cookers.

I would like to add some extra historical threads to the tapestry of food and spices that was so colorfully woven from the East through to Europe through the centuries.

It would appear that the Indians and Arabs were eating noodles some fifty years before Marco Polo ever went to China. It may be that the Mongols spread their popularity in Europe for, when the Mongol empire fragmented, wealthy Europeans took Mongol or Tartar slaves as domestic servants. It seems likely that they brought their own predilection for noodles into the households to whom they were indentured.

Potatoes were brought from the Americas to Europe in the sixteenth century and then to Asia. They never really caught on with the Siamese, who referred to them as *Man Farang*, or foreign root. A latecomer to the Thai culinary scene, coffee, originated in Ethiopia and was brought to Java in the East Indies in the early eighteenth century. It is now a universal Thai beverage.

# ONE
# Life in Thailand

## BANGKOK: "THE CITY OF ANGELS"

There are few cities in the world where the urban dweller considers his city—London, New York, Paris, Berlin, Rome, Rio de Janeiro, Tokyo, Hong Kong—the focus of civilization. Bangkok would head this list: Bangkok is Thailand as Thailand is Bangkok.

This sprawling city is full of contrasts; ugly and noisy with new construction, yet beautiful in the serene pockets of temple complexes and the tree-shaded backwaters of forgotten *klongs*.

The immediate impression which strikes the visitor is not the physical city, however, but the diversity of the people. The crowds are kaleidoscopic: small, dark southern Thai, their flattened features showing a kinship to the Malays; paler skinned Northerners; Chinese merchants; bearded and turbanned Sikhs; saffron-robed monks with shaved heads; aristocrats, whose aquiline features betray an ancient Brahmin heritage, and everywhere, the schoolchildren in spotless uniforms—all represent Bangkok.

The nucleus of the older area of the city, cradled in a curve of the Chao Phya River, is the splendid Grand Palace complex. Separating it from the nearby crowded area of the old city is the large, oval Pramane Ground or *Sanam Luang* —the ancient meeting place, site of festivals, kite-flying contests and the Weekend Market. South and east of the Palace lies the dense mass of Chinatown in the Pahurat and Sampeng area; a vast market of winding lanes lined with stalls and shops.

From the old city, roads radiate north, east and south into the elite suburbs of the wealthy and Westernized sections of Bangkok studded with parks and luxury hotels. Here air-conditioned supermarkets underline the modernization of food marketing as frozen and packaged goods, both local and imported, disappear into the shopping carts of affluent Thai living in Western-style apartments with the luxury of refrigerators and freezers.

The traditional markets still exist, however, fed by a prodigious bounty of food arriving daily from the outlying provinces by barge and sampan, oxcart and truck. The latter monsters of the road scorch along the crown of the highways blowing their horns like Toad's motorcar in *Wind in the Willows.* Thai trucks look very like overgrown escapees from a bumper-car amusement ride and behave in much the same way. The timid motorist, catching sight of one of these chrome-plated leviathans in his rear-view mirror, would do well to pull over and let the monster speed by in a puff of smoke.

Both the land and floating markets of the city bustle with activity from the break of day as mountains of baskets full of food are unloaded and displayed. Delicacies arrive from every region: lobster from Phuket on the Andaman Sea; shrimp and crab from Rayong and Siracha on the Gulf; durian, oranges, mangoes and rambutan from the orchards of Chanthaburi; even edible birds' nests from Chumphon in the south and seasonal strawberries from Chiengmai in the north.

The marketing and the eating go hand-in-hand. The Thai

love to snack and every market is rimmed with rows of restaurants and food stalls. The main meal, however, is eaten in the evening as the hot day cools. It consists of an assortment of curry dishes, soups, salads, vegetables and sauces served simultaneously around a central dish of plain, boiled rice; the Thai colloquial invitation to eat is *kin kao* or "eat rice." Sauces are served as accompaniments to main dishes or as dips for seafood and vegetables. The familiar array of vegetables that Westerners know is often augmented by young leaves off various trees and wayside shrubs as well as water plants, which grow in profusion in the streams and canals. The Thai housewife is lucky—a quick stroll down the lane will result in a free and handsome vegetable dish for dinner.

Thai desserts are generally reserved for formal dinners and a tray of fresh fruit normally suffices to round off a meal. With the fruit tray, small towels soaked in flower water or cologne and iced, are presented to refresh the face and hands of the diner. This custom is followed in traditional restaurants and at formal dinners. (Towel serving, before and after the meal, is certainly a civilized convention and one that we could well adopt.) If, in addition to the fruit, you choose to serve iced towels at your own dinners, try briefly soaking facecloths in diluted cologne, squeezing out the surplus moisture, then folding and stacking them in a freezer for about thirty minutes.

Towels bring a fleeting memory of Bangkok to my mind. In a certain Chinese-Thai restaurant near the boxing stadium in Bangkok, the towels, hygienically sealed in plastic, are brought to the table. They pop open with a satisfying explosion when struck sharply against the palm; an action that few foreigners, adult or child, can resist. These childish antics bring indulgent smiles to the faces of the Chinese and Thai diners.

The Thai are very fond of sweetmeats. There are so many varieties they are almost too numerous to count. Most are available commercially and are sold in the markets for snacks. Many are versions of fragrant custards concocted from coconut cream thickened with tapioca flour or rice starch. Jasmine or rosewater provide flavoring and the little banana-leaf cups in which they are sold often contain sesame or lotus seeds. Other varieties are gelatinous. The Thai use agar-agar to set the mixtures because, unlike our gelatin, it does not melt in the heat and needs no refrigeration. These highly-colored jellies are sweetened with palm sugar and decorated with coconut shreds.

No account of Thai food can be complete without mention of the importance given to food and meal presentation. Decoration and the proper use of dishes and receptacles is a matter for serious consideration. Fruit and vegetable carving is a traditional and highly cultivated art. A Thai will spend hours carving ginger root into detailed shapes of flowers and, even, crabs and whole shrimp. Cucumber skin is fashioned into delicate leaves and dropped into soup for garnish. Fruits, such as melon and pineapple, are carved into boats and bowls to grace buffet tables. Vegetables—carrots, celery, green onions and radishes—are transformed into chrysanthemums and daisies.

When the first large, Western hotel chains opened in Bangkok, the Thai *sous chefs* were introduced to the art of ice and butter carving. The new creative media opened up a dazzling future. Now, magnificent examples of traditional Thai boats, classic figures from Thai mythology and heroic statuary from the *Ramayana* grace hotel buffet tables in glistening impermanence; wilting and dripping in the omnipresent heat, nonetheless, delighting tourists.

After the evening meals, the night is open to entertainment. Both the urban and country Thai are pleasure-loving—delighting in music, dancing and entertainment. The large and lavish movie theaters of Bangkok are like the Western movie palaces of the 1940's and 1950's, but are probably the best attended in the world, playing to packed houses. Thai boxing also attracts crowds of vociferous fans. Bars, massage parlors and nightclubs prosper. The larger hotels boast supper clubs and, in some cases, lavish floor shows. Programs of Thai classical dancing and dramas play at the National Theater and the business and diplomatic circles attend a seemingly endless social round of cocktail parties, receptions and dinners.

## THE ETERNAL VILLAGE

Every visitor to Bangkok should try to get out into the countryside, which reflects the true Thailand, unchanged for hundreds of years. The pace of life is unhurried and peaceful.

Each small village is administrated by a *kamman* or elected headman who arbitrates its affairs and acts as spokesman to the outside world. Village life is insular. Villagers care and know little of the larger events of the nation. Their loyalty is totally to the King and Queen but they are largely unconcerned by the political changes of the country.

The cycle of life is bound to the crops, the harvest and the vagaries of the weather. Village gossip encompasses small romances and intrigues; birth and death. The big events of the country year are the temple ceremonies and fairs, and the occasional traveling shadow puppet show. Buddhism is devoutly observed, but the animistic spirits that pervade river and mountain, tree and house, also must be placated with offerings.

Village songs and stories are many—concerning the harvest, a mythic love affair or a tragic death. Lively country dances, differing sharply from the ritualistic and stylized classical dancing, are performed by most of the village at feasts and festivals.

In central and southern Thailand, where the earth becomes soggy or flooded in the rainy season, the houses are built on high platforms supported by posts. The family lives in the house, livestock shelters beneath. The village houses are simple, devoid of ornamentation. Built of wood, they are thatched with reeds or palm fronds. The steep pitch of the roofs ensures that the rains will run off the overhanging eaves. Small, outlying sheds, built in similar fashion, shelter the rice crop or additional animals.

Country food is hearty. Curries often contain both meat and vegetables. Coconut milk is seldom added because its preparation takes up too much time in the busy day of family life. If the village is near a stream or river, fish become a large part of the diet; every Thai male being a diligent fisherman. Small boats are everywhere, being rowed along the rivers or pulled up onto the bank by the house.

The fast "long tail" boats provide intervillage water transportation. These shallow-draft vessels are the greatest fun to ride as a passenger, but difficult to pilot. The engine is swivel-mounted on the stern, connected by a long pole/driveshaft to the propeller in the water, several feet behind the boat. The pole also acts as the rudder, being moved in the water to steer the craft, or lifted, dripping, into the air to slow the speed or clear patches of water hyacinth or reeds.

A *farang* who lived in Thailand for a number of years shipped a "long tail" back to Florida when he returned to the United States. Having mastered the skill of operating it, I am sure he is the cynosure of the Everglades, where the unique vessel would be completely at home.

In the cities, small towns and villages, the peace of the lanes and byways is regularly broken throughout the day by bells, buzzers and cries of the itinerant food vendors. They bicycle or push their carts up and down the streets calling to the householders to buy their delicacies. Some housewives rarely cook at all, except the mandatory pot of boiled rice, availing themselves of the endless supply of food from the street hawkers. Each vendor gets up before dawn and starts to make his specialty, which he loads and sells from his cart until the last noodle or piece of fruit has disappeared.

My first morning in Thailand, now almost two decades ago, I was awakened early by a noise sounding exactly like golf balls being tossed in a tin tub. The thundering and rolling racket lasted for some time, and when I came down to breakfast I asked the maid what caused my pre-alarm commotion. She told me that opposite our house was a village of wooden houses where the man who sold fish balls lived. As I later discovered, he was preparing fish balls or quenelles to be served in a clear soup. Apparently, he had already mashed the fish with spices, roughly formed it into spheres and was tossing the marble-sized balls repeatedly on something approximating a cookie sheet to compress them and stabilize their shape. I had heard him preparing his day's stock of merchandise before setting out on his rounds!

## CEREMONIALS AND CELEBRATIONS

Like gold and silver threads woven into a length of Thai silk, the many festivals and ceremonials of Thai life light up the fabric of the working year. The Thai love to celebrate and have fun but, on a more serious level, the pageantry and religious ceremonies reinforce their devotion to Buddhism and strengthen the ties of loyalty which bind them to the monarchy. The origins of their ceremonies and festivals are many and varied, but most are intimately connected with their colorful history and the external influences which have shaped the Thai nation.

The chief events in the life of Buddha are commemorated and observed in Thailand today as they undoubtedly were by the Mon, from whom the Thai adopted their form of Buddhism. *Maka Puja,* in February, commemorates the gathering of Buddha's disciples to hear him preach. Prayers are recited and candlelight processions take place around the temples. In May, *Visakha Puja* is celebrated, honoring the birth of Buddha. Thousands of paper lanterns are lighted and crowds join in torchlight processions. July ushers in *Khao Pansa,* the Buddhist Lent. *Asalaha Puja,* at the beginning of the period, is the time when most young Thai men enter the monkhood for a period of between one week to three months.

*Tod Kathin* marks the end of the rainy season when the annual offering of new, saffron-colored robes is made to the monks. Falling in October, this is also the occasion for the Royal Barge Procession when the King journeys down the Chao Phya in traditional, ceremonial pomp to present new robes to the monks of *Wat Arun*, the Temple of the Dawn. Because of restorations to the ancient Royal Barges, this procession has been suspended in recent years, but should be resumed in the near future.

Particularly in the country, the temples are the centers of both religious and social life. The temple fairs throughout the year are events eagerly anticipated. Two of the largest fairs in the Bangkok area, both falling in the dry month of November, are the Festival of the Temple of the Golden Mount, held at the landmark temple in Bangkok, and the Pra Pathom Chedi Fair at Nakorn Pathom, about fifty miles west of Bangkok. The giant *Chedi* of Pra Pathom is the tallest Buddhist monument in the world and is spectacularly outlined in lights for the fair.

The monarchy of Thailand is the most powerful, unifying force which binds the country together. Born in the far-off days of Sukhothai, the tradition of kingship has been perpetuated down through the centuries and reverence is extended to past monarchs as well as the present King. The affection with which the Thai people hold King Bhumibol shows in the fervor with which they celebrate the personal events of his rule.

*Chakri* Day, in April, is the national holiday commemorating the founding of the present dynasty. The Thai visit the Temple of the Emerald Buddha (carved from jasper not emerald), taking flowers and incense to offer in respect to the former kings. May is the occasion of the Coronation Day Anniversary of the present King. Queen Sirikit's birthday is celebrated in August. *Chulalongkorn* Day is on the twenty-third of October, memorializing the death of the great and beloved King Rama V. Thousands flock to his statue in front of the old parliament building in Bangkok to lay wreaths of flowers.

The Trooping of the Colors, an event similar to the British military ceremonial, is held on the eighth of November. The King reviews contingents from all three branches of the armed forces in the Royal Plaza, attracting crowds of spectators. December fifth marks the King's birthday. It is the occasion for mass illuminations of all public buildings in Bangkok, and national flags flutter from every vantage point—a cross between Times Square on New Year's Eve and the Fourth of July. The streets after dark are thronged with pedestrians and car and bus loads of Thai up from the country to view the lights. Street-side food stalls do a roaring business and there is a general air of festivity.

Other festivals and ceremonies show their foreign, historical origins, and some reflect the perpetuation of ancient animistic beliefs which co-exist happily with Buddhism. Their dates are determined by the Thai Lunar calendar and Brahmin priests officiate at the rites of ceremony. The Thai have recently moved their New Year celebration from the time of the Chinese New Year, in February, to the date of Western New Year. The thousands of Chinese in Thailand, however, still celebrate the traditional Chinese New Year with all its attendant customs and foods. New Year's in Thailand is a time for general high spirits, rounds of parties and the universal expression of *Sawadee Pimai,* or Happy New Year. Chiengmai, the northern city, celebrates New Year with a three-day Winter Fair, featuring parades and beauty contests.

Mid-April is *Songkran,* a festival which derives its origins from the Holi Festival in India. Celebrated mainly in Northern Thailand, it is also observed in Laos, Cambodia and Burma. One of the liveliest in the calendar, it is literally a water festival. After offerings are brought to the temples and the Buddha images sprinkled, the young people honor their parents by bathing their hands with perfumed water. After the formalities, the festivities break open with a cheerful and indiscriminate splashing and pouring of water on everybody. One *Songkran,* while in Laos, I spent a breathless hour dodging down side streets trying to protect my camera from groups of noisy revelers intent on dousing me with water from plastic buckets. May is the month of the Ploughing Ceremony, *Raek Na.*

Brahmin priests officiate at this ceremony, which is described in detail later in the book.

November is the month of the *Loy Krathong* festival, one of the most colorful in the calendar and the one most loved by visitors. Thousands of elaborate little boats, constructed either from banana leaves or colored paper, wire and glittering trimmings are fashioned into lotus blossoms, ships or fanciful birds. Each craft carries a candle, incense sticks and a coin. They are launched onto the rivers and *klongs* to honor the water spirits and carry away the sender's sins. Superstition has it that if the frail little craft sails away without getting snagged on the waterweeds or capsizing, wishes are granted and success ensured. Every flowing stream is illuminated by thousands of twinkling lights. Folk songs and dances are performed, snacks and drinks consumed, and it is a time to appreciate the gaiety of the Thai. *Deepvali* or *Devalli,* the Hindu Festival of the Lights, is also celebrated around the same time by the Hindus in Bangkok at the ornate temple on Silom Road.

The Brahmin priests also play a very important part in both Thai wedding ceremonies and the elaborate funeral rites. The actual wedding is a very simple affair—the bride and groom being joined by a symbolic white cord and, then, having lustral water poured over their hands by the wedding guests. A Thai funeral, by contrast, is a drawn-out and very formal occasion marking the rites of passage.

Two further events during the Thai year are colorful spectacles, although they do not qualify as festivals or holidays. The first is the Elephant Roundup, which takes place at Surin, an ancient Khmer site northeast of Bangkok. Held in November, hundreds of elephants take part in this spectacle—Cecil B. DeMille would have loved it. Thousands of tourists and Thai take trains and buses from Bangkok to attend. From mid-February to April, kite-fighting is the big attraction. Held at the Pramane Ground, teams sponsored by government offices and commercial companies compete in contests. Fought by a *chula,* a large kite, against a smaller, called a *pakpao,* the object is for the *chula* to bring the *pakpao* down to earth. Crowds turn out to participate or spectate. Food stalls refresh and chairs are provided for the spectators.

The festivals of Thailand exemplify the spirit of the Thai attitude to life—an attitude which can be summed up in one word, *sanook*. Difficult to translate exactly, it means pleasurable or fun, and it illustrates their conviction about the way life should be lived. It is not a shallow attitude but, rather, a sensible philosophy; a resolve to enjoy their daily existence. It is the reason that factory workers will joke with each other while engaged in the most repetitive tasks or why farm workers will laugh and sing while performing back-breaking labor in the rice paddies. *Sanook* is the resolve to look for the joy in life.

# TWO
# The Thai Kitchen

## FURNISHINGS, UTENSILS, APPLIANCES, IMPLEMENTS

The kitchen in Thailand is a very simple affair. It is generally built away from the main house, as part of the servants' quarters if the family is wealthy. Whether separate or part of the main dwelling, it is a plain room, cement- or mud-floored, with unglazed windows, which might boast the luxury of mesh screens to keep out the mosquitoes.

The stove, around which most of the activity takes place, is generally built-in and constructed entirely of cement or adobe-like materials. It is normally under a window to vent away heat and odors. It has a large aperture below, used to insert and remove the charcoal pot; a funnel-shaped vessel of kiln-baked earthenware, which holds the burning charcoal. When this pot is in place it fits directly under a circular opening in the top of the stove. This range top hole is ringed by flanged superstructures

which hold a wok snugly in place above the burning charcoal in the pot. Extra charcoal is kept in a box or sack beside the stove. Because there are no oven arrangements, there is no baking in the home and, in the entire cuisine, there are few baked dishes.

Next in importance will be a wooden cupboard resembling an old-fashioned meat safe. The back, sides and doors are covered with wire-mesh screens to keep the flies out and allow the air to circulate freely. The wooden legs always stand in saucers of water to discourage marauding ants. This cupboard will house nothing more than some stored garlic bulbs, a bottle of the ubiquitous fish sauce, *Nam Pla,* some dried fish and, perhaps, some precooked, cold rice. Because of the tropical climate and the fact that a Thai kitchen seldom has a refrigerator, marketing is done daily and leftovers are uncommon.

If the kitchen is blessed with running water, there will be a sink. Whether it is plumbed or not, there are always large Ali Baba jars or cisterns covered with rough-hewn wooden lids standing outside the kitchen. These trap rainwater for both cooking and washing up and are kept closed so that mosquito larvae cannot breed inside. A customary and preferred location for Thai houses is on or beside the rivers and canals; these *klong* dwellers merely use the fast-flowing water, practically outside the kitchen door, for their corporal requirements.

If large enough, the kitchen will house a wooden table and a chair or two. Wooden wall shelves provide extra storage and complete the furnishings.

The basic utensils will be one or two woks hanging from nails on the wall, several saucepans, the largest of which will be reserved for cooking rice, and perhaps a multi-tiered aluminum steamer. Made by Chinese tin merchants, the steamer consists of two or three layers of pans, the bottom pan being solid-based and the others having perforations. A close-fitting lid will crown the topmost layer and seal the steamer.

Aside from the wok, the most important implements in a Thai kitchen are the cleavers, cutting board and the mortar and pestle. The Thai mortar is made of heavy, crude earthenware and is deep with a weighted base. The pestle is a chunky affair, carved out of wood. A selection of knives, a ladle and a coconut meat scraper, together with a cane basket for expressing the milk from the soaking coconut flesh, round out the basic Thai cooking implements.

As the skill of the cook increases, and/or the wealth of

the family, so does the complexity of utensils and implements. With the availability of electricity spreading through the small towns and villages, the first status symbol in the kitchen will be a Japanese-manufactured electric rice cooker. This relieves the housewife of the daily chore of preparing the rice, no mean saving in a country in which each person consumes approximately one pound of rice a day; not necessarily all the rice consumption occurs in the household.

In the markets there are stalls which only sell kitchen implements. Fashioned skillfully and attractively from bronze, bamboo or teak, each will serve a specific function—unlike some of our multipurpose utensils. An important adjunct to the Thai kitchen is a large, bamboo handled, shallow, mesh frying basket. This is commonly made from twisted brass or bronze wire and, as the shape closely follows the curve of the wok, is a marvelous way to lower all manner of items into boiling oil for deep-frying. Another mesh implement is the noodle or vegetable cooker. This is also a wire-mesh basket attached to a long bamboo handle but this basket is flowerpot-shaped, deep and about three-and-one-half inches in diameter. It is used to dunk noodles or blanch vegetables in boiling water.

Other implements are more exotic and esoteric. There is a brass cone with a handle. The bottom, smaller end, is pinched to form two pin-hole size openings. This is used for the Thai dessert, *Foi Tong*, where beaten eggs are trickled through the split cone to form threads which cook in boiling syrup. Another bronze or brass implement is a long-handled shell mold. It has a wooden handle from which extend two congruent molds on thin wire stems. These molds, resembling patty shells, are dipped first in batter to coat the outsides and then in boiling oil to form

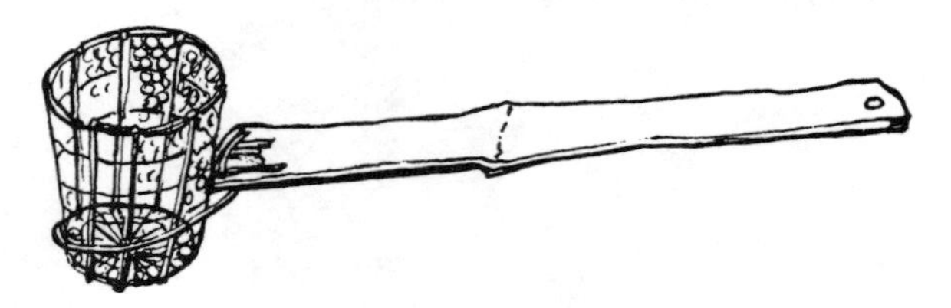

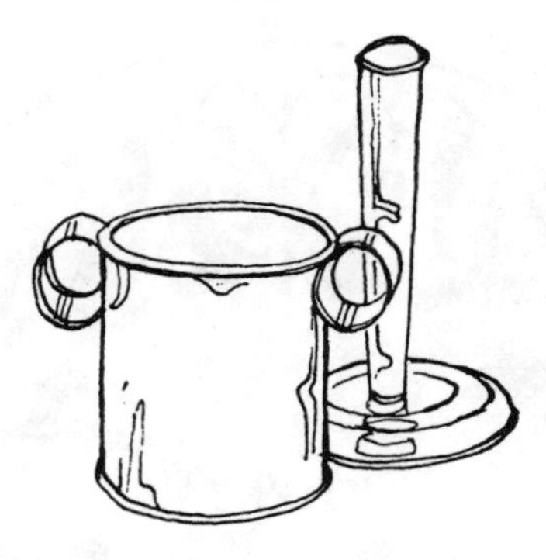

little batter-cups, which are filled for snacks. A *klong krang* board looks rather like a large butter paddle and can be made from wood or metal. Dough is pressed and rolled along the ridges to form shell-like curls which are then deep-fried. There are two interesting presses, one for tapioca, the other mung-bean noodles. The *lachong* press is a perforated metal plate, resembling a cheese grater. Tapioca dough is pressed through the perforations to form sweet noodles. The other press is a handsome and decorative bronze can with a perforated base, into which fits a bronze plunger. A sweet paste of mung-bean flour, coconut milk and palm sugar is extruded from the bottom into a thin syrup flavored with jasmine petals. This delightful dessert is called *Saleem* and the press, appropriately, is a *Saleem* maker.

There are many craftsmen's variations on these implements, most of which are used to make desserts and snacks. Some Thai cookies, *Kanom*, are pressed into cookie molds carved into wooden boards and then steamed or deep-fried. Other cake molds are fashioned from bronze and look far too handsome to be utilitarian. Nearly all these implements, however, are for specialized confections and are not part of an everyday Thai kitchen.

The last cooking aid in a Thai kitchen grows around the house and proliferates the countryside! It is the all-purpose banana leaf: kitchen foil, waxed paper, plastic wrap all rolled into one. Steamed foods are wrapped in it, containers are shaped from it and it is an indispensable part of a Thai kitchen.

## COCONUT AND COCONUT MILK

The coconut, *Maprao,* is woven into the everyday fabric of life in Thailand. Every part of the palm—leaf, trunk, husk, nut—is used somewhere in the culture. It is a staple food and commercial product essential to the Thai economy.

The fibrous, middle covering of the coconut is worked into rope, woven into mats or used for making brushes. The fronds are used for thatching houses, weaving baskets and for clothing. The hard meat of the mature coconut is dried in the sun to make copra, from which coconut oil is expressed for soap, cosmetics, candles—even nitroglycerine! The waste, after the oil is extracted from the meat, is used for cattle fodder. The hard brown shells are turned into cups and ladles, toys and carved into souvenirs; they are also burnt for fuel. Some happy man even discovered that the sap of the palm, allowed to ferment in the sun for a few days, makes a powerful palm wine or toddy.

Dried, flaked meat from mature coconuts has limited use in Thai cooking, being reserved for desserts, sweetmeats and decoration.

Coconut milk, *Nam Katee,* is one of the most important ingredients in Thai cooking. It is a component of almost all Thai foods: curries; meat, vegetable, fish dishes as well as sweets, desserts and beverages.

Coconut milk is the liquid that is expressed from the meat of the mature coconut after soaking it in boiling milk or water. It is not the liquid that is found inside a fresh coconut. That water is only used in tropical beverages, Rum Cocos and Piña Coladas, and does not have the properties of coconut milk.

Throughout the Pacific and Orient, coconut milk is extracted from the meat of mature coconuts. This process entails cracking the nut, prising out the meat and removing the brown outer skin. The meat is then shredded, steeped in boiling water and squeezed to extract the liquid—coconut milk. This primitive process can be accelerated and more efficiently accomplished in food processor or blender.

In the United States, fresh coconuts are not always to be found; when they are, their age and quality vary. I find it preferable to used dried, unsweetened (desiccated) coconut, which is always available either in health food shops or Oriental stores. I use whole cow's milk to extract the coconut essence because it produces a richer milk and cream. However, nonfat, skim milk or water may be substituted with good results, although the resultant "milk" will be somewhat thinner.

When I refer to "thick" coconut milk in a recipe, it is made from the first pressing of the milk or water through the coconut meat. Coconut "cream" is obtained by refrigerating the pressed "thick" coconut milk; it will rise to the top where it can be spooned off. "Thin" coconut milk is the product of repeated pressings of the same coconut meat, using additional liquid.

Following is an approximate table for the preparation of varying amounts of coconut milk. You will find that for each 4 cups "thick" coconut milk, using whole milk, after refrigeration, about ½ cup heavy coconut "cream" will rise to the top. (The amount of "cream" will depend on the butterfat content of the milk and oil concentration in the coconut.) Use this ratio: 8 cups milk will produce approximately 1 cup included "cream."

| YIELD | COCONUT | MILK / WATER |
|---|---|---|
| *2 cups* | *2 cups* | *3 cups* |
| *4 cups* | *4 cups* | *6 cups* |
| *6 cups* | *5 cups* | *8 cups* |
| *8 cups* | *6 cups* | *10 cups* |
| *10 cups* | *7 cups* | *13 cups* |

Scald the milk in a saucepan. Place the coconut in the milk. Stir and remove from heat. Let stand until cooled to room temperature, stirring occasionally. Strain this mixture through a sieve using the back of a spoon to express as much liquid as possible. To retrieve more milk and make it more concentrated, wrap this "used" coconut in muslin, terrycloth or, as one of my students suggested, a nylon stocking, and squeeze out the remaining liquid. (Some liquid will remain in the coconut, therefore the extra milk.) Refrigerate until used.

Coconut milk made in this fashion will behave as dairy milk. It must be refrigerated and will have the same refrigerator life. This milk comfortably fits into the small Ziploc bags in 2-cup amounts. These bags store and stack conveniently in your freezer for future use.

## RICE

Rice is of almost equal importance to Thai cuisine as is coconut milk. The Thai use mainly two varieties of the grain: long, short. Long grain, of various qualities, is used as a basic element served with all meals—white and fluffy. Short grain, or glutinous, replaces long grain as a staple mainly in northern Thailand and neighboring Laos, Cambodia and Burma. It is cooked universally for desserts, often boiled with coconut milk. Glutinous is often referred to as "sticky rice" because of its agglutination and is generally eaten with the hands.

Since the advent of the electric rice cooker, from Japan and widely used in Thailand, cooks produce trouble-free, foolproof rice when the cooking instructions are followed.

Without a rice cooker, following are two methods for producing uniformly good, cooked rice, one for long and the other for short grain. Please note: These methods do not apply to "instant rice." If you are using any "convenience" preparations, follow the instructions on the packet.

To cook rice:

### Long Grain

2 *cups water for the first measured cup rice, 1½ cups water for each additional cup rice, e.g.:*
1 *cup rice = 2 cups water*
2 *cups rice = 3½ cups water*
3 *cups rice = 5 cups water*

### Short Grain

1½ *cups water for the first measured cup rice, 1 cup water for each additional cup rice, e.g.:*
1 *cup rice = 1½ cups water*
2 *cups rice = 2½ cups water*
3 *cups rice = 3½ cups water*

Wash the rice thoroughly in several rinsings of water, agitating the grains with your fingers.

Repeat this process until the water runs clear. In a saucepan, bring the washed rice and water to a rolling boil over high heat. Turn heat to low, cover tightly and simmer for 20 minutes. Remove from heat, uncover to let steam escape and fluff with a fork or chopstick. **N.B.**: Use this washing method also with a rice cooker.

Overcooked rice which is still wet can be resuscitated by spreading out the grains on a platter and drying in a low oven (200° F.), separating from time to time with a fork. Leftover firm cold rice can be refrigerated and, conveniently, frozen for future use. To reheat and revive the texture, place the cold rice in an ovenproof bowl in a steamer, cover and steam until fluffy and hot (about 10 minutes). Without a steamer, you may put the rice in a metal colander, cover and place in a large saucepan over boiling water. Cooked rice, used in fried-rice dishes, behaves better if it has been refrigerated prior to frying.

## GARLIC

The Thai garlic cloves are much smaller than ours and the skin is thinner. The Thai therefore crush them together with the skin and universally use them whole. We do need to peel our tough-skinned garlic and, for the purposes of the recipes in this book, when garlic is specified, it is presumed to be peeled.

When garlic is pounded in a mortar with a pestle, and salt is required, it is recommended they be pounded together to aid in the pulverizing and help extract the garlic juices. It can also be smashed with the flat surface of a cleaver and, then, chopped.

Individual cloves can be peeled ahead of time and stored in an airtight container in the refrigerator. If this method is followed, it is preferable to place a folded paper towel in the bottom of the container to absorb any condensation and help prevent the formation of mold. Whole garlic pods can be kept for long periods (several months) successfully, unpeeled in a cool cupboard with good circulation.

The Thai sometimes use pickled garlic in recipes. It can be added to either *Mee Krob* or any of the fried rice dishes. Pickled garlic is also eaten with Chinese sausages as a snack.

To pickle garlic:

•

**PICKLED GARLIC · KRATIEM DONG**

*1 cup white vinegar*
*4 cups water*
*1/4 cup granulated sugar*
*1 tablespoon salt*
*6 garlic pods (approximately 120 cloves depending on size), peeled*

In a medium saucepan, bring the vinegar, water, sugar and salt to a boil. Reduce heat and simmer for 5 minutes. Drop in the garlic. Return to boil for 1 minute, then remove from heat. Cool, and fill sterilized, screw-top jars. Store in the refrigerator for at least 1 week before eating. Continue to refrigerate, tightly covered, between serving.

## TAMARIND

Tamarind provides the sour flavor in Thai curries, meat and fish dishes. It is the dough-like flesh inside the pods of the tamarind tree (see Glossary, page 281). In recipes, tamarind water is usually specified as it blends more easily than the lumps of fibrous tamarind pulp. There are two principal methods for making tamarind water, the latter by far the most convenient. First, soak a lump of the moist, unrefined tamarind pulp in hot water until it completely dissolves. Stir the lumps to aid dissolution and strain the liquid, "tamarind water," before using. Use about 1 teaspoon tamarind pulp to 2 tablespoons hot water. Second, Indian food stores stock jars of homogeneous tamarind concentrate—a recent, welcome addition to their stocks. Because this concentrate is more refined it is easily dissolved directly in hot water and needs no straining. Generally use about 1 teaspoon concentrate to 3 tablespoons water.

## CHILLIES

Treat all members of the chilli family with extreme care and deference. Not all Thai dishes are incendiary hot, but spiciness, almost overwhelming to the Western palate, is a hallmark.

The amount of spicy "fire" is a matter of individual preference and varies considerably even among aficionados of the cuisine. For instance, there are many Thai who cannot tolerate spicy-hot food. If you or your guests are unused to chilli spiciness, either reduce the chilli proportion or choose the larger, milder varieties; generally the larger the chilli, the milder its taste. For many, heat tolerance builds with familiarity.

When preparing chillies, fresh or dried, always wash your hands several times directly after handling and use a nail brush to remove the oil from under the fingernails. *Do not* put your hands anywhere near your face until you have washed them; the volatile oils play havoc with tender skin and eyes.

There are three stages at which chillies are usually purchased: fresh; immature (green), mature (red and yellow); and dried (deep red and variegated brown to black). To seed a fresh chilli, grasp the stem end firmly in one hand and, using a sharp pointed knife in the other, guide the heel (back of the blade) along your thumbnail to pierce the chilli through both sides. Then, with a smooth, quick motion, draw the knife outward, slicing the fruit down its length to the tip. Scrape out the seeds with the point and heel of the knife. With the blade, shave the ribs and membranes. Dried chillies may be seeded by cutting off the base at the stem and rolling the pod between the thumb and fingers to loosen the seeds. These may be shaken out the open end.

If whole fresh red chillies are specified, usually for decoration, but are not available and a substitution cannot be made, whole, dried red chillies may be partially reconstituted by soaking in hot water for several minutes.

The most commonly specified fresh chilli in recipes is the Serrano. This is partially because it is homologous to certain common Thai chillies not available here and, moreover, produce sections of supermarkets in major cities usually carry this variety.

I find ripening (maturing) my own whole, fresh chillies preferable to depending on the vagaries in produce availability. This can be easily accomplished by setting the fresh, green chillies in the sun for several days.

When storing, I refrigerate them in a covered container lined with a paper towel to help absorb moisture and retard mold formation. Refrigerated chillies remain in good shape for at least one week.

Chillies are a rich source of vitamin C, and in hot climates, when consumed, induce perspiration, which, in turn, cools the body.

It is easy to grow almost any variety of *Capsicum*. The plant is very hardy. It needs sunlight, regular watering and good drainage. It can be grown in a pot on a sunny patio or, even, on a sunlit windowsill. The plant is effective in repelling garden pests. Even when quite small, the plant bears an abundance of fruit if picked regularly. Chillies can be plucked when green or left on the plant to redden (mature).

## CORIANDER

Coriander or cilantro, as it is often referred to in the

southwestern United States, is found fresh in the produce section of supermarkets. In those areas where it cannot be found, it can be ordered in pots from herb nurseries. It grows in the same manner as parsley and is prepared and used in the same way.

The roots, important in Thai cooking, are a culinary ingredient unique to the country. In Thailand, coriander is bought with long, trailing roots, but here the produce managers order them cut off for esthetic reasons. If you pick over all the bunches in the coriander bin, you may find some that sport partial root remnants. Buy these, even extra bunches, because these partial roots, valuable and scarce, can be cut off and stored for future use. When cleaning and despite whatever other use I planned, I immediately cut off the roots and one-quarter-inch of the stem directly above, wash and dry carefully and place in a small freezer container. When frozen and defrosted they appear soggy, but the flavor is not affected. Because of the amount of roots necessary for Siamese Fried Chicken *(Kai Tord)*, for instance, I keep adding to my precious hoard every time I market.

The stems and leaves should be washed to remove any grit or dirt, then shaken dry. They can be kept successfully for a week in the refrigerator, standing in a jar of water and covered with a plastic bag or, merely, placed in a plastic bag and put in the vegetable drawer.

If fresh coriander is not available, dried leaves, available from mail-order sources, can be used in cooked dishes. Fresh parsley or mint can be substituted for garnishes.

## LEMON GRASS

Lemon grass has a marvelous lemony flavor, similar to lemon balm, and is one of the ingredients which gives Thai dishes their characteristic, aromatic, lemon quality. Until a few years ago, it was grown in the United States only in Florida and was available for selected shipment. Now the plant is grown in many other areas because it is easy to propagate. Found fresh almost exclusively in the produce bins in Thai markets, lemon grass has the appearance of an elongated bulb with long, fibrous leaves; slightly larger than a green onion (see Glossary, page 281).

If you wish to grow your own, select fresh plants which have vestiges of roots. The plants so endowed can be put in a jar of water until the roots develop and then planted in large pots—they need room to spread. As they grow, they form side plants attached to a common base. To pick from your own batch, use a sharp knife to section needed stalks, one by one, cutting downward into the soil, leaving the remaining shoots intact.

Where fresh lemon grass is not obtainable, packets of the dried stems or powdered lemon grass may be substituted. The dried pieces should be first soaked in hot water before using; the powder added directly during cooking. These convenient packets can be purchased directly or by mail-order from Thai and Oriental food specialty stores.

## FLOWER FLAVORINGS AND ESSENCES

The Thai have traditionally flavored their sweets and desserts with blossoms or the smoke of scented candles. Cakes and other desserts were either put in a closed container with highly scented flowers, such as jasmine or roses, or placed in a container with a smoking, perfumed candle so the odor permeated the dish.

Some sweets and desserts were originally colored and flavored with a solution of crushed, green Pandanus leaves *(Bai Toey)* and water. *Lamciak, Pandanus Tectorius,* branched screwpine flowers, were also used for perfuming desserts. *Anjan* flowers (I cannot find an English equivalent or scientific name) were mixed with hot water, and the resultant, perfumed extract was kneaded into cake mixtures. *Anjan* produces a blue coloration; cochineal used for red.

We are now lucky to have short cuts available which even the most dedicated purist uses. Besides rose- and orange-blossom water, the Thai stores sell small bottles of other imported flavorings. One, *Yod Nam Nom Maeo,* is amylacetate ester and produces the flavor of old-fashioned pear drops. Another, which I use frequently is *Yod Nam Malee,* or jasmine oil. A few drops will delicately perfume any dessert.

Jasmine is much beloved by the Thai for its fragrance. I have often traveled in Bangkok taxis where the whole of the back windowsills have been strewn with masses of fresh, fragrant jasmine blossoms. Little *leis* or wrist garlands of jasmine are sold to motorists in the streets. Whenever a car stops at the traffic lights, throngs of children run up, their arms laden with dozens of garlands, and bargain vociferously with the motorists. Every taxi or *samlor* has a garland swinging from the rear-view mirror and most drivers replenish their garlands daily.

## ONION FLAKES

Many Thai dishes are garnished with crisp-fried onion flakes or crisp-fried minced garlic. The onerous task of frying these before preparing a recipe was alleviated when I found the Thai stores carry little plastic bags of ready-fried onion flakes. I marveled at the evenness of color and the fact that they were not greasy. Mine never seemed to attain that perfection. One day as I was experimenting in the kitchen, my eye caught sight of a large jar of commercial dried onion flakes, which I keep for occasional shortcuts. I heated a little oil in a frying pan and poured in some flakes. Shaking the pan well as they began to brown, I removed them quickly. Eureka! Perfectly fried onion flakes for garnishes. I discovered the product of my newfound technique would keep well in an airtight jar without refrigeration. As I experimented further, I found it was only necessary to lightly grease the pan, unless onion-flavored oil was also required in a recipe. I recommend removing the dried onions, while still cooking, before they have reached the desired degree of coloring—they continue to brown in the residual heat after removal from the range. I am now using this technique for dried garlic flakes with good results.

## DRIED FISH

Dried fish are considered a staple in a Thai larder. It is one of the few foods which keep without refrigeration in the tropical temperatures and humid climate of Thailand. Small herring-like fish are generally dried in the sun commercially and sold in the markets. They are quite salty and pungent and are eaten flaked and mixed with plain rice. They are also sold smoke-dried.

Dried fish can be bought in Thai stores in the United States. If you own a smoke oven, you may try smoking your own. I do not suggest, however, that you attempt sun-drying your own fish—you will antagonize your neighbors and alienate your family, if not by the unsightliness, certainly by the odor. However, you can achieve a reasonable facsimile by drying fish in an oven on the lowest setting for twenty-four to thirty-six hours.

## EGG THREAD NETS

While the technique of making egg thread nets is used only in four recipes, Pork Bundles, Pork Stuffed Bell Peppers, Shrimp Caught in a Net and Stuffed Eggs in a Net, it is a common and decorative enclosure with widespread applications beyond those I have specified.

Some recipes require the use of the whole, beaten egg, while others use only the yolk. Either way, it requires trailing beaten fresh eggs or their yolks with your fingers to produce a web or net in hot oil (instructions follow). I recommend, if you have the time, that you practice this technique in advance to develop your dexterity and discover the proper temperature.

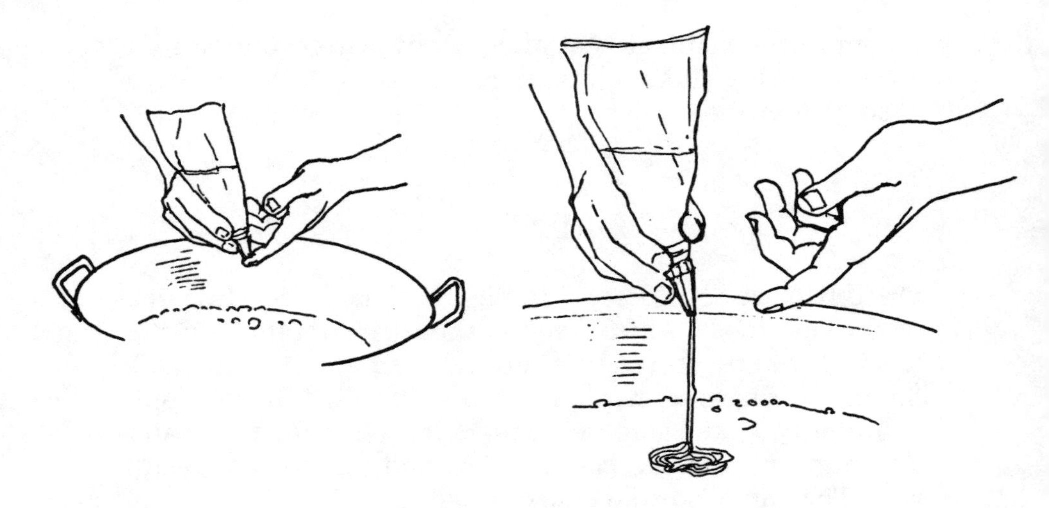

The temperature, of course, is of primary importance. Similar to making crepes, the first attempts are discarded while you modulate the heat. What you are trying to achieve is firmly set, just-cooked-through, yellow, elastic webbing. If the temperature of the oil is too high, the eggs will cook too quickly, the layers will not adhere to each other and will, probably, brown or darken. If too cool, the eggs will not cook through (reducing their elasticity) and may tend to disperse and coalesce, producing egg blobs with holes. I have not specified an exact oil temperature because (a) there is a wide range of oil temperatures that can produce successful nets, and (b) the temperature of the eggs (are they just out of the refrigerator?) affects the cooking time required and, in some cases, the results. Suffice it to say, you must repeatedly adjust and readjust the heat.

The process of trailing the eggs in the hot oil with your hands and fingers is of next consequence. When you are ready to begin and the oil is up to temperature, hold the bowl containing the eggs near, almost over, the heated oil. Dip your fingers, partially closed in a fist, in the eggs and in an even, unhurried motion, draw your hands across the oil, gradually releasing your fist and extending your fingers. Each finger will leave at least one egg trail, which begins to cook as it touches the oil. Quickly repeat this motion with any remaining in your hand and/or dip your hand back in the eggs, but change direction, at first, at least 90°. Continue this procedure until you have about four layers, doing your best not to burn your fingers in the oil. Remove the completed net with a spatula and drain on paper towels until ready to begin wrapping.

# FOUR
# Fruit and Vegetable Carving

The Thai are a very artistic race and have a deep appreciation for beauty and ornamentation. This is evident in the elaborate costumes of the classical Thai dancers and the intricate adornment of their temples. The presentation and decoration of dishes in a Thai meal is innate to the culture. It is an adaptation of the magic Japanese art of *Yasai.* Their salads, fresh vegetable dishes and fruit presentations are works of art transforming humble harvests into incredible edibles.

They fashion banana leaves into baskets and cups for food and use them for platters. Pumpkins and other gourds, melons, pineapples and papayas are carved in traditional designs and hollowed out to become containers for fruit salads, fried rice or sauces. When assembling a platter of raw vegetables for a party, the Thai will carve them into flowers, leaves and even fish and crab shapes. With the occasional, discreet application of food coloring, the whole array will then be assembled with the loving care and artistry implicit in a formal flower arrangement.

If you are skillful with your hands, you might like to try some decorative shapes for yourself. You will need a large bowl of iced water, a very sharp paring knife, a vegetable peeler and a substantial supply of time and patience.

CAUTION: There is no successful way to carve without using your hands in close proximity to a knife. From personal experience, I can attest to the acute danger even a small slip can pose. Please be extremely careful, or do the carving next door to an emergency room.

Here are some ideas:

## CUCUMBERS

Of course, the whole fruit can be halved and hollowed to make boat-like containers and the meat, after the seeds are removed, makes a nice medium for smaller carvings. However, the peel can be cut into interesting shapes for garnishing soups.

Using a vegetable peeler, carefully pare away a large section of skin. Cut it into rectangles approximately 2″ × 1″ and cut out of each a simple, pointed leaf shape. Draw the knife point down the center to approximate the main rib of the leaf. Then make shallow cuts on each side to simulate secondary ribs. Embellish the edges of the "leaf" with a series of serrations and drop it into a bowl of iced water until use.

The unpeeled cucumber can also be cut into decorative slices for garnish. With the tip of a knife, cut long, shallow *V*-shaped incisions down the entire length. These incisions should be spaced about one-quarter inch apart. When the *V* cuts have been completed around the circumference and the fruit is green-and-white striped, slice it into thin cross sections, which will then have attractive serrated edges. A quicker process to produce serrations is by firmly scoring the skin, lengthwise, with the tines of a fork. This, obviously, produces less dramatic results.

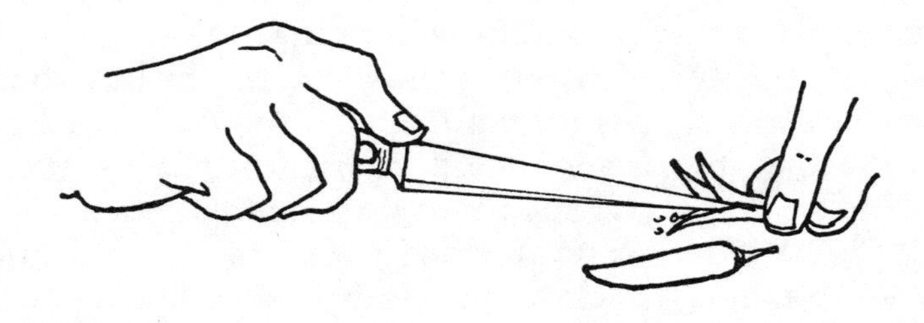

## CHILLIES

Chillies, cut into flower shapes, are a most common and popular garnish in Thai cooking. There are a handful (pun intended) of ways to accomplish this but I recommend, not necessarily use, the following: place any variety of pointed, fresh chilli on a cutting board. Secure the stem with your fingers and insert the point of a knife, with the blade outward, at the base, less than ⅛″ of the distance from the stem, and slice to the point of the fruit. Rotate the chilli 90° and repeat the slice. Remove the seeds. You will now have 4 pointed spears. To produce more slivers, bisect the existing 4 to 8 to 16, etc., until you have exhausted your patience or produced a fine, artist's brush. Drop your "flower" into iced water. After a few minutes you will notice the strands or "petals" curling outward. Usually the thinner the "petals," the more they will curl. Before attempting chilli "flowers," please read about chilli handling and seeding, chapter 3, "Fundamentals."

## RADISHES, TURNIPS AND CARROTS

These can be cut into daisies, even chrysanthemums, with skill and patience. Using a vegetable peeler, make a series of thin parings all the way around the root from the top almost to the bottom, leaving them connected at the base. Drop the vegetable into iced water and leave until the parings have started to curl away from the tip. When a layer of parings has curled, exposing the inside, remove it from the water and start a second, inner circle of parings

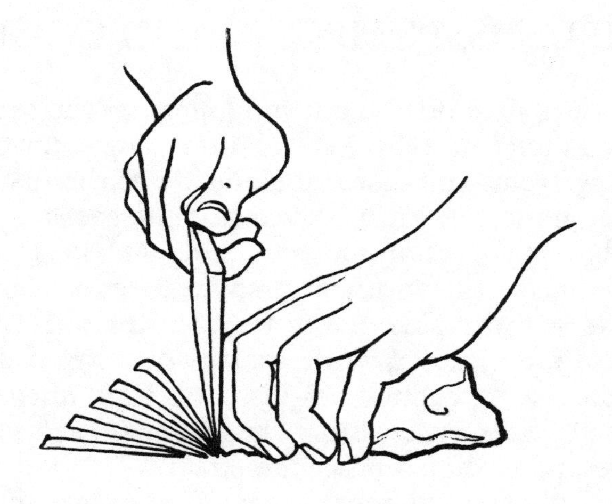

around the inner cone. Place the root back in the water until these, also, have curled. Repeat until the tip is reduced to a thin stick. This tip can be quartered lengthwise. Carefully place the completed flower in the water until ready to use.

## GREEN ONIONS

White or green, or double-ended, white/green tassels like party favors may be produced depending on (a) what color balance you desire for each dish and (b) the proportion of the bulb end to shoot on the individual onion. Use the same technique to produce onion tassels as in making chilli flowers, i.e., slicing, rotating, etc. For instance, to produce white tassels, clean the onion in the customary fashion by removing the outer layer and squarely slicing off the roots and some bulb. Now, where the white bulb begins to turn green, cut and discard the dark green ends. Presuming the greener portion is analogous to the stem end of a chilli, proceed repeatedly with the slicing and rotating. Finally, again, drop in iced water. After about 15 minutes in water you will have a miniature, white, curly chrysanthemum.

## MELONS, PUMPKINS AND GOURDS

Take a thin slice off the bottom (opposite the stem) so the fruit will stand upright. Section off one-quarter of the top, including stem, and discard. Hollow out the inside with a spoon or grapefruit knife, discarding the seeds. Around the top ridge make contiguous, equal *V*-shaped serrations. Adjust the depth, width and angle to suit your creative instincts and the size of the fruit. In a continuous circle around the perimeter, with the tip of a knife, below the serrations, score a circle of *V*'s. Continue until you have decorated the entire skin. The rings of scoring can be staggered producing a pinecone effect.

If you choose to be more creative, alternate the *V*'s with large curves. A brief study of traditional Thai design will yield endless suggestions; for instance, the lotus motif, relatively easy to execute and a predominant Thai form. Decorations are more visually effective when there is good contrast between the skin and meat.

When completed, cover and chill until ready to fill.

## PINEAPPLES

If you examine a pineapple carefully, you will see that the brown tufts on the rind are arranged in symmetrical rows which spiral around the fruit from bottom to top. These tufts can be excised and the fruit decoratively carved and peeled by cutting a shallow *V*-shaped furrow, following each spiral from bottom to top until that diagonal row of tufts has been removed. Start again at the bottom with the next spiral and continue until all the rows of tufts have been removed and the meat exposed. The pineapple will now be deeply carved in winding spiral cuts and ready to grace a fruit centerpiece. Alternatively, the fruit can be beheaded, hollowed out and filled with fried rice or some other interesting mixture.

FIVE

# Memo to the Cook

The art of Thai cooking is essentially one of creation, experimentation and improvisation. It has always been an oral tradition, handed down from family to family through generations. There are as many ways to make a dish as there are cooks to cook it. The recipes in this book will produce authentic and genuine Thai food. They will not, however, produce the exact replica of a specific dish which you ate last night in your favorite Thai restaurant. All Thai cooks are fiercely individualistic and creative and, after adhering to the basic principles, produce their own versions—hopefully a masterpiece. As you become more familiar with Thai food, both by eating out and by creating in your own kitchen, you will be able to detect the subtle changes and nuances in each dish. "Ah! He put a little *Ka* (see Glossary: Galangal) in the *Panaeng Neua*" and praise the ingenuity of the cook rather than damning the dish because it did not taste as you expected.

Unless you are steeped in the methods of Thai and Oriental cooking, I urge you to read this, along with the following segments before you embark on your first Thai cooking experience: Fundamentals, Pronunciation Guide, Vocabulary, Glossary, Sources and Suppliers—for information which will be *essential* to you. If you have difficulty locating any of the ingredients indicated in a recipe, consult the Glossary or "Fundamentals" for substitutes, which should prove satisfactory.

Although the preparation of Thai food is basically simple, the treatment and ingredients are somewhat unique. While, at first, the recipes herein seem difficult because of the number of ingredients and their unusual names, you will find that familiarity breeds affection. After a few attempts at the exotic, you will become friendly with methods, ingredients and dishes.

As with any cuisine, allowances should be made for the individual size, freshness, texture and quality of ingredients. We can emulate Thai shopping methods: if it is in season and looks fresh and appetizing, buy and cook it; if not, substitute ingredients or recipes. In my classes, I seldom plan the menus more than one week in advance because the excellence of the dish depends on the quality of the foodstuffs available. The difference in size between our super-fed, super-cosseted vegetables and the more skinny and hardy ones in Thailand is marked. In translating and reworking recipes I have had to make allowances for these biformities. In some cases I have indicated substitutions. If you want to improvise on a recipe, make sure you are familiar with the effect of the new ingredients, know the quantity to use, and are acquainted with the taste of the finished dish. By all means, use your "kitchen common sense": allow for inevitable differences between your stove (range) and mine; your refrigerator and mine; your pans and mine, etc.

For the proper use, care and preparation of your utensils (wok, cleaver, mortar and pestle, etc.), see the *Chinese Village Cookbook*, Taylor & Ng, Box 200, Brisbane, California (distributed by Random House), by Rhoda Yee, and *The Wok: A Chinese Cookbook*, Nitty Gritty Productions, Concord, California, by Gary Lee.

Because of local variations in age and quality, allowances must also be made in the cooking times of various ingredients, such as meat, fish and vegetables. If the meat or fish appears it will become overcooked to your taste, remove it and continue with the next steps before putting it back into the wok toward the end of the cooking period. There is no substitute for plain common sense and experience in a kitchen. If you have a favorite and well-tested cooking principle, do not hesitate to experiment and try it in a recipe. From my students, I have learnt many marvelous tips and tricks that I include. Each recipe is merely a starting point of a journey, hopefully, into the sublime.

I caution you, as I do my students, to thoroughly read each recipe in its entirety before starting, then methodically arrange and order the ingredients, with whatever preparation they require. Carefully check the list of ingredients to make sure you have not omitted anything—when you are in the middle of a fast stir-fry, it is too late to leave the wok and hurriedly peel and chop garlic.

To paraphrase Edison, the division of labor for a Thai meal, from refrigerator to serving is "Ten percent inspiration (improvisational cooking), ninety percent preparation." This formula, of course, does not include the sometimes considerable effort that may be required to locate and acquire certain esoteric ingredients.

Many students tell me they love cooking Thai food but how can they possibly put a Thai meal together on a working night? Careful study of the recipes and menu-planning will provide the answer.

Most dishes can be semiprepared in advance and finished assembly/cooking accomplished just before serving. Examine the recipe carefully for a convenient breaking-off point, prepare to that point and set aside for final cooking. For instance, with *Mussaman* Curry (page 137), make the Paste in the morning, boil the beef and seasonings until tender, cover and refrigerate until the evening's meal. Or you may remove the beef and reduce the gravy (a lengthy, tedious process), recombine the meat and refrigerate until recommencing. There are usually several options in any recipe to discontinue the cooking and these, if chosen, can substantially reduce your last-minute flurry.

I recommend the following for those who cannot or do not choose to spend extravagant amounts of time in the kitchen: salads can be arranged and refrigerated the night before, then tossed in their dressing and sprinkled with preprepared garnishes; curries macerate nicely during overnight refrigeration and become more flavorful in the process; cold, cooked rice and vegetables can be smartly revitalized in a steamer; coconut milk freezes conveniently for future use (the small, Ziploc bags comfortably contain two cups liquid and freeze and stack neatly); ample amounts of Curry Pastes, made in advance, tightly covered, store well for over a month in the refrigerator.

A few words about my basic terminology: when I refer to garlic, onions or shallots, I assume they will have been peeled first. Unless otherwise specified, conclude the use of the whole stalk of lemon grass but, only the first one-third or one-half of a green onion. My spelling for hot, *Capsicum* peppers is "chilli" to differentiate from the American/ Mexican Chile and Chile Con Carne mixtures and because it is common spelling in the Far East. Coriander is always the fresh plant unless seeds are specified.

I think it was Shaw who referred to England and America as "two countries, separated by the same language." While translating the Thai into English, I have also had to translate my English into American!

I sincerely hope you will have as much fun in preparing and eating these recipes as I have in cooking and teaching them.

## METRIC CONVERSIONS

When I began to prepare this table, I became aware that conventional mensuration equivalents from, heretofore considered, reliable sources would not be sufficient or appropriate. Apart from the fact that many references were grossly inaccurate and disagreed with each other, none of them specifically applied to the volumetric/weight conversions of unusual ingredients which are called for in this book.

Therefore, except for the standard, simple arithmetic conversions (1 liter equals 1.05671 quarts, etc.), I have empirically tested *all* the conversions and, where applicable, rounded them off to the nearest 5 grams—one gram is the weight of a small fingernail clipping! (All conversions are approximate except where indicated by a decimal point.)

Please use your kitchen common sense when converting: (1) as stated before, consistent with the Thai philosophy of experimentation and improvisation, these recipes and the amount of the individual ingredients should act as a starting point to begin your own catalog of Thai cuisine, and (2) the conversions are open for interpretation—you may tamp your bean sprouts more firmly in a cup before weighing them than I did.

Here, then, are my tables; tailored exclusively for each recipe:

## GENERAL

### *Liquid and Dry Volume*

United States

| | |
|---|---|
| 1 U.S. tablespoon | =3.0 U.S. teaspoons |
| 2 U.S. tablespoons | =1.0 U.S. ounce |
| 8 U.S. ounces | =1.0 U.S. cup |
| 48 U.S. teaspoons | =1.0 U.S. cup |
| 16 U.S. tablespoons | =1.0 U.S. cup |
| 2 U.S. cups | =1.0 U.S. pint |
| 2 U.S. pints | =1.0 U.S. quart |
| 4 U.S. quarts | =1.0 U.S. gallon |

## International System (Metric)

| | |
|---|---|
| 1 U.S. teaspoon | =5 milliliters |
| 1 U.S. tablespoon | =15 milliliters |
| 1 U.S. cup | =¼ liter or 250 milliliters |
| 1 U.S. pint | =0.4732 liters |
| 1 U.S. quart | =0.9463 liters |
| 1 U.S. gallon | =3.7853 liters |
| 4 U.S. cups | =1 liter |

## *Temperature*

$\frac{(F^\circ - 32)}{9} \times 5 = C^\circ$ is the formula for the exact conversion of Fahrenheit to Celsius. Following are the most frequently occurring equivalents.

| | |
|---|---|
| 185° F. | = 85° C. |
| 200° F. | = 93° C. |
| 350° F. | = 177° C. |
| 375° F. | = 190° C. |
| 450° F. | = 232° C. |

## *Weight (Avoirdupois)*

For quick conversions I use 30 grams/ounce, 450 grams/pound and 2¼ pounds/kilogram. However, I have listed the exact equivalents for the curious.

| | |
|---|---|
| 1 ounce | = 28.34952 grams |
| 1 pound | = 453.59237 grams |
| 2.20462 pounds | = 1 kilogram |
| 1000 grams | = 1 kilogram |

*Linear*

For absolute precision, use 2.540005 × no. inches = centimeters.

| | |
|---|---|
| 1/8 inch | = 3/10 centimeter |
| 1/4 inch | = 3/5 centimeter |
| 1 inch | = 2½ centimeters |
| 2 inches | = 5 centimeters |

## SPECIFIC

*United States Liquid and Dry Volume to Metric Weight*

| | |
|---|---|
| 1 cup sliced, diced or ground meat | = 220 grams |
| 1 generous cup green (raw), medium shrimp, shelled and deveined | = 180 grams |
| 1 generous cup cooked Bay shrimp | = 160 grams |
| 6 ounces (avoirdupois) cooked Bay shrimp | = 170 grams |
| 1 cup cooked, shredded crabmeat | = 210 grams |
| 1 cup raw fish fillets | = 180 grams |
| 1 cup granulated sugar | = 220 grams |
| 1 cup coarse brown or palm sugar | = 160 grams |
| 1 cup desiccated, flaked coconut | = 65 grams |
| 1 cup desiccated, sweetened flaked coconut | = 75 grams |
| 1 cup long grain or glutinous rice | = 220 grams |
| 1 cup all-purpose, rice or tapioca flour | = 170 grams |
| 1 cup roasted, pounded peanuts | = 180 grams |
| 1 cup sunflower seeds | = 140 grams |
| 1 cup roasted sesame seeds | = 160 grams |
| 1 cup raisins | = 160 grams |
| 1 cup bean curd, drained | = 120 grams |
| 1 cup bamboo shoots, drained and sliced | = 170 grams |

| | |
|---|---|
| 1 cup dried onion flakes, fried | = 130 grams |
| 1 cup bean sprouts, washed and drained | = 80 grams |
| 1 cup fresh green beans, chopped | = 115 grams |
| 1 cup cabbage, shredded and firmly packed | = 110 grams |
| 1 cup fresh broccoli, sliced | = 100 grams |
| 1 cup cauliflower, cut into flowerets | = 125 grams |
| 1 cup Chinese snow peas | = 100 grams |
| 1 cup corn kernels | = 125 grams |

# SIX
# Menus

Thai food, like most Oriental food, does not lend itself easily to portion counting. It is not the Thai way of hospitality. If extra guests are expected to dinner, extra dishes are cooked; the amount of rice increased. This philosophy is evident in the menus I have suggested.

For Western cooks, however, I have indicated the number of portions to each recipe. The lower value indicates the servings when the dish is accompanied merely by rice and perhaps one other dish. The higher suggests the servings when the meal is four or five dishes. Of course, there are other variables such as appetites, capacities and the chilli heat of the food. The hotter the dish, the more rice consumed and the smaller the serving.

For *hors d'oeuvres* and snacks, I would allow at least two to three per person; more if no additional *hors d'oeuvres* are served. Allow one cup of soup, including solids, per person; less, if the soup is served as part of a large meal.

When serving curries, cook about one-quarter to one-third pound of meat or other solids per person. The Thai

# COMPOSITION OF A CLASSIC THAI MEAL

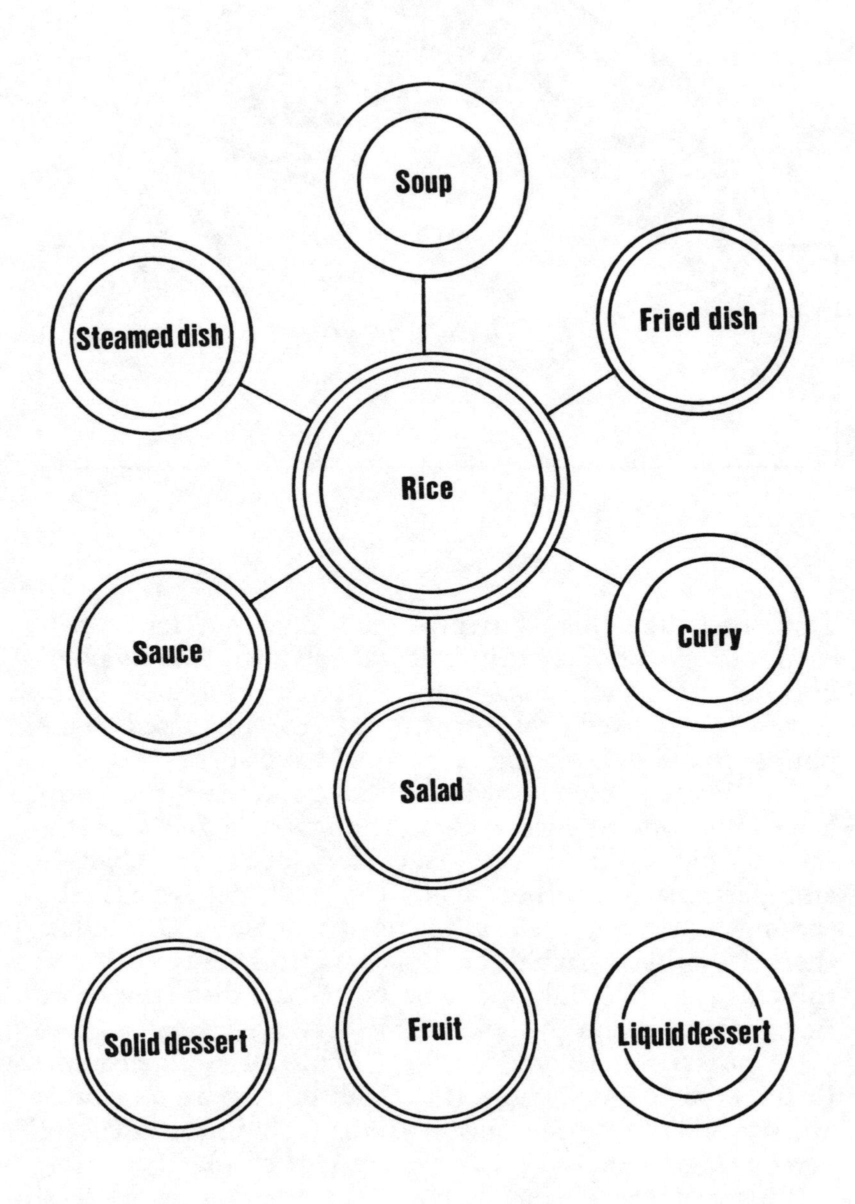

would use less per person but there would be an abundance of hot, spicy gravy and the eaters would fill up with rice. Adopt this portion rule to other meat dishes.

When a whole fish is served, people will tend to help themselves to about one-quarter pound each. If the fish is filleted, people tend to eat more. A good rule for salads is about one-third cup per guest. The equivalent of one cup per person seems to be adequate for noodle dishes. Thai sauces are concentrated and pungent. I have observed that my students will help themselves to between one teaspoon and one tablespoon during the meal. Desserts, of course, will depend on whether your guests have a sweet tooth. Allow more for young adults.

## THAI MEALS

| | |
|---|---|
| Dinner for 4, I | Green Curry of Duck, GAENG KEO WAN PET 140 |
| | Steamed Yellow Fillets, PLA NERNG LEUNG 184 |
| | Combination Thai Fried Rice, KAO PAD 104 |
| | Fresh Fruit Platter |
| Dinner for 4, II | Hot and Sour Shrimp Soup, DOM YAM GUNG 110 |
| | Chilli Chicken, PANAENG KRUANG DON 165 |
| | Rice, KAO 44 |
| | Siamese Watercress Salad, PAK SIAM 204 |
| | Chilled Lichees in Custard, LEENCHEE LOI MEK 253 |

| | |
|---|---|
| Dinner for 4, III | Fried Fillets in Tamarind Sauce, PLA CHIEN 182<br>Stuffed Zucchini or Cucumber, FAN TIENG 238<br>Korat Beef Curry, GAENG PED KORAT 144<br>Rice, KAO 44<br>Thai Coffee, CA FE 265 |
| Dinner for 4, IV | Thai Beef Salad, YAM NEUA 199<br>Fried Pork and Long Beans; MOO PAD TUA FAK YAW 160<br>Steamed and Fried Crab Cakes, POO CHA 189<br>Sweet and Hot Chilli Sauce, SAUS PRIK 224<br>Rice, KAO 44<br>Thai Coffee, CA FE 265 |
| Dinner for 6, I | Thai Muslim Curry, GAENG MUSSAMAN 137<br>Rice, KAO 44<br>Thai Crisp-Fried Noodles, MEE KROB 232<br>Papaya and Shrimp Salad, SOM TAM 202<br>Chicken with Ginger, GAI KING 169<br>Tapioca and Coconut Creams, TAKAW 256 |
| Dinner for 6, II | Fish Curry Soup, NAM YAR PA 193<br>Fried Rice with Chicken, KAO PAD GAI 105<br>Chopped Beef with Garnishes, LAAP ISSAN 152<br>Steamed Stuffed Onions, HUA HOM SOD SAI 240 |

| | |
|---|---|
| | Mangoes and Sticky Rice, MAMUANG KAO NIEO 251 |
| | Thai Coffee, CA FE 265 |
| Dinner for 6, III | Stuffed Chicken Wings, PEEK GAI YOD SAI 96 |
| | Bamboo Shoot and Pork Soup, GAENG CHUD NO MAI 112 |
| | Bangkok Noodles, SEN MEE KRUNG THEP 229 |
| | Oyster and Chilli Salad, PLA HOY NARNG ROM 207 |
| | Baked Custard Squares, KANOM MO KAENG 255 |
| Dinner for 6, IV | Red Beef Curry, GAENG PED NEUA 132 |
| | Rice, KAO 44 |
| | Siamese Fried Chicken, GAI TORD 167 |
| | Thai Hot Sauce, NAM PRIK 217 |
| | Korat Marinated Shrimp, KOI GUNG 190 |
| | Sautéed Greens, BAI GUP KAO 239 |
| | Thai Fried Bananas, KLUAY TORD 261 |
| A Formal Thai Dinner | Flim-Flan Fish, PLA SAMPANTAMIT 185 |
| | Chicken and Coconut Milk Soup, GAENG DOM YAM GAI 121 |
| | Beef Balls in Peanut Sauce, PANAENG NEUA 79 |
| | Shrimp and Cucumber Curry, GAENG PED TAET 135 |
| | Gala Salad, PAK SOD 208 |
| | Hot Sauce Dip, NAM PRIK ONG 221 |

Rice, KAO 44
Thai Silk, FOI TONG 257
Bananas in Coconut Milk, KLUAY BUAT CHEE 252
Fresh Fruit Platter

A Thai Buffet

Sate, SATAY 80
Sweet and Sour Fresh Cucumber, TAENG KWA BRIO WAN 245
Galloping Horses, MA HO 82
Fried Rice with Pineapple, KAO PAD SUPPAROT 106
Steamed Fish Curry, HAW MOK 183
Roast Red Pork, MOO DAENG 157
Fried Stuffed Prawn (Shrimp), GUNG TIPAROT 195
Cucumber Boats, YAM NEUA LAE TAENG KWA 206
Three Chum Cakes, KANOM SAM KLOE 259
Fresh Fruit Platter

*Family reunion:*
*Evening cicadas*
*Starting up in the trees*
NAKAMURA KUSADAO

SEVEN

# Appetizers and Snacks

## GUP KLEM, KONG TAN LEN

The Thai love parties and celebrations. In the large and closely knit family clans, there is always someone having a birthday, there is a visitor to be entertained or a festival to be celebrated.

As the day begins to cool, tables are set up in the garden and spread with snacks. Tin tubs, filled with clinking bottles of soda pop and beer resting on ice, are brought out and the party begins. If it is any sort of occasion there are always long speeches punctuated by enthusiastic applause and much laughter. The eating and drinking continues. The daughters of the house run in and out replenishing the trays of food. The menfolk gather around the table, which carries the Singha beer, Amarit lager and Mekong or White Cock local whiskies. Soon there is music, either from the radio or, if it is a grand occasion, musicians will begin to play. Everyone dances, except the family matriarchs sitting on the perimeter in a dignified cluster, hands folded on laps and legs sedately crossed at the ankles. They keep up a running commentary on the party, interspersed with gossip and fortified by glasses of Green Spot orange soda pop. Distant cousins cross over to pay their respects to elder relatives, hands raised in a *wai,* palms together in front of the face. This gesture is accompanied by a respectful bow of the head to the senior family member.

As the lights or lanterns are lit, the mosquitoes and gnats arrive and hover in swarms, but no one seems to notice or mind. The dancers are joining in a *Ram Wong,* a traditional dance where the couples rotate around each other, never touching, while progressing in a large circle. Even the children join in. Now a young man requests that the musicians play some Occidental songs and a few young couples shyly take to the floor. The party continues until late and someone's uncle has to be gently supported home, having drunk too much Mekong. Gradually it ends and people make their farewells, emptying the garden and leaving it to the mosquitoes, crickets and croaking bull-frogs in the nearby river.

The Thai eat when they are hungry and will snack five or six times throughout the day. Most of the snacks are bought from the food vendors who appear at the garden gate at regular and exact times during the day. Each vendor has his own call or sound that he makes to alert the community of his arrival. A stentorian cry of something that sounds like *"OW KEP POO MALAKAAP"* announces the arrival of the fruit vendor selling luscious slices of papaya. The soup vendor clacks hollow pieces of bamboo together; the cake man rings his bicycle bell. This succession of cries and noises breaks the early-morning quiet of the lanes and pierces the afternoon siesta.

My own children soon learnt the processional order and besieged the house with requests for "Just three baht, Mummy!" then they would scamper out of the gate to stand in a cluster with the Thai children round the vendor's cart, devouring such delicacies as sour mango dipped in sugar and pepper or sticky and highly colored sweets; sweet mangoes and glutinous rice or sticks of *Satay,* complete with little plastic bags of cucumber relish. Even the bags that the snacks are placed in are a fascinating item as recycling is the order of the day. Your bag can be fashioned from a page of someone's homework book, while mine is a highly colored comic strip of the exploits of a Thai hero. Life is never boring, even to the house-bound. A whole colorful pageant passes by every day, right outside the garden gate.

•

## FRIED MEAT BALLS · TORD MAN NEUA

*4 Servings*

- 1 *cup ground pork*
- ½ *cup ground beef*
- 10 *black peppercorns or ½ teaspoon cracked black pepper*
- 4 *coriander roots*
- 6 *cloves garlic, chopped*
- ½ *teaspoon ground nutmeg*
- 2 *green onions, finely chopped*
- 2 *tablespoons fish sauce* (Nam Pla, *see Glossary)*
- 2 *tablespoons coriander leaves, finely chopped*
- 2 *eggs, beaten*
- *Flour for coating*
- *Vegetable oil for deep frying*

In a bowl, mix together the two meats until well blended.

In a mortar, pound together the peppercorns, coriander roots and garlic into a juicy paste. Add this mixture to the meats in a bowl. Stir in the nutmeg, green onions, fish sauce, coriander leaves and beaten eggs. Knead all these ingredients thoroughly. Form into firm balls, 1" in diameter. Lightly dust the balls with flour.

Heat the oil in a wok until a haze appears and fry the balls, three or four at a time, until golden brown. Drain on paper towels and serve hot on toothpicks with homemade chilli or the commercially available *Siracha* sauce for dipping.

## PORK AND SHRIMP TOAST · KANOM PAN NAR MOO

*8 to 10 Servings*

Our cook in Thailand introduced me to this snack and I found it delightful. It was also an instant hit with my children. When two of my students here got married last year, they requested that I cook Thai food for the wedding reception. This was one of the dishes that I chose and it was rewarding to see all the relatives and guests, most of whom had probably never tasted Oriental food before, let alone Thai, consuming the *Kanom Pan Nar Moo* with gusto.

2 *tablespoons coriander, including roots, finely chopped*
1 *teaspoon ground black pepper*
3 *cloves garlic, finely chopped*
1 *pound ground pork*
½ *cup cooked Bay shrimp, finely chopped*
3 *green onions, including tops, finely chopped*
1 *tablespoon shrimp powder*
1 *tablespoon fish sauce* (Nam Pla)
½ *teaspoon salt*
1 *egg, beaten*
10 *slices stale bread, crust trimmed*
*Vegetable oil for deep frying*
*Coriander sprigs for garnish*

In a food processor or mortar grind or pound together the coriander, black pepper and garlic until the mixture becomes a paste. Turn the paste into a large bowl and add the pork, shrimp, green onions, shrimp powder, fish sauce, salt and the beaten egg.

Knead and squeeze the mixture thoroughly until all the ingredients are completely combined and the mass has a paste-like consistency. Cover the bread slices with the pork/shrimp mixture to the depth of about ½", making sure the mixture is evenly spread to the edges of the bread. Cut the spread bread into squares or triangles. Heat the vegetable oil until almost smoking, or 375°F., in a wok and fry the bread pieces, two or three at a time, introducing them into the oil meat side down.

Fry on each side until crisp brown and remove with a slotted spoon, shaking well and draining over the wok before draining on a dish lined with paper towels.

The pork toasts should retain no grease; this can only be achieved by letting the oil come back to full temperature each time and draining and blotting well.

After frying each lot, place in a dish in a warm oven and serve hot, garnished with coriander sprigs.

•

## BEEF BALLS IN PEANUT SAUCE · PANAENG NEUA

*4 to 6 Servings*

*Panaeng Neua* is sold by the Thai street vendors as an occasional snack. It is also commonly served as one of the dishes to complement a Thai dinner. This rich curry/peanut sauce transforms the plain meatballs into a savory delight. It is delicious and *farangs,* Westerners living in Thailand, find it a popular cocktail *hors d'oeuvre.*

- 1 *pound medium lean ground beef*
- ½ *cup all-purpose flour*
- 2 *tablespoons vegetable oil*
- 4 *cloves garlic, coarsely chopped*
- 2 *tablespoons red curry paste* (Krung Gaeng Ped)
- 1 *cup "Thick" coconut milk*
- 2 *tablespoons chunky peanut butter or ground peanuts*
- 1½ *tablespoons granulated sugar*
- 2 *tablespoons fish sauce* (Nam Pla)
- 1 *teaspoon fresh mint or sweet basil leaves, chopped*

Shape the beef into small, firm balls about 1" in diameter. Press and roll the balls in the flour, dusting off the excess. Heat the oil in a wok until a haze forms and fry the garlic for 1 minute. Add the floured meatballs and continue frying until brown, stirring and tilting the wok to cook the balls uniformly. Remove with a slotted spoon and drain on paper towels. In the remainder of the oil in the wok, fry the Red Curry Paste for about 2 minutes, stirring well to prevent sticking. Add the "Thick" coconut milk and stir in the peanut butter. Continue cooking and stirring until you have a smooth, uniform consistency. Season with sugar and fish sauce. Return the meatballs to the sauce and simmer over low heat for 5 minutes or until they return to temperature. Remove to a serving dish and garnish with mint or sweet basil sprinkled over the top.

•

## SATE · SATAY

*6 Servings*

The generic term Sate refers more to a fashion of cooking, barbecued on skewers, rather than a specific dish or food.

Southeast Asians, as other Orientals, have great difficulty pronouncing any two consonants together, particularly *s* in conjunction with *t* or *p*. (The popular soda pop in Thailand, Green Spot, generally is heard as "Galeen Supot.") The common reference is that the name *Satay* is merely a corruption stemming from Asian attempts at the word "steak." *Satay* is indigenous to Indonesia but this way of cooking has spread up through Malaysia and is commonplace in Thailand. Thai restaurants, here in the United States, almost universally feature *Satay* on their menus, causing many Americans to believe that it is an original Thai specialty.

1 *pound beef, pork or chicken, very thinly sliced and cut into strips ½" wide × 2" long*

### *Marinade*

2 *cloves garlic, smashed and chopped*
½ *onion, chopped*
1 *tablespoon palm or brown sugar*
*Juice of 1 lime*
1 *tablespoon fish sauce* (Nam Pla)
½ *teaspoon tamarind pulp, dissolved in 2 tablespoons hot water*
1 *tablespoon vegetable oil*

### *Sauce*

8 *tablespoons crunchy peanut butter*
1 *onion, finely chopped*
1 *cup "Thick" coconut milk*
1 *tablespoon palm or brown sugar*
1 *teaspoon red chilli powder (Cayenne)*
1 *stalk lemon grass, finely chopped*
1 *tablespoon fish sauce* (Nam Pla)
1 *tablespoon dark, sweet soy sauce*

Place all the Marinade ingredients in a food processor or blender and process or blend until smooth. Thread the meat strips like a ribbon on 12" wooden skewers, 3 or 4 to each stick, and place in a large, shallow dish. Pour the Marinade over the *Satay* and let stand for 30 to 60 minutes, rotating each stick occasionally.

If cooking over charcoal, light the coals and let them come to a temperature that creates a white, chalky film. If using a broiler, turn it on and let it come to a full heat for at least 10 minutes before you start to grill or broil. The *Satay* should be grilled, barbecued or broiled near high heat.

In a saucepan, combine all the Sauce ingredients and bring to a boil, stirring. Remove from heat and pour into small bowls for accompaniment.

Remove the *Satay* from the Marinade and cook fiercely and quickly. (The cooking time will vary with the type and density of meat used, the amount of heat and proximity thereto, but should never exceed a total of 5 minutes for all sides.)

Serve with the Sauce, and side bowls of *Taeng Kwa Brio Wan.*

•

## GALLOPING HORSES · MA HO

*8 to 10 Servings*

This delightful snack makes a popular treat, both here and abroad. *Ma Ho* is an interesting contrast in both color and texture between the fruit segments and pork/peanut mixture topped with the chillies and coriander or mint.

- 3 *tangerines, peeled and separated into segments**
- 2 *tablespoons peanut oil*
- 4 *cloves garlic, finely chopped*
- 2 *shallots, finely chopped*
- 1 *pound ground pork*
- 1 *teaspoon salt*
- 1 *teaspoon ground black pepper*
- ¼ *cup granulated sugar*
- ½ *cup roasted peanuts, coarsely pounded*
- 2 *red Serrano chillies, seeded and cut into slivers*
- *Mint or coriander leaves for garnish*

Remove the pith and white fibers from the tangerine segments. Cut each down the back, as if deveining a shrimp, splitting it so it opens into a connected circle. Lay the tangerine circles on a platter.

In a wok, heat the oil and fry the garlic and shallots until light brown. Add the pork, salt, pepper and sugar and stir-

*An equivalent amount and size of canned or fresh pineapple is frequently substituted in Thailand.

fry until the pork is cooked through (about 4 to 5 minutes).

Stir in the peanuts and mix thoroughly. Remove from heat. Place a heaped teaspoonful of the pork/peanut mixture on each segment. Decorate with chilli slivers and a sprig of mint or coriander leaves.

Chill until ready to serve.

•

## FAT HORSES · MA UON

*4 to 6 Servings*

*Ma Uon* is a classical Thai snack. Authentically, cups are fashioned from banana leaves and the meat mixture is steamed therein. Small paper, plastic or Pyrex cups can be substituted.

- ½ *cup ground pork*
- 1 *whole chicken breast, skinned, boned and finely chopped*
- ½ *cup cooked crabmeat, shredded*
- 1 *tablespoon coriander roots, chopped*
- 1 *teaspoon black peppercorns*
- 4 *cloves garlic, chopped*
- 1 *tablespoon palm sugar*
- 1 *tablespoon fish sauce* (Nam Pla)
- 2 *tablespoons coconut "Cream"*
- 2 *eggs, beaten until foamy*
- 1 *green onion, finely chopped*
- *Coriander leaves for garnish*

In a food processor, process the meats together until they have a smooth, even consistency. In a mortar, pound together the coriander roots, peppercorns and garlic to a juicy paste. Add the contents of the mortar to the processor along with palm sugar, fish sauce, coconut "Cream" and eggs, reserving 1 tablespoon of the egg mixture. Give the processor a few more turns to completely blend everything together. Heap the contents of the processor into whichever receptacles (greased) you have chosen and brush the top of each lightly with the reserved egg. Sprinkle the cups with green onion.

Heat the water in a steamer until boiling and arrange the cups inside. Steam until the mixture is set and firm. (The length of time will depend on the size of the cups and amount of mixture in each.) Cool.

Invert the cups over a platter and tap gently to remove the little cakes. Garnish with coriander leaves and serve.

•

## PORK BUNDLES · RUM

*4 to 6 Servings*

*Rum* is a delicious finger food with the added piquancy of pickled garlic. As regards pickled garlic, this is one instance where I recommend store-bought over homemade for its texture and the authenticity it brings to the recipe (see "Fundamentals," chapter 3).

- 1 *tablespoon peanut oil*
- ½ *pound ground pork*
- 2 *tablespoons fish sauce* (Nam Pla)
- 1 *tablespoon superfine granulated sugar*
- 3 *tablespoons vegetable oil*
- 4 *eggs, beaten*
- 20 to 30 *coriander leaves*
- 3 *red Serrano chillies, seeded and cut into slivers*

1 *pod of pickled garlic, cut into paper-thin slices*
*Coriander sprigs for decoration*

Heat the peanut oil in a wok and fry the pork until brown. Stir in the fish sauce and sugar. Mix thoroughly, then turn the mixture onto a plate to cool. Wipe out the wok, pour in the vegetable oil and bring to medium heat. Dip your fingers in the beaten eggs and quickly trail them across the oil, first in one direction and then repeat, crossing the first threads at right angles. Continue until you have 4 layers and use a spatula to remove the netting and drain on paper towels. Repeat making nets until the eggs are used up (see "Fundamentals," chapter 3).

Take a teaspoon of the cooked pork mixture and lay it on the center of a net. Place a few coriander leaves on top and a slice of pickled garlic. Follow with 2 strips of chilli forming an *X*.

Carefully fold the net around the pork to form a small bundle, like a parcel. Continue making bundles until all the pork is utilized. Lay the bundles on a serving dish and decorate with coriander sprigs.

•

## STUFFED EGGS PRATOOM · KAI KWAM PRATOOM

*4 to 6 Servings*

Pratoom was my first Thai maid. She had a round, dimpled, smiling face, a mop of unruly black curls, and a quick wit.

When I first arrived in Thailand, I lived in an enormous house, joining families with my mother's existing household. Pratoom applied for the position of second maid and was brought in by virtue of the fact she was the Number One maid's younger sister. When I set up my own household and moved down the lane to a smaller house, Pratoom, affectionately abbreviated to "Toomie," was installed in splendor as Number One and, although she had never mentioned she could cook, developed considerable talents in that direction and was soon setting both European and Thai dishes before us with equal aplomb. Toomie's fried, stuffed eggs appeared on the first occasion we entertained and were a regular favorite after that, particularly with Jonathan, my son.

½ *cup all-purpose flour*
½ *cup water*
2 *teaspoons vegetable oil*
½ *teaspoon salt*
8 *eggs, hardcooked, peeled, halved, yolks and whites separated*
1 *cup cooked crabmeat*
1 *cup ground pork, cooked*
1 *tablespoon coriander leaves, finely chopped*
½ *teaspoon ground black pepper*
½ *teaspoon salt*
1 *teaspoon granulated sugar*
1 *tablespoon fish sauce* (Nam Pla)
2 *tablespoons coconut "Cream"*
*Oil for deep-frying*

In a bowl, mix together the flour, water, oil and salt, beating into a smooth batter. Set aside.

Scoop the egg yolks into another bowl and mash with a fork adding the crabmeat, pork, coriander leaves, pepper, salt, sugar and fish sauce.

Mix together well, pouring in the coconut "Cream" to bind it.

Fill the egg halves with the crab/pork mixture, mounding and forming into the shape of a whole egg.

Heat the deep-frying oil in a wok to 375° F. Dip each egg shape in the batter and deep-fry until golden brown and blistered. When you initially introduce them in the oil, begin frying, filling side down.

When the eggs are cooked, never more than two or three at a time, remove with a slotted spoon and drain on paper towels.

Serve warm or cold, either as a cocktail snack or side dish. Any of the *Nam Prik* sauces may be used as an accompaniment.

•

## SALTED EGGS · KAI KEM

A Thai way to preserve eggs without refrigeration, *Kai Kem* are sliced and used for garnish or as part of an *hors d'oeuvre* tray. The yolks are also a component of *Prik King*, a highly flavored dry curry. These eggs are preserved raw and, then, hardcooked before use.

- 1 *cup salt*
- 4 *quarts water*
- 12 *large whole eggs*

In a large saucepan, bring salt and water to a boil. Remove from heat and cool until lukewarm. Place the eggs in a large earthenware crock with a lid, or in a large glass jar. Pour the saltwater over the eggs, covering them completely. Cover the jar or crock and let stand in a cool place for at least 1 month.

## QUAIL EGG FLOWERS · DOK MAI KAI NOK KRA TA

*4 to 6 Servings*

6 *small, egg or pickling, cucumbers or 6 zucchini*
3 *tablespoons white vinegar*
2 *tablespoons granulated sugar*
1 *teaspoon salt*
½ *cup water*
1 *teaspoon garlic, finely chopped*
1 *teaspoon black peppercorns*
1 *teaspoon coriander roots*
1 *tablespoon vegetable oil for frying*
4 *tablespoons dark soy sauce*
1 *tablespoon granulated sugar*
12 *fresh quail eggs, hardcooked and peeled, or 12 canned, cooked quail eggs*

Cut 1" off from both ends of the cucumbers or zucchini and discard the center section. Hollow out these ends with a sharp paring knife. Cut large *V*-shapes around the edge so the vegetable ends look like flowers or sepals, 4 or 5 "petals" to each.

Combine the vinegar, sugar, salt and water in a bowl and drop in the cucumber "flowers" to marinate for at least 10 minutes.

In a mortar, pound the garlic, peppercorns and coriander roots to a paste. Using a wok or small saucepan, heat the oil and fry the paste for 1 minute, stirring. Add the soy sauce and sugar, continue on heat and when the mixture bubbles, put in the eggs and shake the pan so the eggs are coated with the sauce and turn a rich brown. Remove the pan from heat and set aside to cool.

To assemble the "flowers," place an egg inside each hollowed cucumber and pierce them through the bottom with a toothpick to form a stem and hold the two together.

**N.B.** This recipe can be adapted to hen's eggs, using larger, more commonly available cucumbers.

## SHRIMP CAUGHT IN A NET · LA TIENG

*4 to 6 Servings*

The preparation of the nets for this *hors d'oeuvre* is the same as the *Rum* bundles but the filling is shrimp-flavored with coriander and black pepper.

- 1 *tablespoon coriander roots, chopped*
- ½ *teaspoon black peppercorns*
- 1 *tablespoon peanut oil*
- ½ *pound green (raw) shrimp meat, finely chopped*
- 1 *tablespoon fish sauce* (Nam Pla)
- 3 *tablespoons vegetable oil*
- 4 *eggs, beaten*
- 20 to 30 *coriander leaves*
- 3 *red Serrano chillies, seeded and cut into slivers*
- 2 *limes, cut into wedges*
- *Coriander sprigs for decoration*

Pound the coriander roots and peppercorns into a fine paste in a mortar. Heat the peanut oil in a wok and fry the paste for 1 minute. Add the shrimp and stir for less than 1 minute. Stir in the fish sauce then remove the mixture to a plate to cool. Wipe out the wok, pour in the vegetable oil and bring to medium heat. Make egg nets as in "Fundamentals," chapter 3.

Fold the nets around individual portions of the shrimp filling (approximately 1 tablespoon) with coriander leaves and 2 chilli slivers inside.

Arrange the bundles on a platter and garnish with lime wedges and coriander sprigs. Serve hot or cold.

•

## STUFFED EGGS IN A NET · KAI KWAN

*6 to 8 Servings*

- 1 *tablespoon vegetable oil*
- 4 *tablespoons ground pork*
- 2 *tablespoons cooked shrimp or crabmeat, finely chopped*
- 6 *Chinese mushrooms, soaked in hot water, stems removed, finely chopped*
- 1 *teaspoon black peppercorns*
- 1 *tablespoon coriander roots, chopped*
- 3 *cloves garlic, chopped*
- 1 *tablespoon fish sauce* (Nam Pla)
- 1 *teaspoon granulated sugar*
- 12 *eggs, hardcooked, shelled and halved, yolks set aside*
- ½ *cup vegetable oil*
- 2 *eggs, beaten*
- 4 *red or green Serrano chillies, seeded and cut into flowers*
- *Coriander sprigs for garnish*

Heat the *1* tablespoon of vegetable oil in a wok and stir-fry the pork, crabmeat and mushrooms until the pork begins to brown. Remove wok from heat.

In a mortar, pound the peppercorns, coriander roots and garlic to a juicy paste. Add the cooked mixture from the wok, spoonful by spoonful, pounding with each addition to make the mixture smooth and uniform. (Alternatively, you may use a food processor for this step, after pounding the peppercorn/coriander root/garlic mixture in the mortar.)

Stir into this the fish sauce and sugar. Add the hard-cooked yolks and continue to pound or process to a uniform purée. Fill the egg halves with this purée to replace the yolks and press the egg halves back together, securing with toothpicks.

Heat the ½ cup oil in a wok and fry the reconstructed eggs, one by one, until each is golden brown and blistered.

Remove to a plate lined with paper towels and drain. Bring the oil remaining in the wok up to heat and, dipping the fingers in the beaten eggs, form two or three egg nets (see "Fundamentals," chapter 3).

Place the fried eggs on a platter and cover them with the nets. Decorate with chilli flowers and tuck sprigs of coriander leaves into the dish at random to garnish. Serve hot or cold with a side bowl of soy sauce.

•

## STEAMED STUFFED EGGS · KAI TIAN

*8 to 10 Servings*

The Thai enjoy a little prank with *Kai Tian.* If properly prepared, they appear to be untouched, simple hard-cooked and peeled eggs and the savory filling surprises the diner at first bite.

| | |
|---|---|
| *10+* | *extra large eggs* |
| | *Bowl of cold water* |
| *10* | *peppercorns* |
| *4* | *cloves garlic* |
| *1* | *tablespoon coriander roots* |
| *½* | *cup ground pork* |
| *½* | *cup cooked crabmeat, shredded* |
| *1* | *teaspoon granulated sugar* |
| *1* | *tablespoon fish sauce* (Nam Pla) |
| *4* | *fresh red chillies, cut into flowers* |
| | *Coriander leaves for garnish* |

In a saucepan, soft-cook the eggs for about 1½ minutes and plunge them directly into cold water. Carefully peel away an irregular section of shell about the size of a dime at the pointed end of each egg. With the point of a sharp knife, cut a conical plug of white from the peeled section. Arrange the plugs in an orderly fashion so they can be reassembled with their corresponding egg. Pour the contents of the eggs, uncooked white and yolk, in a bowl and set aside. Repeat with all the eggs and set aside.

Place the peppercorns, garlic and coriander roots in a mortar and pound to a paste. In a processor, place the pork, crabmeat, sugar, fish sauce and the contents of the mortar and grind until well mixed, no more than 1 minute. With the handle of a spoon, stuff the mixture from the processor into each egg to almost full. To help seal the plug, brush the top of the stuffing and edges of the opening with some of the reserved, uncooked egg white. Now replace the plugs. Place the eggs, plug side up, in suitable ovenproof containers. (You can fashion small nests, about 2″ diameter, from aluminum foil to support each egg upright.)

Heat the water in a steamer and when it is boiling, steam the eggs for 12 minutes.

Remove the eggs from the steamer and cool until they can be handled. Gently peel off the shells and arrange on a platter, garnishing with red chilli flowers and coriander leaves. Serve for a snack or as *hors d'oeuvres.*

## SON-IN-LAW EGGS · KAI LOOK KOEI

*8 Servings*

I have been unable to find the exact origin of this title but it is interesting to speculate. From the grins of the Thai, I know that it has something to do with a mother-in-law who doesn't have a high opinion of her son-in-law! However, just when you think there cannot possibly be a new approach to egg cooking in the entire lexicon, here is a real original, and it is delicious.

*Oil for deep-frying*
8 *hardcooked eggs, peeled and halved*
1/4 *cup palm sugar, or sticky brown sugar*
4 *tablespoons fish sauce* (Nam Pla)
2 *red or green Serrano chillies, seeded and cut into slivers*
3 *tablespoons dried onion flakes, fried crisp-brown in a little oil, drained**
*Sprigs of coriander to garnish*

Heat the oil in a wok and deep-fry the eggs, *flat side down,* until the outsides are golden and blistered.

Lift with a slotted spoon from the oil and put on a plate, lined with paper towels, to drain, yolk uppermost. Pour all the oil except 2 tablespoons from the wok, and in it melt the palm sugar, stirring constantly. Add the fish sauce, still stirring. Reduce heat and let the sauce simmer for about 5 minutes until it is thick, brown and well-blended.

The sauce should taste sweet/salt, in a balanced combination. Place the eggs, yolk uppermost, on a platter and mask them with the sauce.

Sprinkle the chilli slivers and fried onion flakes over the top and garnish with coriander sprigs.

Serve with toothpicks at the side as an unusual *hors d'oeuvre.*

*See Chapter 3, Fundamentals.

## SHRIMP ROLLS · HAE KOON

*8 to 10 Servings*

Traditionally, in Thailand, *Hae Koon* are made with dried bean-curd sheets, softened with water, filled and steamed. I break with tradition because I prefer the convenience and texture of ready-made wrappers. Depending on the size of the completed roll, you may desire to use egg roll (largest), spring roll or Won-Ton (smallest) wrappers.

*Filling*

- 2 *tablespoons peanut oil*
- 3 *cloves garlic, chopped*
- ½ *teaspoon ginger, minced*
- ½ *cup ground pork*
- 1 *tablespoon fish sauce* (Nam Pla)
- ½ *teaspoon ground black pepper*
- ½ *teaspoon salt*
- ½ *teaspoon cornstarch*
- 1½ *cups cooked Bay shrimp, minced*

*Rolls*

- 1 *packet spring rolls (20 per packet)*
- *Vegetable oil for deep-frying*
- 1½ *teaspoons cornstarch dissolved in 2 tablespoons water*

*Filling*

In a wok, heat the peanut oil over medium heat. Slowly fry the garlic and ginger until the garlic is golden. Add the pork and stir-fry it for about 1 minute. Now add the fish sauce, black pepper, salt and cornstarch. Stir until the cornstarch begins to thicken the mixture. Drop in the shrimp, remove from heat and set aside to cool.

*Rolls*

Separate the sheets and set aside. Begin heating

the frying oil in a wok, saucepan or fryer. Regulate to at least 375° F., the desired frying temperature.

*Assembly*

Arrange the individual spring roll to be filled so as you face it, it appears as a baseball diamond from the press box.

Baste the perimeter with about 1" ribbon of the diluted cornstarch. Place a spoonful of the filling between home plate and the pitcher's mound. Roll the "backstop" flap over the filling. Fold the first and third base points to meet in the center. Continue rolling and seal the outfield flap with additional cornstarch/water if necessary. Repeat with each wrapper and set aside in a stack.

The finished rolls should have a uniform, cylindrical shape. Fry the rolls, several at a time, until each is crisp-golden. Drain and serve with *Saus Prik*.

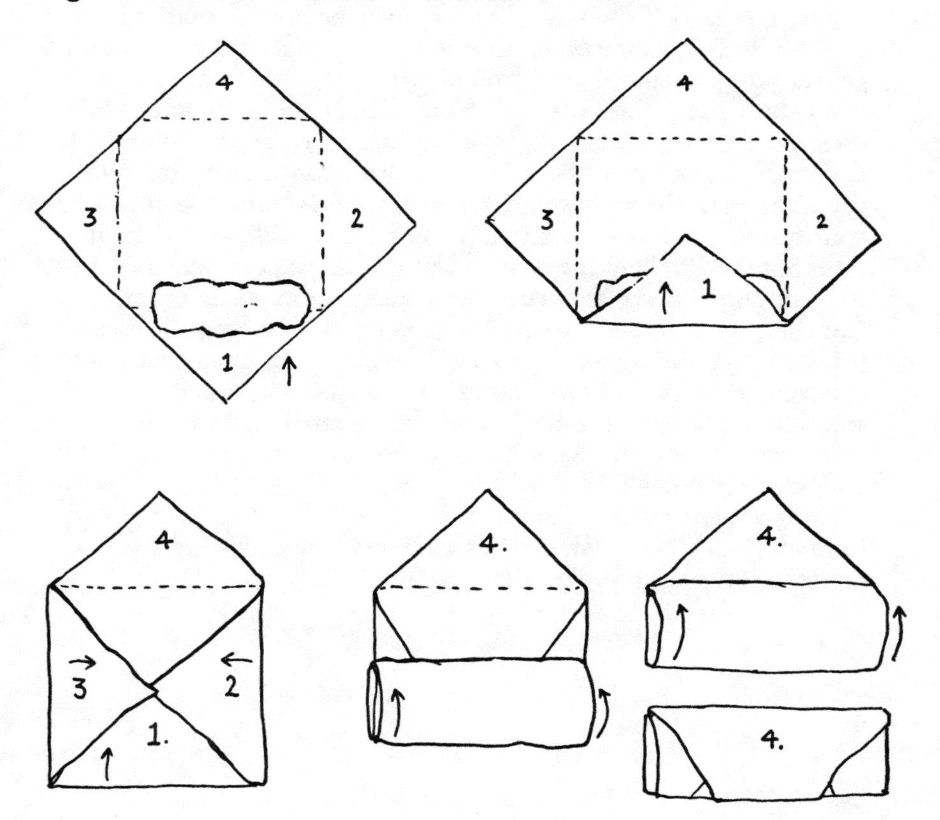

## STUFFED CHICKEN WINGS · PEEK GAI YOD SAI

*5 to 6 Servings*

To embark on this adventure you need several important things: a very sharp knife, several chicken wings (some for experimentation because you will inevitably muck-up a few), one ton of patience. Make no mistake about it—boning a chicken wing is a tedious, difficult task requiring about 10 to 20 minutes of arduous scraping and slicing per wing.

Let me offer several suggestions about boning: (1) Wings taken from your own whole chicken are easier to bone because you can arrange the original tendon separation. (2) Before skinning, bend the two wing joints backward (against their normal motion) to loosen the bones and tendons. (3) Using a paring knife (again sharp), cut and recut a ring around the top of the largest bone (the one that separates from the body of the bird). (4) With the blade of your knife, scrape and cut the meat and skin down the first bone to the joint, turning back the skin over the unboned portions like a glove as you progress. (5) When it is completely exposed, break off the first bone from the next two smaller ones at the joint. (6) Insert your thumbnail just under the skin and gently move it completely around the joint; detaching the skin from the underlying flesh and bone. (Study the outside of your own elbow to see how the skin is caught in at the joint.) (7) Carefully, so as not to puncture the skin, continue to roll back the skin over the two smaller bones (this is part of a regular, continuing process of cutting, scraping and sliding that facilitates boning). (8) Peel the flesh back from the exposed ends of the two smaller bones and cut them apart from each other. (9) Continue to roll the skin back, scraping and cutting the flesh, primarily on the dorsal side of the larger bone, until you have exposed most of the two bones. (10) Break the bones off (the smaller one is easier) from the remaining cartilage and skin that comprise, in fact, the wing tip and turn the skin right side out, checking for holes and punctures.

Congratulations, you now have a boned chicken wing. The following ingredients should make about 5 or 6 (depending how densely you pack them) stuffed wings.

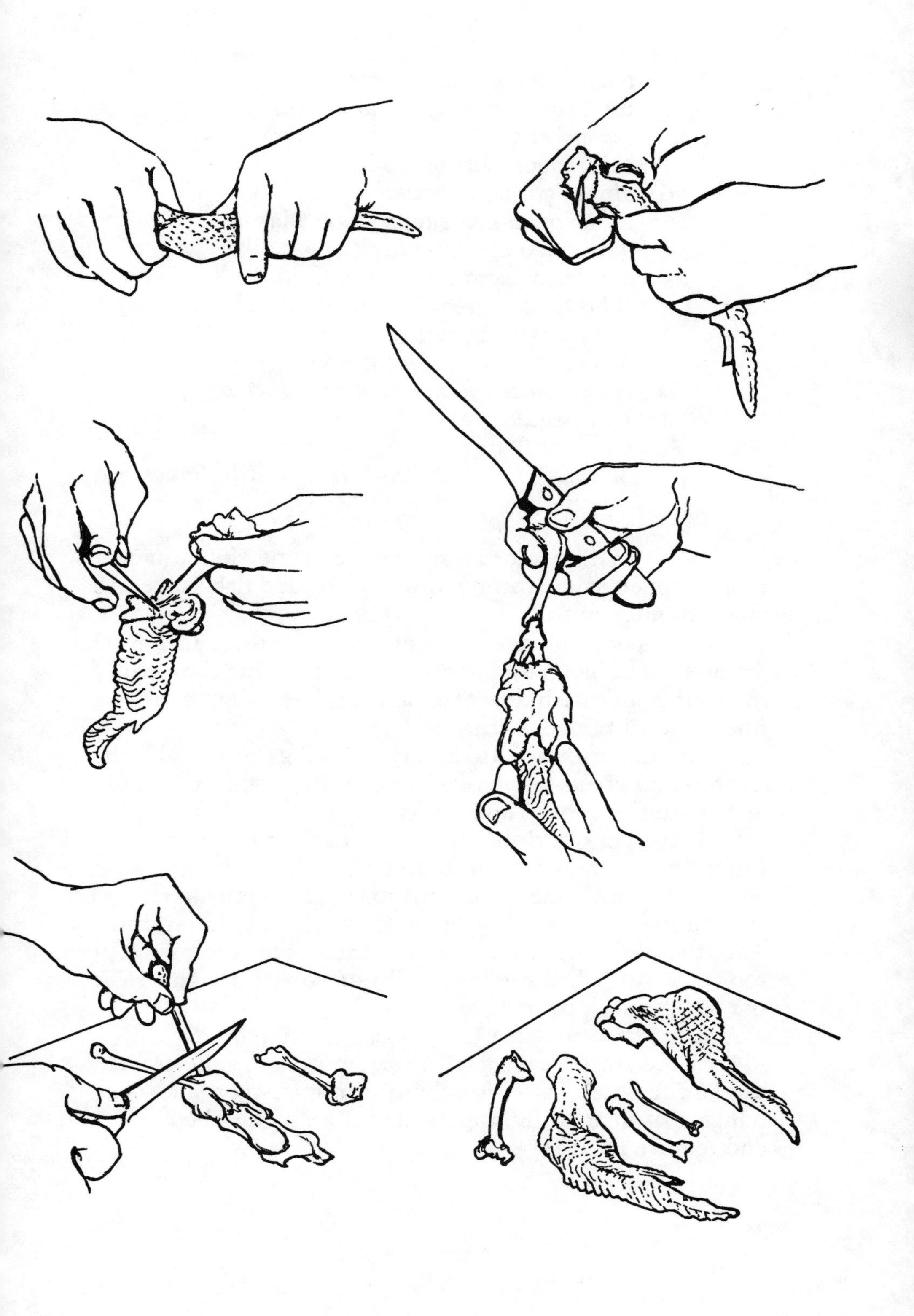

1 *teaspoon coriander roots*
1 *tablespoon freshly ground black pepper*
1 *teaspoon salt*
1 *tablespoon shrimp powder*
6 *cloves garlic, chopped*
1 *tablespoon fish sauce* (Nam Pla)
1 *pound lean ground pork*
4 *ounces cooked Bay shrimp, minced*
2 *tablespoons green onions, minced*
6 *boned chicken wings*
3 *cups vegetable oil for frying*
⅛ *teaspoon red food coloring (optional)*
1 *egg, beaten*
¼ *cup rice flour*
Siracha *or Sweet and Hot Chilli Sauce for dipping*

With a mortar and pestle, grind the coriander roots, pepper, salt, shrimp powder, garlic and fish sauce to a smooth, juicy paste.

Put the pork and the contents of the mortar in a food processor and blend for about one minute. This thoroughly mixes the pork with the spices and renders the mixture to a fine paste suitable for stuffing.

Place this mixture in a large mixing bowl, add the shrimp and green onions and knead thoroughly to evenly distribute the shrimp and onion.

Stuff the pork/shrimp mixture in each wing, using your thumb to tamp and force the stuffing. The chicken skin will behave like sausage casing, expanding considerably to accommodate amazingly large quantities of the stuffing. About ⅙ of the mixture will be sufficient for each wing (if too fully stuffed, the wings will not cook through). Heat the oil in a wok or fryer to 375° F.

Add the food coloring to the egg and whip briefly.

Coat the stuffed wings with rice flour, dip in the colored egg and fry each in oil for about 5 minutes per side. (The wings will float to the top of the oil like a beached whale and require turning.)

Recommend you fry no more than two wings at a time and, when they are done, remove and drain.

Serve with chilli sauce, using the wing tips to hold and dip.

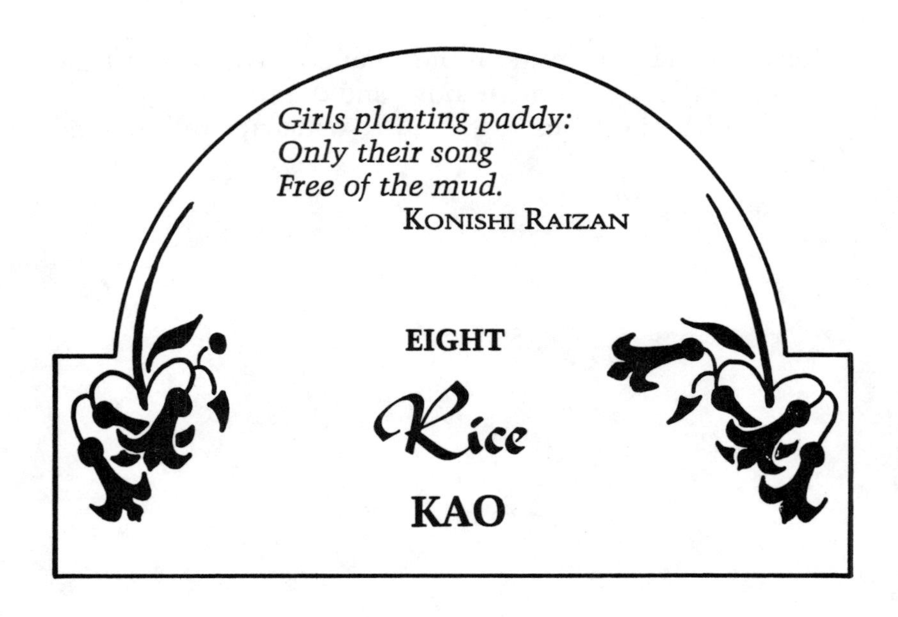


Rice is the all-important food in Thailand. Meals revolve around it, culture and traditions celebrate it and the monsoon climate causes it to flourish.

Food historians have always believed that rice originated in either China or India, but recent archaeological digs at Ban Chien, Northeastern Thailand, have turned up rice grains dating to 3500 B.C. This predates the earliest known evidence of rice in China by seven hundred years.

A Frenchman, Laloubere, writing about the Kingdom of Siam in the late 1700's, remarked that: "A Siamese makes a very good meal with a pound of rice a day, which amounts not to more than a farthing . . ." Today the rice is certainly a few "farthings" more, but the estimation of a pound of rice per person per day is still accurate.

In the middle of Bangkok, just by the Grand Palace, is a large, open area called the Pramane Ground. Until recently, on weekends it was the site for the colorful "Sunday Market" and, historically, was the saddling area for the riding elephants. Nowadays it is used for sports and ceremonies, including the Ploughing Ceremony, which is held in the spring before rice planting. The Ceremony placates the gods so they will guarantee a good rice harvest, and also predicts the plentitude of the new crop. At dawn, in the presence of the King, a procession bearing sacred images enters the Pramane Ground. Candles and incense are lighted and food offerings made to the gods. Two caparisoned white oxen with uniformed attendants then slowly pull a ceremonial plough round the Ground three times, while drums beat and women scatter rice from golden pails. When three circles have been completed, the oxen stop before the King and are offered a choice of different foods and liquor. The excellence of the next harvest depends on which they choose and liquor augurs the worst harvest! After the ceremony has ended and the King has gone, the crowds rush onto the Ground and scramble frantically for the grains of rice that have just been sown. The farmers believe that this rice, mixed with their own, will ensure a good harvest when they have taken it back to their farms.

The Thai prefer to eat polished rice, tending to look down on untreated rice as inferior. While the polishing and washing removes most of the vitamins, particularly the B family, the side dishes and sauces that are served with the rice are extremely rich in vitamins and more than replace the deficiency. Rice is never salted in the cooking. The ubiquitous *Nam Pla,* or fish sauce rich in salt, is seasoning enough.

Rice is sold in Thai markets from enormous sacks; you bring your own container into which portions are scooped according to your needs. There are many grades of rice, particularly long grain, and I find the grading system seems to be based on the proportion of broken grains in the sack. Besides the long grain, there are grades of short grain, glutinous or sticky rice, often referred to as sweet rice. The Thai reserve this mostly for sweets and desserts, unlike the hill tribes and Laotians, who use it as a staple with their meat dishes.

The recipes in this chapter deal with variations of the

fried rice dishes which are universally popular throughout Thailand. Fried rice serves as a gentle introduction to Thai cuisine for the gastronomically timid and those unused to highly spiced foods. *Kao Pad,* fried rice, is eaten for a quick meal at any time of the day. I remember on one occasion sitting down to a memorable dish of *Kao Pad* at daybreak on the Thai bank of the Mekong River while waiting to cross into Laos.

We had driven up north from Bangkok all through the night and as portions of the road had been washed away with recent rains, the trip was full of tension. We arrived hungry and tired at Nong Khai, the little border town, at five thirty in the morning. We found the immigration and customs offices closed so we went to look for a restaurant. The saffron-robed monks were walking down the streets with their food bowls, into which the villagers would put offerings of food thereby "making merit" for the day. Apart from the monks, the only living creatures visible on the beaten earth streets were the dogs; slinking around the wooden houses in search of breakfast. So were we. We were fortunate to find a little food shop with a friendly owner just taking down the wooden shutters. We sat on rickety chairs on an uneven cement floor, gazing out under the carved eaves of the balcony at the broad, still river. The early mists were rising and the sun was turning everything pale gold.

Fortified by steaming glasses of Thai coffee sweetened with condensed milk, we appreciated the marvelous smells of frying garlic and chicken, accompanied by scraping noises as the owner deftly tossed the rice in a wok for the smells and sounds signaled the imminent arrival of our food. In about ten minutes she placed platters in front of us, piled high with a mélange of glistening rice, peppers, green onions, chillies and chicken. This was served with bowls of *Nam Prik,* hot sauce, and thin cucumber slices steeped in vinegar, sugar and tiny, hot green chillies. Breakfast never tasted so good—not even in the finest hotels in the world. The bill for this feast, reluctantly presented, was twenty *baht,* one dollar!

For basic rice preparation, see Fundamentals, Chapter 3.

•

## PLAIN (RED) FRIED RICE · KAO PAD TAMADA

*3 Servings*

This is the quickest and easiest of all the fried-rice dishes. It gets its red color from tomato ketchup. If you think it odd that ketchup is used, believe me, it is authentic and used widely in Thailand today. It is even bottled locally. I once had a Thai cook who had to be gently but firmly restrained from adding it to every dish that she cooked for us. She reasoned that if we liked it once, we would like it every time!

*3 tablespoons vegetable oil*
*3 cloves garlic, finely chopped*
*1 onion, finely chopped*
*1 cup cooked shrimp*
*2 tablespoons fish sauce* (Nam Pla)
*3 cups cooked rice, chilled*
*3 tablespoons tomato ketchup*

*Garnish*

*6 green onions, cut into tassels*
*1 small cucumber, peeled and sliced*
*3 tablespoons coriander leaves, chopped*

Heat the oil in a wok. Lightly brown the garlic. Add the onions and stir-fry until golden. Add the shrimp and fish sauce and heat through. Stir in the rice and toss until everything is well mixed.

Pour in the ketchup and stir well. Remove to a platter. Garnish with the green onion tassels, ring with cucumber slices and sprinkle the coriander leaves over the top.

## COMBINATION THAI FRIED RICE · KAO PAD

*4 Servings*

While *Kao Pad* is normally eaten by itself as a complete one-dish meal (allow 1 cup cooked rice per person), it can also be served as a central buffet dish.

4 *tablespoons vegetable oil*
2 *medium onions, finely chopped*
2 *cloves garlic, finely chopped*
½ *pound lean pork, diced*
4 *eggs, beaten and seasoned with salt and pepper*
4 *cups cooked rice, chilled*
2 *tablespoons fish sauce* (Nam Pla)
1 *tablespoon chilli sauce (Siracha or other good quality commercial sauce)*
1 *green bell pepper, seeded and finely chopped*
1 *tomato, chopped*
5 *green onions (including green), finely chopped*
½ *pound cooked Bay shrimp or cooked crabmeat (additional, optional ingredients include diced, cooked ham, sliced Chinese sausages or diced, cooked chicken)*

*Garnish*

2 *green onions, cut into tassels*
1 *cucumber, sliced decoratively*
3 *tablespoons coriander leaves, chopped*
1 *lime, cut into wedges*

Heat the oil in a wok or large frying pan and fry the onion and garlic until the latter is golden. Add the pork and stir-fry until it is just cooked through. Make a hole in the center of the pork, pour in the seasoned, beaten eggs and scramble. Toss in the rice and stir well. Sprinkle the fish and chilli sauces over the mixture. In order, add the green pepper, tomato, 5 green onions and shrimp, stirring between each addition to heat the new ingredients thoroughly. Transfer to a large platter and garnish attractively with green onion tassels, cucumber slices, coriander and lime wedges. Serve at once accompanied by extra fish and chilli sauce.

## FRIED RICE WITH CHICKEN · KAO PAD GAI

*3 to 4 Servings*

- 2 *tablespoons vegetable oil*
- 3 *cloves garlic, finely chopped*
- ½ *packet bean curd (approximately ⅔ cup), drained and cut into ½" cubes*
- ½ *chicken breast, cut into thin strips ½" wide × 1" long*
- ½ *pound lean pork, cut into thin strips ½" wide × 1" long*
- 2 *tablespoons fish sauce* (Nam Pla)
- ½ *teaspoon red chilli powder (Cayenne)*
- 1 *teaspoon dried shrimp powder*
- 3 to 4 *cups cooked rice, chilled*
- 1 *lime, halved*
- 1 *egg, beaten with 1 teaspoon water, fried as an omelet and cut into thin strips*
- 3 *red Serrano chillies, seeded and cut into strips*
- 2 *tablespoons coriander leaves, chopped*

Heat the oil in a wok and fry the garlic until golden. Add the bean curd and fry until brown.

Now add the chicken and pork and stir-fry until both are cooked through. Season with fish sauce and stir in the chilli and dried shrimp powders. Place in the rice and stir until uniform and the rice is heated through. Turn onto a platter and squeeze the lime halves over the top, discarding the lime. Decorate the rice with the omelet strips. Sprinkle the platter with red chilli strips and coriander leaves.

•

## FRIED RICE WITH PINEAPPLE · KAO PAD SUPPAROT

*3 to 4 Servings*

This dish is very decorative and makes an attractive centerpiece for a Thai buffet. If a whole, fresh pineapple cannot be obtained, drained, canned pineapple can be used in the preparation. Omit filling the pineapple container, and merely place the Fried Rice with Pineapple on a platter and then garnish.

- 3 *tablespoons vegetable oil*
- ½ *cup pork, diced*
- 1 *medium onion, finely chopped*
- 6 *ounces cooked shrimp (whole)*
- 1 *tablespoon dried shrimp powder*
- 1 *tablespoon fish sauce* (Nam Pla)
- 1 *tablespoon soy sauce*
- 3 *cups cooked rice, chilled*
- 1 *large pineapple, tufts cut off,* hollowed and flesh cut in cubes and reserved*
- 1 *fresh Serrano chilli, seeded and cut into slivers*
- *Sprig of coriander or parsley*

Heat the oil in a wok. Stir-fry the pork and onion until brown. Add the shrimp and shrimp powder and warm through. Stir in the fish and soy sauces. Add the rice and mix thoroughly. Add the pineapple cubes and stir-fry for 2 more minutes. Fill the pineapple with the mixture

* See Chapter 4, Fruit and Vegetable Carving.

from the wok, taking care that some pineapple pieces and shrimp appear on top. Decorate the filling with chilli slices and a sprig of coriander or parsley. Serve hot.

•

## CHILLI FRIED RICE · KAO PAD PRIK

*4 Servings*

Most Thai fried-rice dishes are mild. For this reason they are popular with children and tourists. This dish, however, is intended for the aficionado as it is quite spicy!

- 3 *tablespoons vegetable oil*
- 1 *large onion, finely chopped*
- 2 *fresh Serrano chillies, seeded and finely chopped*
- 1 *tablespoon red curry paste* (Krung Gaeng Ped)
- 4 *tablespoons pork or ham, diced*
- 4 *cups cooked rice, chilled*
- 3 *eggs, beaten*
- 1 *cup cooked shrimp*
- 3 *tablespoons fish sauce* (Nam Pla)

*Garnish*

- 4 *green onions (including green), finely chopped*
- 2 *tablespoons coriander leaves, finely chopped*
- 4 *fresh red chillies, seeded and cut into flowers*

In a wok, heat the oil and fry the onion and Serrano chillies until the onion is soft. Add the red curry paste and fry for 3 minutes or until the oil starts to separate around the edges.

Add the pork and stir-fry for 2 minutes. Now add the rice and stir and toss thoroughly until the rice is colored with the paste and heated through.

Make a hole in the center of the mixture and pour in the eggs, letting them set slightly, then mixing them evenly through the rice. Stir in the shrimp and sprinkle with fish sauce. Remove from heat and transfer to a platter. Decorate with the Garnish and serve.

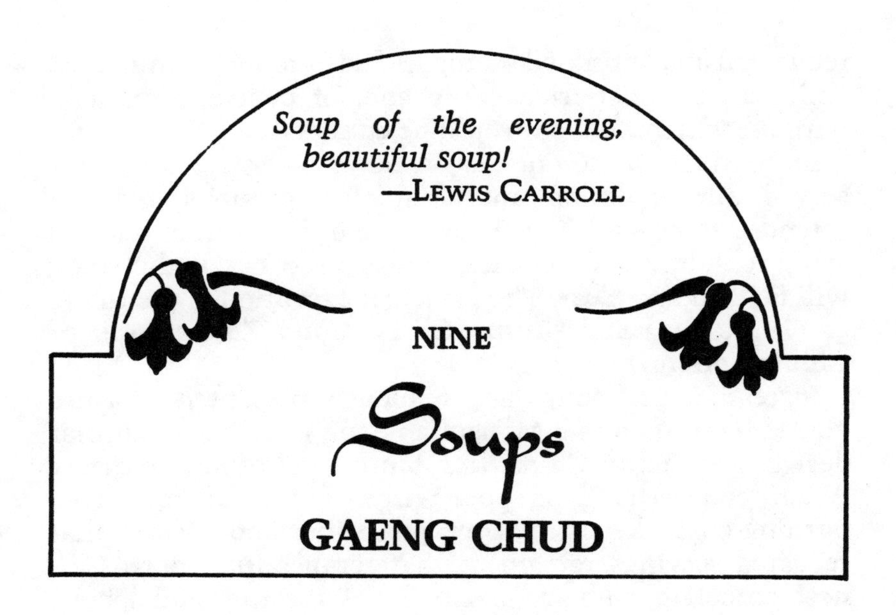


NINE

# Soups

# GAENG CHUD

Soups are included in almost every meal in Thailand. Breakfast will commonly start with a bland rice soup followed by small selections of whatever the eater desires. At a full meal, the soup is served together with the other dishes, not before, as Western custom dictates.

Virtually all over Thailand, the light midday meal or snack will be a hearty bowl of the substantial *Gwaytio*, noodle soup purchased from a traveling soup vendor or in an open-fronted soup kitchen. Instead of Styrofoam, the fast-food soup entrepreneur uses large, off-white porcelain bowls with crude pink or blue imitations of the Chinese Willow Pattern, mass produced in little local ceramic factories. The bowl will contain a thin chicken- or beef-based broth with a good measure of wide or narrow noodles and some hard, compacted meat or fish balls, pieces of red-edged, spiced pork or squares of any kind of innards, including tripe. The brimming bowls are garnished with chopped green onions, coriander leaves and whole, incendiary red or green chillies. Optional trimmings usually requested and sprinkled on top include ground peanuts, red chilli flakes, crisp-fried garlic and, of course, *Nam Pla,* without which no dish would be complete.

In contrast to the one-dish meal of *Gwaytio,* the soups served during dinner are of smaller portions and not intended to be so filling. They range in flavor from hot and spicy to subtle and delicate and, in most cases, the stock will be thin and clear. The principal exception is the thick, gruel-like corn and shrimp *Gaeng Chud Kaopot Aun* of Chinese origin.

In restaurants, soups are frequently presented in a fire pot, known to us as a Mongolian Soup Pot. Pots of similar design are used in China, *dah-bin-lo,* and other Southeast Asian countries. This pot, with its central funnel of burning coals, keeps the soup piping-hot and ensures that repeated servings remain at that temperature. Both Chinese porcelain soup spoons and our Western metal spoons are used by the Thai. There is certainly comforting, tactile reassurance to the experience of using a porcelain spoon.

•

## HOT AND SOUR SHRIMP SOUP · DOM YAM GUNG

*6 to 8 Servings*

The best known and loved of Thai soups, *Dom Yam Gung,* is a marvelous combination of tender shrimp floating in a rich broth, liberally spiced with chillies and tangy with lemon grass, lime juice and citrus leaves.

1 *tablespoon vegetable oil*
*Shells from shrimp (see below)*
8 *cups chicken stock*
1½ *teaspoons salt*
3 *stalks lemon grass, cut into 1" lengths*

4 *citrus leaves*
1 *teaspoon lime zest, slivered*
2 *green Serrano chillies, slivered*
2 *pounds fresh (green) shrimp (approximately 20 count per pound), shelled and deveined*
1 *tablespoon fish sauce* (Nam Pla)
*Juice of 2 limes*
1 *red Serrano chilli, slivered*
2 *tablespoons coriander leaves, coarsely chopped*
3 *green onions (including some green), coarsely chopped*

Heat the oil in a saucepan and fry the shells until they turn pink. Add the chicken stock, salt, lemon grass, citrus leaves, lime rind and green chillies. Bring to a boil, cover, reduce heat and simmer for 20 minutes. Strain the mixture through a sieve, return the liquid to a saucepan and bring to a boil. Add the shrimp to this boiling "stock" and cook them for 2 to 3 minutes. Reduce heat to simmer and add the fish sauce and lime juice. Stir and immediately remove from heat to prevent overcooking. Pour the soup in a tureen, sprinkle with red chillies, coriander leaves and green onions. Serve piping-hot.

•

## CORN AND SHRIMP SOUP · GAENG CHUD KAOPOT AUN

*3 to 4 Servings*

A very quick and easy soup, commonly served in Chinese/Thai restaurants in Bangkok. Often made with shredded crabmeat instead of shrimp, the soup has been adapted from the Chinese. I specify canned, creamed corn for texture and convenience. You may use canned or frozen, plain corn or, for the ambitious, strip fresh kernels from the cob. If fresh corn is used, increase the cooking time by two minutes.

1 *tablespoon vegetable oil*
5 *cloves garlic, minced*
3 *shallots, minced*
3 *cups chicken stock*
2 *tablespoons fish sauce* (Nam Pla)
½ *pound cooked shrimp or crabmeat*
1 *large can creamed corn*
½ *teaspoon cracked black peppercorns*
1 *egg, beaten*
2 *tablespoons coriander leaves, chopped*

In a large saucepan, heat the oil and fry the garlic and shallots until light brown. Add the chicken stock, fish sauce, shrimp or crabmeat, corn and black pepper. Bring to a boil. Pour in the beaten egg and stir to break up the egg in the soup. Boil for 1 more minute. Pour into a soup tureen and sprinkle with coriander leaves.

•

## BAMBOO SHOOT AND PORK SOUP · GAENG CHUD NO MAI

*4 Servings*

This soup comes from Northern Thailand and is also commonly eaten across the border in Laos. The Mekong River forms the geographic border between the two countries but, until recently, the Thai and Laotians fished side by side on the river, and freely traveled back and forth to trade. Similarly, the two cultures blended in this area and both language and cuisine intermingled.

2 *tablespoons vegetable oil*
1 *clove garlic, crushed*

½ *teaspoon ground coriander seeds*
¼ *teaspoon ground black pepper*
1 *tablespoon fish sauce* (Nam Pla)
1 *cup lean pork, thinly sliced into strips, ½" × 1½"*
1 *tablespoon granulated sugar*
4 *cups stock (chicken, beef, pork)*
1 *15-ounce can bamboo shoots, drained and thinly sliced*
2 *green onions, chopped*

In a large saucepan, heat the oil and fry the garlic, coriander and pepper, stirring until the garlic is golden. Add the fish sauce. Introduce the pork strips and stir-fry until brown. Add the sugar and pour in the stock. Lower the heat and simmer for 15 minutes. Now add the bamboo shoots and bring the soup back to the boil. Correct the seasoning with additional pepper and fish sauce, if necessary. Pour into a soup tureen, garnish with green onions and serve.

•

## CHICKEN AND MUSHROOM SOUP · GAENG CHUD GAI GUP HED

*4 Servings*

This soup has the characteristic Thai flavor combination of garlic, coriander roots and peppercorns.

3 *cloves garlic, chopped*
1 *tablespoon coriander roots*
8 *black peppercorns*
1 *tablespoon vegetable oil*
1 *cup chicken meat, sliced into bite-sized pieces*
4 *cups chicken stock*
5 *dried Chinese mushrooms, soaked in hot*

*water, stemmed and halved*
1 *tablespoon fish sauce* (Nam Pla)
*The skin of 1 cucumber**
4 *green onions, cut diagonally into thirds*

In a mortar, pound the garlic, coriander roots and peppercorns into a paste. Heat the oil in a saucepan and fry this paste, stirring, for 1 minute. Add the chicken stock, Chinese mushrooms, chicken meat and fish sauce. Bring to a boil, cover and reduce heat to low. Simmer for 15 minutes. Meanwhile take a sharp knife and cut the cucumber peel into leaf shapes.* Carve about 8 to 12 leaves. When the simmering is complete, uncover the soup, add the cucumber leaves and the green onions. Simmer for 1 more minute. Correct the seasoning with a little fish sauce if necessary, then serve.

•

## SHRIMP AND MUSHROOM SOUP · GAENG CHUD GUNG GUP HED

*4 Servings*

4 *cups chicken stock*
8 *dried Chinese mushrooms, soaked in hot water, stemmed and cut into thin strips*
1 *tablespoon black peppercorns*
1 *tablespoon coriander roots*
6 *cloves garlic, chopped*
1 *tablespoon vegetable oil*
12 *ounces small shrimp, shelled and cleaned (deveining optional)*
2 *tablespoons fish sauce* (Nam Pla)

* See Chapter 4, Fruit and Vegetable Carving.

Heat the chicken stock in a saucepan. Add the mushroom strips and simmer for about 10 minutes over low heat. In a mortar, pound together the peppercorns, coriander roots and garlic to a paste. Heat the vegetable oil in a small frying pan and fry the paste until it is light brown. Transfer the paste to the stock. Bring the combination to a boil and cook for 1 minute. Add the shrimp to the liquid and cook for 2 more minutes. Season with fish sauce and serve immediately.

**N.B.** Frozen, cooked shrimp, defrosted and drained, can be used for this soup. They will not require any further cooking but should just warm through.

•

## RICE SOUP · KAO DOM

*4 Servings*

An easily digestible and nutritious soup which is often given to children and invalids in Thailand, *Kao Dom* is also eaten for breakfast.

- 4 *cups chicken stock*
- ½ *cup ground pork*
- 1 *cup cooked rice*
- 2 *tablespoons fish sauce* (Nam Pla)
- 1 *small egg for each serving*
- 1 *tablespoon ginger, minced*
- 1 *tablespoon dried onion flakes, fried until golden and drained**
- 1 *tablespoon coriander leaves, chopped*
- 3 *green onions, finely chopped*
- 1 *teaspoon dried red chilli flakes (optional)*

Heat the chicken stock in a saucepan. Add the ground pork and bring to a boil, stirring to break up the pork. Reduce heat to simmer. Add the rice and cook for 2

* See Chapter 3, Fundamentals.

minutes. Season with fish sauce. Break an egg into each soup bowl and pour the boiling soup over the top. Sprinkle each bowl with the ginger, onion flakes, coriander leaves, green onions and dried red chilli flakes.

Alternatively, the last 5 ingredients could be separated into individual bowls, the pork/stock liquid kept hot in a tureen with the diners helping themselves.

•

## CHICKEN AND RICE SOUP · KAO DOM GAI

*4 to 6 Servings*

Another rice soup with a mild flavor. One of my mother's favorites: her Thai cook served it as a regular Sunday night supper with crackers and cheese to round out the meal, the latter additions catering to my mother's British tastes.

1 *pound chicken, boned, skinned and minced*
4 *cups chicken stock*
2 *cups cooked rice*
2 *tablespoons fish sauce* (Nam Pla)
4 *lettuce leaves, shredded*
¼ *teaspoon ginger, minced*
2 *green onions, finely chopped, including tops*
¼ *teaspoon monosodium glutamate (optional)*
¼ *teaspoon ground black pepper*

*Garnish*

8 *cloves garlic, finely chopped and fried in 2 tablespoons peanut oil*

Form (roll) the chicken into balls about 1" in diameter. In a saucepan, bring the stock to a boil and carefully drop in the chicken balls. Add the rice and season with fish sauce. Cook until the chicken balls are firm, no more than 10 minutes. Take the pan off heat and stir in the lettuce, ginger and green onion. Add the monosodium glutamate and black pepper. Serve accompanied by small bowls of the garlic in its oil, to be spooned over the top of the soup.

•

## NOODLES AND PORK SOUP · SEN MEE NAM GUP MOO

*4 to 6 Servings*

*Sen Mee Nam Gup Moo* is commonly served in the Thai equivalent of soup kitchens. The customers specify which kind of noodles they prefer in the basic soup, i.e., egg or rice, wide or narrow, etc.

4 *cups chicken stock*
4 *tablespoons ground pork*
2 *bundles (hanks) rice vermicelli noodles (6 to 8 ounces approximately)*
1 *cup bean sprouts*
3 *cloves garlic, minced and crisp-fried*
2 *tablespoons fish sauce* (Nam Pla)
2 *lettuce leaves, shredded*
2 *green onions, finely chopped, including tops*
1 *tablespoon coriander leaves, chopped*
½ *pound pork loin, cooked and thinly sliced**
1 *tablespoon dried red chilli flakes*
1 *tablespoon granulated sugar*
1 *heaped tablespoon ground roasted peanuts*

In a saucepan, heat the chicken stock. Add the ground pork and simmer for 3 minutes, stirring to break up the pork. Drop in the noodles and bean sprouts, increase the heat and boil for 5 minutes or until the noodles are tender.

* Roast Red Pork or Sweet Pork are recommended for color and flavor although plain, cooked pork slices are common.

To the boiling mixture, stir in the fried garlic, fish sauce and shredded lettuce, green onions, and coriander. Remove from heat and pour into a large serving bowl or tureen. Garnish with green onions, coriander and pork slices. Sprinkle over the chilli flakes, sugar and peanuts and serve immediately.

•

## BEEF NOODLE SOUP · GWAYTIO NEUA NAM

*6 to 8 Servings*

This delicious, brawny beef soup with noodles is a standard (fare) in the smaller restaurants in Bangkok. *Sen Mee,* rice vermicelli noodles, can be substituted for the wide *Gwaytio,* fresh rice noodles. I prefer the rib-sticking qualities of the latter. If *Sen Mee* are used, they must be presoaked.

- 2 *tablespoons peanut oil*
- ½ *pound round steak (approximately ½" thick), fat removed, thinly sliced into strips*
- 5 *cloves garlic, chopped*
- ¼ *pound ground beef*
- 2 *stalks celery, sliced into 1" lengths obliquely (Chinese style)*
- 2 *green onions, thinly sliced including some green*
- 1 to 1½ *quarts beef stock (fresh or canned)*
- 1 *teaspoon ground black pepper*
- ½ *teaspoon ground cinnamon*
- 3 *tablespoons fish sauce* (Nam Pla)
- ¾ *pound wet noodle sheets (½ packet),* Gwaytio, *cut into strips (width to your preference)*
- 1 *cup bean sprouts*

*Garnish*

2 *tablespoons coriander leaves, chopped*
1 *tablespoon dried red chilli flakes, soaked in 2 tablespoons white vinegar*

Heat the oil in a large saucepan over medium high heat and quickly brown the beef slices. Remove with a slotted spoon and set aside. In this same pan, while still on heat, fry the garlic until golden.

Continuing, add the ground beef, celery and onions. Cook, stirring, until the beef just changes color. Pour in the stock and add the pepper, cinnamon and fish sauce. Bring to a boil and add the noodles. When the mixture again returns to a boil, add the bean sprouts. To provide a good serving temperature without overcooking the bean sprouts, immediately pour the soup into a large tureen or individual serving bowls. Decorate with the browned beef strips and coriander. Serve accompanied with a bowl of the chilli-vinegar sauce for individual embellishment.

•

## ORANGE (SOUR) SHRIMP CURRY SOUP · GAENG SOM KAREE

*4 to 6 Servings*

This dish falls somewhere between a curry and a soup. It can be served as a soup in bowls or spooned over rice. The *Krung Gaeng Som* paste (see "Curries," chapter 10) is one of the simplest, containing very few ingredients. The flavor complements both seafood and pork.

1½ *cups water*
2 *cups chicken stock*
*Shells from shrimp (see below)*
1 *pound medium shrimp (31 to 40 count per*

*pound), shelled, cleaned and deveined (reserving the shells)**

- 1 *tablespoon orange curry paste* (Krung Gaeng Som)
- ½ *teaspoon tamarind concentrate, dissolved in 2 tablespoons water*
- 2 *tablespoons fish sauce* (Nam Pla)
- 1½ *tablespoons granulated sugar*
- *Juice of 2 limes*
- 4 *small zucchini, halved lengthwise and sliced (or equivalent amount of cabbage, squash or cauliflower)*
- 2 *tablespoons dried shrimp powder*

In a wok or saucepan, bring the water to a boil. Add the shrimp shells, turn heat to medium, cover and simmer for about 5 minutes. Strain the liquid and discard the shells. Return the strained liquid to the wok, add the chicken stock and increase the heat to boil. When boiling, drop in the shrimp and cook for 1 minute. Remove the shrimp to a bowl with a slotted spoon and reduce heat to medium. Stir *one* teaspoon of the orange curry paste into the shrimp. Add the remainder of the paste to the stock in the wok together with the tamarind, fish sauce, sugar and lime juice. Place the zucchini in the stock and continue cooking over medium heat until the zucchini is tender. Stir in the shrimp powder and return the shrimp/paste to the wok and cook for 1 additional minute. Pour into a large serving bowl and serve immediately.

•

* 1 pound of medium shrimp, when cleaned and shelled, yields about ½ pound or, approximately, 1 cup, which is the desired volume.

## CHICKEN AND COCONUT MILK SOUP
## GAENG DOM YAM GAI

*6 to 8 Servings*

A lovely lemony, creamy soup, *Dom Yam Gai* calls for chicken pieces cut through the bone with a heavy cleaver, Chinese style.* If you find gnawing on chicken pieces and delicately trying to remove the bone, vainly searching for a place to deposit it, inhibiting your dinner conversation, you may debone the bird and substitute chicken pieces. In either case, use both dark and light meats for color and nutrition.

- 5 *cups "Thin" coconut milk*
- 1 *small chicken, sectioned and cut into bite-sized pieces (bone in)**
- 3 *stalks lemon grass, bruised and cut into 1" lengths*
- 2 *teaspoons Laos powder* (Ka)
- 3 *green onions, finely chopped*
- 2 *tablespoons coriander leaves, chopped*
- 4 to 6 *fresh Serrano chillies, seeded and chopped*
- *Juice of 2 limes*
- 3 *tablespoons fish sauce* (Nam Pla)

In a saucepan, bring the "Thin" coconut milk to a boil. Add the chicken pieces, lemon grass and Laos powder. Reduce heat and simmer until the chicken is tender, about 15 minutes. Do not cover as this will tend to curdle coconut milk. When the chicken is tender, add the green onions, coriander leaves and chillies. Bring the heat up just below boiling. Remove the pan from heat, stir in lime juice, fish sauce and serve.

**N.B.** Beef, cut into thin strips or firm white fish pieces may be substituted for chicken.

•

*A whole breast, for instance, should yield 12 pieces when chopped.

## FISH QUENELLES AND MUSHROOM SOUP · GAENG CHUD LOOK CHEEN

*6 to 8 Servings*

At noontime in Thailand, everyone stops and flocks to the little food shops or patronizes the food vendors who pull or pedal their carts along the lanes; each time they stop, collecting a crowd of eager, hungry customers. *Gaeng Chud Look Cheen,* with variations, is among the most frequently ordered soups during these lunchtime breaks.

Fish quenelles (usually labeled "fish balls") can be found in Oriental markets, either in cans or packets. They can easily be made at home by pounding white fish to a paste, mixing with beaten egg white, forming into balls and simmering in either water or stock. Shrimp are a popular substitution for white fish. Whether store-bought or freshly made, white fish or shrimp, the quenelles can be conveniently frozen for future use.

If you prefer a more substantial soup (read: you want the soup to go further), plan on adding noodles of almost any variety after the pork and mushrooms. The soup should then be simmered until the noodles are cooked before proceeding farther.

- *1 tablespoon vegetable oil*
- *6 cloves garlic, finely chopped*
- *5 to 6 cups chicken stock*
- *½ pound lean pork, cut into thin strips*
- *8 dried Chinese mushrooms, soaked in hot water and stemmed*
- *8 to 10 quenelles*
- *½ teaspoon black pepper, coarsely ground*
- *3 tablespoons fish sauce* (Nam Pla)
- *4 green onions, including tops, chopped*
- *½ cup coriander (leaves and stems), chopped*

In a saucepan, heat the oil and fry the garlic until golden. Add the stock, bring to a boil and add the pork strips. Reduce heat to medium and simmer for 5 minutes. Add the Chinese mushrooms and simmer for 5 more minutes. Place in the quenelles and bring back to the boil. Now add the pepper and fish sauce. Remove from heat and stir in the green onions. Pour the soup in a tureen, sprinkle with coriander and serve.

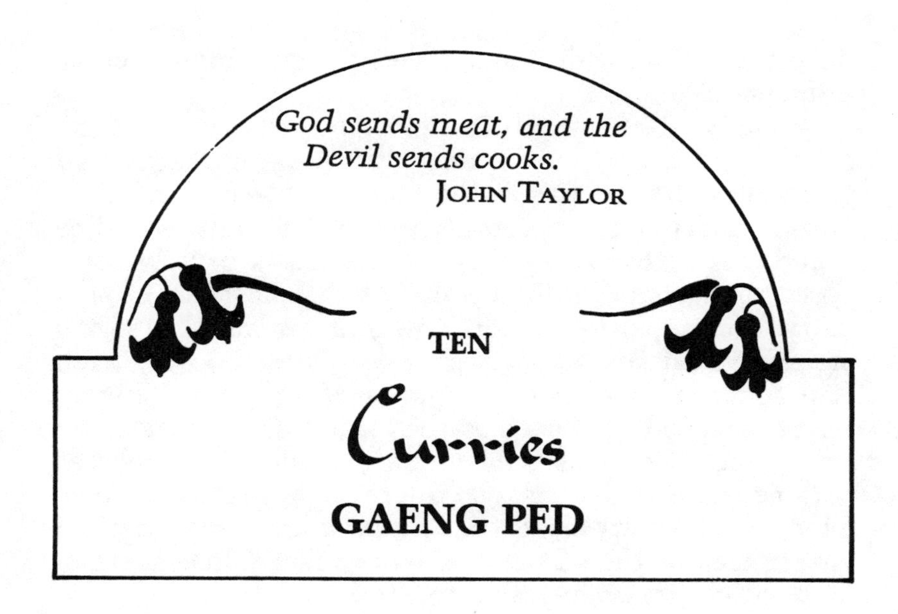

*God sends meat, and the*
*Devil sends cooks.*
JOHN TAYLOR

TEN

# Curries

# GAENG PED

Curries are eaten and enjoyed throughout the world but are considered native to India, Pakistan, Sri Lanka (Ceylon), and Southeast Asia. There are many theories about the origin of the word "curry." Two of the most tenaciously held are that the word derives from the Tamil *kari,* for sauce, or that it stems from the name of the wok-like, metal implement in which curries are cooked in India, a *karahi.* It does seem, though, as if the British helped evolve the word to its present spelling and pronunciation.

There are so many misconceptions about curries in general that it seems a worthy exercise to attempt to define the term. Curry is a fashion of cooking: a process whereby meats, fish, vegetables or even fruit are cooked in varying combinations of ground herbs and spices, known as curry pastes, to produce a stew-like dish. All dishes that are hot and spicy are not necessarily curries, nor are all curries fiery hot. Notwithstanding, the use of commercial curry powder does not produce a curry. Curry powder is an amalgam of some "Indian" spices best applied to the flavorings of curry dips and dishes where a hint of curry influence is desired.

In Thailand, the word *Gaeng,* liquid, is used to define curries and soups but, mainly, curries. The suffix *ped* means hot to the taste in the incendiary sense and Thai curries, practically by definition, are definitely hot! The liquid, *gaeng,* in which they are cooked is usually composed of coconut milk together with spices. In a Thai curry, the proportion of solids to liquid is small. As they are always eaten over large mounds of steamed rice, just a few solids suffice and the flavor of the spicy, highly flavored gravy is extended by the bland rice. The budget of the average Thai household does not include the purchases of large quantities of meat so their recipes make a little go a long way. For my classes and in these following recipes, I have increased the amounts of meat slightly to accommodate our greater meat-eating appetite.

The types of spices in Thai curry pastes are the most distinctive feature of their curries. A curry paste, *Krung Gaeng,* of any variety should be a marvelous, aromatic mixture of freshly ground herbs and spices. Each dish dictates a particular combination that will best complement the solid ingredients. Every person who cooks in Thailand has their own traditional favorites, handed down through the family. There are, however, several main categories of pastes.

The red curry paste, *Krung Gaeng Ped (Daeng),* is searingly hot and takes its name from the quantities of dried, red chillies that give it its ruddy hue. It is used mainly for beef curries and dishes which demand a strong, hot flavor.

Green curry paste, called *Krung Gaeng Keo Wan,* is usually incorporated in poultry curries. The green caste is from the dark herbs and green chillies, but do not be fooled into thinking it is mild—it's not. The little green chilli peppers called *Prik e Noo* are the hottest of the lot and are only for the *aficionado* with an asbestos palate.

Another distinctive paste is *Krung Gaeng Som* or Orange Curry Paste used in Orange (Sour) Shrimp Curry Soup. *Som* generally means sour and occurs in the Thai words for vinegar, oranges and in *Som Or* (pomelo), a rough-skinned fruit very like a grapefruit. It also signifies the color orange [sic].

The *Mussaman* curry paste originated in India, the name being the Thai corruption of the word "Muslim." It was probably introduced into the country by the many Muslim clerks and minor officials that worked in government departments. As further indication of its foreign origin, *Mussaman* curry also uses spices which are absent from the Thai culinary repertoire, such as cinnamon, nutmeg and other sweet spices.

The Thai also offer a yellow curry paste, *Krung Gaeng Karee (Leung),* used for chicken and beef curries. It is very close to the *Mussaman* paste so I have not included it as a separate entry. A satisfactory (preferable?) approximation is to use red curry paste with the addition of large amounts of turmeric.

There are many other combinations of herbs and spices incorporated in *Gaeng* dishes and many lengthy discussions between respected cooks as to their amounts and application. Taking a basic recipe and attempting to maintain authentic continuity, I always modify the balance of the paste ingredients to please my own palate and those of my guests. There is no dogma with Thai cooking—originality and improvisation are appreciated and encouraged.

Ready-made curry pastes are commercially produced and sold in Thailand and are exported to the United States. The manufacturers tend to skimp on the variety of ingredients and compensate by increasing the amounts of chillies. It is advisable to have a few packets or jars as a back-up for emergencies but, when using them, augment with additional ingredients. In any case, it is far more rewarding to make your own. Amounts can be doubled or trebled and that portion not immediately required packed in a jar, tightly sealed and stored in the refrigerator for months.

When preparing a curry paste, it is definitely preferable to first use a mortar and pestle with the hard or fibrous ingredients rather than including them with other ingredients in a food processor or blender. The pounding of the pestle crushes the husks and fibers releasing the oils and juices, whereas the processor and blender merely cut the spices. Pounding a mortar with a pestle is also a great way to release hostilities! In Bangkok, every morning, one of the first sounds heard is the "thunk, thunk" of wood hitting earthenware or stone as the day's spice pastes are prepared. Perhaps this is one of the reasons the Thai are referred to as "happy and smiling."

For the modern kitchen and the appliance-minded cook with no time to spare, a food processor can be used in conjunction with an electric spice or coffee-type grinder. This does not eliminate the requirement for a mortar and pestle; for mashing moist herbs like lemon grass, garlic and shallots there is no substitute. However, the whole, dried spices (chillies, anise, caraway, cloves, etc.) give out their best aroma if attacked and thoroughly pulverized by a good grinder before being incorporated in the main mixture. When you are preparing a paste, single out the hard and dried spices and pound or grind them first before proceeding further.

When I require poultry cut into "curry pieces," I refer to a size, generally larger than bite-sized. A whole chicken leg, for instance, should be split into thigh and drumstick and both cut in half through the bone with a heavy, sharp cleaver. The rest of the chicken should be cut into pieces of similar size with the bone in. Sometimes in curries the poultry may be left in larger pieces, like the parts (wings, breasts, etc.) or sections we buy in trays in the supermarkets, but the smaller pieces cook faster, more uniformly and are easier to eat. The Thai seldom skin their fowls because they are frugal and use all the meat they pay for, but you may for esthetic and dietary reasons. Beef and pork for curries is usually thinly sliced and cut into rectangles ½″ × 2″. Fish, unless otherwise specified, is to be cut into the same size pieces. This makes the amount of meats go further as well as reducing the cooking time.

A few of the "dry" Thai curries will use other media

instead of coconut milk. Tamarind juice and fish sauce are the most common substitutes. When this is the case, the curry paste is generally fried in vegetable oil instead of reduced coconut milk. The bulk of curries, however, are made with coconut milk and it seems to mellow the fierce attack of the raw herbs and spices on the palate. When a dish contains coconut milk or cream, it is generally simmered uncovered, as covering tends to curdle the milk (presuming milk-based rather than water-based coconut milk is used). An occasional exception is if additional coconut milk/cream is to be added later in the recipe. Covering may be required and when more milk/cream is added, it slightly reduces the temperature and reverses the curdling process.

Simmering coconut milk gravies causes oils to rise and separate into beautiful red or green whorls colored by the chillies, as the mixture thickens. This surface appearance is characteristic of Thai curries and may indicate a further step or readiness to serve.

Thai curries use enormous amounts of coconut milk and cream and your food cupboard should contain some cans of coconut milk for emergencies. The best brands come from the Philippines and, oddly enough, the Thai do not can it for export. For regular use, however, stock up on bags of unsweetened dried coconut to make your own milk. These bags can be obtained from Thai and Indian stores and from health food shops; they substantially reduce the cost per finished pint over the commercial variety.

When making your own coconut milk, in addition to the cost saving and the benefit of being able to control the richness and uniformity, you have the opportunity to make additional amounts for future use. (For Coconut Milk, see "Fundamentals," chapter 3). I wholeheartedly endorse this practice—when I get the "curry hungries," I can pluck a premeasured amount of coconut milk from the refrigerator or freezer and, together with my preprepared curry paste, whip together a superb, textbook curry in less than fifteen minutes!

# PRINCIPAL CURRY PASTES

•

## RED CURRY PASTE · KRUNG GAENG PED

*Yields 3 tablespoons, approximately*

Red curry paste may be bought in jars or packets in the larger Oriental markets but the homemade version is milder and more aromatic, using a fuller spectrum of spices. If you do not have an electric coffee grinder and a food processor or blender, prepare to spend more than an hour vigorously pummeling a pestle into a mortar with first the dry and then the moist ingredients to achieve a respectable paste (not an endorsement, merely a *caveat).*

I recommend you evenly multiply the amounts of the ingredients (this recipe yields about 3 tablespoons) and store in the refrigerator in an airtight jar for future use. It will keep well for at least 1 month.

- 14 *medium dried red chillies, seeded or 1 tablespoon ground red chilli powder (Cayenne)*
- 3 *shallots, minced*
- 1 *teaspoon caraway seeds or 1 teaspoon ground caraway*
- 1 *tablespoon whole coriander seeds or 1 tablespoon ground*
- 8 *pieces Laos* (Ka), *chopped or 1 tablespoon Laos powder*
- 2 *tablespoons coriander roots, minced*
- 1 *teaspoon salt*
- 1 *lime zest, minced*
- 1 *stalk lemon grass, minced*
- 1 *teaspoon whole black peppercorns or 1 teaspoon freshly ground black pepper*
- ½ *teaspoon Kaffir lime powder* (Pew Makrut)
- 1 *tablespoon garlic, minced*
- 1 *teaspoon shrimp paste* (Kapee)
- 4 *tablespoons vegetable oil*

Place the whole dried spices (chillies, caraway, coriander, Laos and peppercorns) in an electric spice grinder or mortar and grind or pound to a powder. Omit this step if ground spices are used. Empty this powder into the food processor—if not available, continue with the mortar and pestle. Add the remaining ingredients, including the oil, and process or pound to a smooth, even paste.

•

## GREEN CURRY PASTE · KRUNG GAENG KEO WAN

*Yields 6 to 8 tablespoons, approximately*

The green curries *(Krung Gaeng Keo Wan* is the standard) are the hottest in the Thai spectrum of spiciness. To achieve this color and incendiary hotness, there is an extraordinarily large portion of whole, fresh, green chillies (with seeds) included in the paste. Adjust the amounts of chillies to suit your own spice-heat tolerance and that of your guests. The paste will keep for at least 1 month in an airtight container in your refrigerator.

- 3 *pieces dried Laos* (Ka), *chopped or 1 teaspoon Laos powder*
- 1 *teaspoon dried lesser ginger* (Krachai), *or 1 teaspoon powdered lesser ginger*
- 1 *teaspoon coriander seeds or 1 teaspoon ground coriander*
- 1 *teaspoon caraway seeds or 1 teaspoon ground caraway*
- 12 *black peppercorns or 1½ teaspoons ground black pepper*
- 4 *whole cloves or ¼ teaspoon ground cloves*
- 1 *whole nutmeg pod or 1 teaspoon ground nutmeg*
- 2 *stalks lemon grass, minced*
- 2 *tablespoons coriander roots, chopped*
- 2 *tablespoons garlic, chopped*
- 2 *tablespoons shallots, chopped*

1 *teaspoon lime zest, minced, or ½ teaspoon dried Kaffir lime rind, soaked in hot water until soft, then minced*
8 *whole green Serrano chillies, stemmed and minced*
1 *teaspoon shrimp paste* (Kapee)
1 *teaspoon salt*
4 *tablespoons vegetable oil*

Place the whole, dried spices (Laos, lesser ginger, coriander, caraway, peppercorns, cloves and nutmeg) in a mortar or electric spice grinder and pound or grind to a smooth, somewhat stringy, powder. (If using a spice grinder, because of its size, this will require repeated steps.) Omit this exercise if ground spices are used. Empty the powder into a food processor; if not available, continue with the mortar and pestle. Add the remaining ingredients, including oil, and process or pound to a smooth, even paste.

•

## ORANGE CURRY PASTE · KRUNG GAENG SOM

*Yields 4 to 5 tablespoons, approximately*

10 *medium dried red chillies, seeded, soaked in warm water and finely chopped*
1 *teaspoon salt*
2 *tablespoons of the outer layers of a peeled red onion, chopped*
1 *tablespoon shrimp paste* (Kapee)
1 *teaspoon rice vinegar*

In a mortar, pound the chillies with the salt until they are completely pulverized. Add the red onion and continue pounding until it is macerated. Spoon in the shrimp paste and vinegar and pound until the resultant mixture is smooth and uniform.

•

## ROASTED CURRY PASTE · NAM PRIK PAO

*Yields 6 to 8 tablespoons, approximately*

Because it is precooked, this curry paste is used mainly for flavorings, garnishes and as a component of sauces.

8 *dried, red chillies, seeded*
2 *tablespoons shallots, chopped*
5 *cloves garlic, chopped*
2 *tablespoons vegetable oil*
2 *tablespoons dried shrimp powder*
1 *tablespoon granulated sugar*
1 *tablespoon fish sauce* (Nam Pla)

Tear off a square of aluminum foil and place the chillies, shallots and garlic in it, wrapping tightly into a sealed package. Place the package directly on a stove burner set to medium low and cook for 2 minutes on either side, turning with tongs. Allow to cool, unwrap and transfer the contents to a mortar and pound to a paste, adding oil if necessary.

Heat a small frying pan with the 2 tablespoons of vegetable oil and add the paste, stir-frying until brown. Add the shrimp powder, sugar and fish sauce, stirring. Remove from heat and use the paste immediately or refrigerate in a capped jar. Use within 3 days.

•

# CURRIES

•

## RED BEEF CURRY · GAENG PED NEUA

*6 to 8 Servings*

*Gaeng Ped Neua* originated in Northeast Thailand, although it is widely eaten throughout the country.

- 2 *cups "Thick" coconut milk*
- 2 to 3 *tablespoons red curry paste* (Krung Gaeng Ped)
- 2 *pounds round steak, sliced into thin strips 2" long × ½" wide*
- 2 *cups "Thin" coconut milk*
- 2 *young citrus leaves, fresh picked and torn into strips*
- 1 *teaspoon salt*
- 2 *tablespoons fish sauce* (Nam Pla)
- 2 *red Serrano chillies, seeded and sliced into strips*
- 1 *teaspoon dried sweet basil*
- 1 *tablespoon coriander leaves, chopped for garnish*

In a wok or saucepan, simmer the "Thick" coconut milk over low heat, stirring, until it thickens and oil appears around the edges. When the milk thickens to a cream and is oily, increase heat, add the red curry paste and fry for 5 minutes. There will be a noticeable color and odor change as this mixture becomes properly cooked. Add the beef, "Thin" coconut milk and the remaining ingredients except the coriander leaves. Quickly bring to a boil, reduce heat and simmer until meat is tender. Pour into a serving dish, sprinkle with the coriander leaves and serve.

•

## GREEN CHICKEN CURRY · GAENG KEO WAN GAI

*6 to 8 Servings*

This curry should properly contain pea eggplants, *Makeua Pong* (see Glossary, page 281), a tiny, bitter vegetable of the eggplant/tomato family slightly larger than a pea. It is not commercially obtainable in the United States at this time, but it is being experimentally grown and should be available in Thai markets shortly. Some Thai restaurants substitute green peas for appearance.

- 2½ to 3 *pounds frying chicken, boned, skinned and cut into small chunks*
- 2 *cups "Thick" coconut milk*
- 2 *tablespoons fish sauce* (Nam Pla)
- 3 *pieces dried Laos* (Ka)
- 3 *tablespoons green curry paste* (Krung Gaeng Keo Wan)
- 2 *cups "Thin" coconut milk*
- ½ *cup fresh sweet basil leaves (1 tablespoon dried may be substituted)*
- 6 to 8 *young citrus leaves*
- 2 to 3 *pea eggplants* (Makeua Pong) *(optional)*
- 6 *green Serrano chillies*

In a wok, boil together the chicken, "Thick" coconut milk, fish sauce and Laos until the meat is tender. Remove the chicken to a plate with a slotted spoon and continue boiling until the milk thickens and becomes oily. Add the curry paste and continue cooking, stirring to help mix the paste, for a few more minutes. Return the chicken to the wok when the mixture is smooth and the paste has released its aroma. Pour in the "Thin" coconut milk and return to the boil. Reduce heat and simmer for 5 to 10 minutes. Add the basil and citrus leaves, pea eggplant, and chillies. Increase heat and boil again for 5 minutes. Serve over rice.

•

## PRINCESS'S CURRY · GAENG NEUA KUN YING

*6 to 8 Servings*

*Gaeng Neua Kun Ying* is an adaptation from an old recipe probably created in one of the royal palaces by a princess in honor of the monarch. *Kun Ying* is a term denoting one of the royal ranks of princess.

*Paste*

- 7 to 9 *medium dried red chillies (use canned ortegas and/or reduce the number if a milder paste is preferred)*
- 1 *teaspoon freshly ground black pepper*
- 1 *teaspoon ground caraway seeds*
- ½ *teaspoon lime rind (green zest), chopped*
- 1½ *teaspoons coriander roots, chopped*
- 1 *teaspoon salt*
- 1 *stalk lemon grass, minced*
- 1 *tablespoon Laos powder* (Ka)
- 2 *tablespoons fresh garlic, chopped*
- 2 *tablespoons shallots, chopped*

*Curry*

- 4 *cups "Thick" coconut milk*
- 2 *pounds beef, chuck or stewing, cut into 1" cubes*
- 4 *tablespoons fish sauce* (Nam Pla)
- 8 *young citrus leaves*
- 2 *cups "Thin" coconut milk*
- 1 *teaspoon dried sweet basil (8 leaves, if fresh)*
- 2 *green Serrano chillies, seeded and cut into strips*

*Paste*

Place all the Paste ingredients in a mortar or food processor and pound or grind into an even paste.

*Curry*

In a wok or large saucepan, bring the "Thick" coconut milk to a boil, stirring, and add the beef. Continue to boil, uncovered, until the amount of liquid reduces somewhat, thickens and oil begins to appear at the edges. The milk will feel soapy and cling to the spoon as it thickens. Stir and cook until the beef is tender. Add the Paste, fish sauce and citrus leaves. The mixture will immediately thicken when the Paste is added. Continue cooking and stirring for 5 minutes and pour in the "Thin" coconut milk. Reduce heat and simmer uncovered for 20 minutes. The Curry will again thicken and some oil will float on the surface. Now add the sweet basil and green chilli strips. Mix well and pour into a serving bowl. Serve accompanied by plain, cooked rice.

•

## SHRIMP AND CUCUMBER CURRY · GAENG PED TAET

*4 to 6 Servings*

The slightly sour taste of the sauce complements seafood beautifully in this unusual curry. The tamarind flavor contributes a sour tang to the sauce. (For Tamarind, see "Fundamentals," chapter 3.)

*Paste*

1 *teaspoon powdered Laos* (Ka)
1 *stalk lemon grass, minced*
1 *teaspoon ground turmeric*
3 *cloves garlic, finely chopped*
5 *dried red chillies, chopped (including seeds)*
½ *teaspoon ground black pepper*
1 *teaspoon ground coriander*
1 *teaspoon ground cumin*

1 *teaspoon shrimp paste* (Kapee)
2 *shallots, finely chopped*
¼ *teaspoon ground cinnamon*
¼ *teaspoon ground nutmeg*

*Curry*

½ *cup coconut "Cream"*
1½ *cups "Thick" coconut milk*
2 *large cucumbers, peeled, seeded and cut into 1" cubes*
1 *pound medium raw shrimp (31 to 40 count per pound), shelled, cleaned and deveined*
2 *green Serrano chillies, seeded and finely chopped*
1 *teaspoon tamarind concentrate, dissolved in 2 tablespoons hot water*
3 *tablespoons fish sauce* (Nam Pla)
2 *teaspoons granulated sugar*

*Paste*

In a food processor or mortar, grind or pound the Paste ingredients to a smooth mixture.

*Curry*

In a wok or heavy saucepan, bring the coconut "Cream" to a boil, stirring constantly until it reduces, becomes thick and oil forms around the edges. Add the curry Paste and fry until the color and odor change, stirring to prevent sticking. Place in the "Thick" coconut milk and return to a boil. Add the cucumber pieces and cook for 3 minutes, stirring. Reduce heat to low, add the shrimp and simmer until the shrimp are just cooked, about 2 minutes. Add the chillies. Stir in the tamarind liquid, fish sauce and sugar. Return, again, to a boil and remove at once. Pour into a bowl and serve with rice.

•

## THAI MUSLIM CURRY · GAENG MUSSAMAN

*4 Servings*

As can be seen from the ingredients, the use of cinnamon, cloves and nutmeg marks *Gaeng Mussaman* with origins outside Thailand. The aromatic spices are akin to the *Garam Masala* spice mix added to Indian curries, usually during the later cooking stages.

There is Thai historical reference to a feast for King Rama I, circa 1809, during which an Indian curry was served. It is believed the curry was brought by Muslim officials employed in the Harbor Department in Bangkok.

*Paste*

- 7 *dried red chillies, seeded*
- 2 *teaspoons dried Laos* (Ka), *sliced (Laos powder may be substituted)*
- 1 *stalk lemon grass, minced*
- 5 *cloves*
- 2" *stick cinnamon*
- 6 *cardamom seeds*
- ¼ *teaspoon ground nutmeg*
- 4 *bay leaves*
- ½ *teaspoon shrimp paste* (Kapee)
- 7 *cloves garlic and 7 shallots, chopped and fried in 1 teaspoon oil until just brown, then drained*
- ½ *teaspoon salt*

*Curry*

- 1½ *pounds beef (chuck, round or other inexpensive cut), trimmed of most fat and cut into 1" cubes*
- 4 *cups "Thick" coconut milk*
- ½ *cup roasted, salted peanuts*
- 3 *tablespoons fish sauce* (Nam Pla)
- 2" *stick cinnamon*
- 8 *cardamom seeds*

1 *tablespoon tamarind concentrate, dissolved in 3 tablespoons hot water*
*Juice of 1 lime*
2 *tablespoons palm sugar*

*Paste*

Over high heat in a small fry pan, cook the chillies, Laos, lemon grass, cloves, cinnamon, cardamom, nutmeg and bay. You may bake these in the oven but, either method, be careful not to burn or blacken the dry ingredients.

Place all the Paste ingredients, toasted, dried and moist, in a mortar and pound to a juicy, pungent puree. To expedite this (save pounding) and make a more uniform paste, I recommend the cooked spices be put first in an electric spice grinder and ground to a coarse powder before adding to the mortar. In any event, when you have completed the pounding, set the Paste aside for use in the Curry.

*Curry*

Place the beef, coconut milk, peanuts and fish sauce in a wok or saucepan. Boil over medium heat, stirring, until the beef is tender (approximately 20 minutes). Remove the meat with a slotted spoon to a plate, continue to boil and reduce the sauce to one half by volume. Add the paste, stir and return the meat to the boiling sauce.

Put in the cinnamon stick and cardamoms. Reduce heat and simmer for 5 minutes. Stir in the tamarind liquid, lime juice and palm sugar. The gravy should remain thick but still liquid. Remove the cinnamon stick and serve immediately with rice.

•

## PORK AND VEGETABLE CURRY · GAENG PED MOO

*4 Servings*

This curry is often prepared by the farm people in the little villages. It is one of the few Thai curries which does not require coconut milk. Because of this the preparation time is short; the curry is cooked after work when everyone comes home from the fields.

- ¼ *cup vegetable oil*
- 3 *tablespoons red curry paste* (Krung Gaeng Ped)
- 1 *cup lean pork, loin or butt, cut into thin slices ½" × 2"*
- 2 *tablespoons fish sauce* (Nam Pla)
- 1 *stalk lemon grass, chopped*
- ½ *cup cabbage, chopped and soaked in cold water*
- ½ *cup green beans, cut into 1½" lengths, soaked in cold water*
- 1 *cup dried Chinese mushrooms, soaked in hot water, stemmed and cut into strips*
- 5 *fresh, red Serrano chillies, seeded and cut into strips*
- 2 *teaspoons granulated sugar*
- 12 *mint leaves, chopped*

Heat the oil in a wok and fry the red curry paste for 3 minutes, stirring until color and odor change. Add the pork, fish sauce and lemon grass. Stir-fry for 5 minutes. Drain the cabbage, beans and mushrooms and add them to the wok. Fry for a further 3 minutes. Sprinkle with chilli strips. Stir them into the mixture and fry for another minute. Sprinkle with sugar, stir and remove to a serving bowl. Garnish with mint leaves and serve.

•

## GREEN CURRY OF DUCK · GAENG KEO WAN PET

*6 to 8 Servings*

Duck is widely used in Thailand, primarily for special occasions. The indigenous birds are smaller and skinnier than ours; also considerably cheaper. In the predominantly Chinese sections of Bangkok, rows upon rows of duck hang in the markets, clean plucked but with heads and feet. The Chinese-Thai feature a form of roasted duck with spice sauce (barbecued *Pei Par Ngap)* but this *Gaeng Keo Wan Pet* is original and authentically Thai.

- 1 *cup coconut "Cream"*
- 5 *tablespoons green curry paste* (Krung Gaeng Keo Wan)
- 3 *pounds (approximately) roasting duck, cut into curry-size pieces*
- 2 *cups "Thin" coconut milk*
- 2 *cups "Thick" coconut milk*
- 8 to 10 *fresh citrus leaves (optional)*
- 1 *teaspoon salt*
- 2 *tablespoons fish sauce* (Nam Pla)
- 3 *green Serrano chillies, slivered*
- 2 *tablespoons fresh sweet basil leaves, chopped (1 tablespoon dried may be substituted)*
- 2 *tablespoons coriander leaves, finely chopped*

Spoon the coconut "Cream" into a wok. Fry, stirring, over medium heat until it reduces by ¼, thickens and the coconut oil begins to separate and bubble.

Add the green curry paste and continue frying for approximately 5 minutes or until the mixture changes color and odor. While still on heat, add the duck pieces and coat thoroughly with the cream/curry paste. Reduce heat to low, cover and continue cooking for an additional 15 minutes, stirring occasionally to prevent burning and sticking. Remove the accumulated fat in the wok with a bulb baster.

Now add both the "Thin" and "Thick" coconut milks,

citrus leaves, salt and fish sauce and bring to a boil. Immediately reduce heat to simmer and cook, uncovered, for 30 to 40 minutes or until the duck is tender and begins to shrink from the bones.

Again, skim off any accumulated fat and stir in the chillies, sweet basil and coriander.

Simmer for 5 more minutes, until all the ingredients are heated through, adjust the seasoning *(Nam Pla)* and serve.

•

## STEAMED CHICKEN CURRY · HAW MOK GAI

*4 Servings*

In Thailand, *Haw Mok Gai* is steamed in a dish fashioned from banana leaves. Substitute a baking dish lined with foil if you do not have a banana tree at the bottom of your garden.

- 3 *whole chicken breasts, boned and thinly sliced*
- 1 *cup "Thick" coconut milk*
- 8 *dried red chillies, seeded and finely chopped*
- ½ *teaspoon ground black pepper*
- *Zest of 3 limes, finely chopped*
- 3 *cloves garlic, finely chopped*
- 3 *shallots, finely chopped*
- ½ *teaspoon shrimp paste* (Kapee)
- 1 *stalk lemon grass, thinly sliced cross-wise*
- 2 *teaspoons coriander roots, finely chopped*
- ½ *teaspoon salt*
- ½ *cup "Thin" coconut milk*
- 4 *citrus leaves, shredded*
- 4 *inner lettuce leaves, cut into 1" pieces*
- 8 *fresh sweet basil leaves or 1 teaspoon dried basil*

Place the chicken in a bowl and pour in the "Thick" coconut milk, reserving 1 tablespoon. Mix the chicken and milk together and let it stand. In a mortar pound together the chillies, pepper, lime zest, garlic, shallots, shrimp paste, lemon grass, coriander roots and salt into a fine, juicy paste. Stir the "Thin" coconut milk into this paste until a smooth sauce is formed. Pour over the chicken and stir in the citrus leaves. Line a baking dish with a piece of foil large enough to be folded over the contents. Layer the lettuce leaves and sweet basil in the bottom. Pour in the chicken mixture and sprinkle with the reserved tablespoon of "Thick" coconut milk. Fold the foil over the top, sealing completely. Bring the water in a steamer up to boiling. Place the dish inside and steam for 30 to 40 minutes or until chicken is firm and tender. Cut away the surplus foil from the top and serve.

•

## CRISP CURRY · PRIK KING

*4 to 6 Servings*

A great favorite with the Thai, *Prik King* is a dry curry with a concentrated and piquant flavor. A scant two spoonfuls will flavor a heaped plate of rice. Although fish predominates, there is no noticeably fishy flavor.

*Paste*

*4 stems lemon grass, finely chopped*
*6 large, dried, red chillies, seeded and chopped*
*1 boned, smoked kipper, flaked (½ cup of similar boned, smoked fish may be substituted)*
*6 shallots, chopped*
*8 cloves garlic, chopped*
*1 tablespoon Laos powder* (Ka)
*1 teaspoon salt*
*1 teaspoon shrimp paste* (Kapee)

*Zest of 2 limes, chopped*
2 *tablespoons coriander roots, chopped*

*Curry*

4 *tablespoons vegetable oil*
4 *tablespoons granulated sugar*
3 *tablespoons fish sauce* (Nam Pla)
*Yolks of 10 hardcooked, salted eggs* (Kai Kem) *(plain, hardcooked eggs may be substituted)*
3 *herring fillets, fresh or canned, crisp-fried in 1 tablespoon oil (1 cup boned mackerel or tuna may be substituted)*
½ *cup sunflower seeds, crisp-fried*
½ *cup fresh green beans, cut into 1" lengths*

*Paste*

Place all the Paste ingredients into a mortar or food processor and pound or grind into an even paste.

*Curry*

In a wok or large saucepan, heat the vegetable oil and fry the Paste until color and odor change. Add the sugar and fish sauce and stir until the mixture is quite dry. Stir in the hard egg yolks, one at a time, then add the herring pieces and sunflower seeds. Stir well to mix everything and add the green beans. Turn the heat to low and cook for 6 minutes, stirring continuously. The green beans should be tender but still crisp. Transfer to a serving dish and serve with rice.

•

## KORAT BEEF CURRY · GAENG PED KORAT

*4 to 6 Servings*

*Gaeng Ped Korat* comes from Nakhon Ratchasima (Korat), northeast of Bangkok. Although many will remember the name from the large air base outside the little town, the people are still country folk and this is a simple country curry.

If using whole, dried spices in the recipe *(Krachai,* peppercorns, chillies), put them into a mortar or electric spice or coffee-type grinder and pound or grind to a coarse powder before adding them to the rest of the paste ingredients. Whole, freshly ground spices add more bouquet to dishes.

- 1 *stalk lemon grass, minced*
- 1 *teaspoon Laos powder* (Ka)
- 4 *shallots, chopped*
- 1½ *teaspoons shrimp paste* (Kapee)
- 1 *teaspoon Lesser Ginger* (Krachai), *powdered or whole*
- 1 *teaspoon ground black pepper or equivalent amounts whole peppercorns*
- *Zest of 1 lime, minced*
- ½ *teaspoon salt*
- 1½ *teaspoons red chilli powder (Cayenne) or 6 dried, red chillies, chopped*
- 1 *tablespoon vegetable oil (optional)*
- 1 *pound lean ground beef*
- 1 *tablespoon vegetable oil for frying*
- 1½ *cups water*
- 2 *tablespoons fish sauce* (Nam Pla)
- 4 *citrus leaves, shredded*
- 4 *basil leaves, shredded*

In a mortar or food processor, pound or grind together the lemon grass, Laos powder, shallots, shrimp paste, lesser ginger, black pepper, lime zest, salt and chilli powder to a paste. If using the processor, add some or all of the optional oil to achieve the proper consistency. In a bowl, mix this paste with the ground beef until the meat is thoroughly coated. Heat the cooking oil in a wok over low heat. Gently stir-fry the beef/curry paste until the beef releases its moisture. Add the water and bring to a boil. Reduce heat and simmer until beef is tender. Stir in the fish sauce, citrus and sweet basil leaves. Simmer for 5 more minutes and serve hot, accompanied by plain rice.

•

## CRAB CURRY · GAENG POO TA LAY

*4 to 6 Servings*

The little beach restaurants lining the Gulf of Siam naturally use freshly caught crab for this curry. However, I have adapted this recipe to accommodate precooked crab, which is more readily available in our seafood shops.

7 *medium dried red chillies, seeded and chopped, or 1½ teaspoons red chilli powder (Cayenne)*
2 *pieces Laos* (Ka), *chopped, or 1 teaspoon Laos powder*
½ *teaspoon whole, black peppercorns or ½ teaspoon ground black pepper*
4 *cloves garlic, chopped*
5 *shallots, chopped*
5 *coriander roots, chopped*
½ *teaspoon lime zest, minced*
1 *stalk lemon grass, minced*
½ *teaspoon salt*
1 *teaspoon shrimp paste* (Kapee)
2 *cups "Thick" coconut milk*
2 *tablespoons fish sauce* (Nam Pla)
1 *tablespoon palm sugar*
*The cooked body and claw meat (as intact as possible) from 2 Dungeness crabs (2½ pounds each before shelling)*

6 *citrus leaves*
1 *tablespoon coriander leaves, finely chopped*

Place the whole dried spices (red chillies, Laos and peppercorns) in an electric spice grinder or mortar and grind or pound to a powder. Of course, omit this step if ground spices are used. Empty this powder into the food processor; if not available, continue with the mortar and pestle. Add the garlic, shallots, coriander roots, lime zest, lemon grass, salt and shrimp paste and process or pound into a smooth, even paste.

In a wok or saucepan, simmer the "Thick" coconut milk over low heat, stirring, until it reduces by at least one half and becomes thick and oily. Transfer the paste from the processor or mortar into the thickened coconut milk and stir constantly until the mixture changes in odor and becomes properly cooked (about 5 minutes). Season with the fish sauce and palm sugar and stir until the sugar is dissolved. Add the crab meat and citrus leaves and stir gently until the crab meat has warmed through. Transfer the mixture to a heated serving bowl and sprinkle with the chopped coriander leaves. Serve immediately.

•

## CHICKEN CURRY WITH TOMATOES · GAENG PED GAI GUP MAKEUATAET

*6 to 8 Servings*

This savory, red chicken curry uses the most common techniques for curry-making: frying the cream briefly and adding the paste. To ensure enough cream, I recommend you make your "Thick" coconut milk at least one day in advance and refrigerate overnight. (The fraction of cream that rises to the top depends on the butterfat content of your milk and the oil richness of your coconuts. See "Fundamentals," chapter 3.) The Thai seldom skin or seed their tomatoes before cooking and, although the result may not be esthetically appealing to some, I am sure that the fiber is good for the digestive system!

*1 teaspoon shrimp paste* (Kapee)
*1 stalk lemon grass, minced*
*3 shallots, chopped*
*4 cloves garlic, chopped*
*7 dried red chillies, chopped*
*7 coriander roots, chopped*
*1 teaspoon ground cumin*
*1 teaspoon freshly ground black pepper*
*1 teaspoon Laos powder* (Ka)
*½ cup coconut "Cream"*
*2½ to 3 pounds frying chicken or equal weight of chicken parts, boned and cut into 2" cubes (approximately), e.g., the whole breast will be cut into 6 pieces*
*1½ cups "Thin" coconut milk*
*4 beefsteak tomatoes or 6 small tomatoes, coarsely chopped*
*1 tablespoon fish sauce* (Nam Pla)
*1 teaspoon tamarind concentrate dissolved in 2 tablespoons hot water*
*1 tablespoon granulated sugar*

In a mortar or food processor, pound or grind the following ingredients to form a smooth, even paste: shrimp paste, lemon grass, shallots, garlic, red chillies, coriander roots, cumin, pepper, Laos. Heat the "Cream" in a wok over moderate heat, stirring, until oil forms around the edges. Stir in the paste from the mortar or processor and fry until it changes color and becomes less pungent. Put the chicken pieces in the paste and stir until the pieces are well coated. Pour in the "Thin" coconut milk and stir until the gravy has thickened. Reduce heat to low and simmer until chicken is tender (approximately 20 minutes). Now add the tomatoes, increase heat and bring to a boil. Reduce heat and simmer for 5 minutes. Add the fish sauce, tamarind liquid and sugar. Stir and simmer for 5 more minutes. Pour into a serving bowl.

*I want there to be no peasant in my realm so poor that he will not have a chicken in his pot every Sunday.*
ATTRIBUTED TO HENRY IV OF FRANCE

ELEVEN

# Meat and Poultry

## NEUA, GAI LAE PET

A visit to the meat section of a Thai market is not for the squeamish, nor for the average American accustomed to hygienically packaged pieces of carefully butchered meat, classified and labeled. This is a jungle and a celebration of meat; large slabs of flesh, unidentifiable to the novitiate. The beef is stacked in great, Elizabethan hunks of fresh, red meat, untouched by red dye number two, or any of the numerous, modern food preservatives. The pork is a monument to good living. Beautiful, delicate pink chunks of lean meat and long strips of loin, seldom seen in our markets, nestle alongside such esoteric delicacies as shell-thin pig's ears and rows of neat little pig's trotters.

Chickens hang in chorus lines, chicken-pimple bare or bedraggled feathers. They probably stopped squawking mere minutes ago. They are the thin, scrawny maiden aunts to our plump, force-fed, battery babies, but undoubtedly spent their days pecking and scratching in the lush grass and their spare flesh has a superb flavor in consequence.

Ducks are there also; purveyed by the Chinese, who click up the prices with computer-like rapidity on their abaci. These are the true relatives of the wild duck. No pampered, cosseted fowl, these. True, it takes two of them to equal an expensive, American, supermarket duck in size, but the cost of a bird will be but a fraction of the price.

Watch that plump Thai housewife over there; her flowered blouse and much-washed black *pasin* stretched over her ample frame. She is bargaining hard and seriously over the price of a kilo of beef (two and one quarter pounds). The discussion is taking at least five minutes. She has pinched and poked every piece of beef on the slab and is standing squarely in front of the counter, hands clasping an already bulging string bag of vegetables. The vendor questions; the housewife nods and a sharp knife splits the beef, accurately cutting off the exact amount. The housewife shifts her stance and peers anxiously at the old-fashioned scales. The meat is weighed. This is serious business as scales have been known to be unfairly weighted. The transaction is concluded in an outbreak of smiles all round and a series of good-natured jests from neighboring vendors, whose wares were not patronized. The meat is wrapped in a big piece of banana leaf, then in newspaper, and off goes another satisfied customer.

With all this plentitude, one can still reflect that the Thai are essentially a fish-eating nation. Meat is for high days and holidays. That housewife who was so absorbed in her purchase, was probably planning a family feast for visiting relatives; a fifth-cycle birthday celebration for her mother (sixty years, which is an enviable pinnacle in life), or perhaps a special meal in honor of her favorite nephew who was entering the Buddhist monkhood for his obligatory three-month sabbatical.

Meat is a special high point of the average meal. A little goes a long way, helped along by myriad herbs and spices, swimming in coconut-milk gravy and served over steaming mounds of white rice. Fish is the everyday stuff of life; meat is the treat. The Thai hill-tribes—Lahu, Mien, Karen and Kammu—will sacrifice a pig for a special village feast, or hunt and kill a wild deer. However, like most other Thai villagers, this is something to be talked about and remembered as the event of the month, if not the season.

As well as headlining a special meal, meat composes several delicacies of which the Thai are very fond. One is *Nem,* a fragrantly spicy sausage. It is made of shreds of preserved pork and skin, heavily spiced with garlic and black pepper, the whole morsel being wrapped in banana leaf. This delicious savory harbors a fiery-hot, green chilli in its bosom, cunningly hidden from view as many an unwary tourist has found out. Barbecued and spiced pork is another: a delicatessen-like prize of Chinese origin. The pork loin is slow-roasted, after being marinated in Five Spice powder and tinted pink with Chinese food coloring. Slices of this adorn many a fried-rice dish and also make an appetizer to accompany ice-cold bottles of *Singha* beer or *Amarit* lager, both indigenous to Thailand.

Chicken is much more commonplace than beef in the diet of the Thai. Acetylene flares or strings of generator-driven light bulbs illuminate hundreds of little street stands at night, around which the Thai cluster to buy barbecued chicken. The flesh of this chicken is smoked and barbecued after being dusted with spices, or marinated in a mixture of black pepper, garlic and pounded coriander roots. At the *Chai Talay,* a large and well-known Chinese-Thai restaurant near the boxing stadium in Bangkok, the several floors are packed nightly with families wolfing down incredible amounts of the house speciality, a barbecued chicken. This speciality is accompanied by a sweet, hot pepper sauce, the fame of which is celebrated beyond the shores of Thailand. The owners will not give you the recipe, but they will sell bottles of the sauce. I have experimented with the sauce and in chapter 14, "Sauces," have given an approximate recipe.

The Thai, being Buddhist, do not kill animals, so the meat butchering is left to the Muslims and Chinese. The beef animal is the buffalo and its meat is surprisingly tender, being indistinguishable from prime beef, in the hands of a good cook. This treatment of buffalo is the same also in India. In our family there is an amusing story about my mother who, although British, was born in India. Returning to England as a young bride, on her first foray to an English butcher she asked for a cow's hump and was very upset when the butcher did not understand what she meant. She complained about the incident to my father when he returned from work and was mortified when he laughed until the tears rolled down his cheeks. He then explained to her gently that the cows in England did not have humps!

This illustrates the point that Oriental butchering is not the same as ours. *Caveat emptor!* Meat in Thailand is bought by the piece (cut unknown) in the markets, and the shopper will specify whether the meat should include fat or not and if it is wanted whole, or ground. More detailed requests are seldom made. The Chinese and Thai markets in the United States also sell meat in the same fashion, and the novice can be intimidated by large, unfamiliar chunks sitting on unrefrigerated trays behind the counter. Do not be put off by this seemingly casual presentation. The meat is generally of very high quality. It is lean, suitable for most stir-fried dishes and you merely specify by weight how much you want. The beef corresponds in quality to *sukiyaki* beef. The same superior quality applies to the pork. It is frequently butt or loin, but usually cheaper, pound for pound, than supermarket cuts.

Frying or roasting chicken is best for Thai chicken recipes—at least those in this book. I have already made allowances for the difference in tenderness between their birds and ours by reducing the cooking time. Chicken may be served cut into parts, bone-in, or into small, bite-sized pieces with or without bone. Either have your butcher cut it for you or, if chopping it yourself, use a large, heavy and sharp Chinese cleaver. Do not use a small cleaver. It does not have the weight to carry it through the bone and the cutting edge will be damaged. Whether or not you skin your chicken is up to you. The Thai do not, nor do I. Do cut off surplus fat, however, as most dishes already contain oil or coconut cream at the frying stage.

## CHOPPED BEEF WITH GARNISHES · LAAP ISSAN

*3 to 4 Servings*

This Thai version of Steak Tartare, *Laap,* comes from the Thai Issan Restaurant beside the market on Thaan Road, Udon, in Northeast Thailand. In its original form, raw buffalo meat and blood are used because water buffalo is the "beef" animal of Thailand.

Since most United States supermarkets do not have a "water buffalo" section, I have suggested a common cut of beef steak.

If you are not a raw-beef lover, you may modify the recipe by lightly poaching the ground steak in boiling water until the meat just changes color, then follow the rest of the cooking instructions. You may find you prefer this interesting combination of beef and seasonings to the traditional Steak Tartare!

- *1½ tablespoons long or short grain rice*
- *4 small dried red chillies, seeded*
- *1 pound top round, finely ground*
- *Juice of 2 limes*
- *3 stalks lemon grass, finely minced*
- *1 large red onion, finely chopped*
- *1 large bell pepper, cored, seeded and chopped*
- *30 (approximately) mint leaves*
- *2 tablespoons fish sauce* (Nam Pla)

In a small dry frying pan, over medium heat, roast the rice and chillies, shaking the pan, until the grains are brown and the chillies are darkened. Remove the rice and chillies to a mortar and pestle or electric grinder and pound or grind until you have the consistency of coarse sand.

Place the ground steak in a bowl and mix, with your hands, adding the ground rice and chillies, lime juice, lemon grass, red onion and green pepper. Chop one half the mint leaves and stir them into the mixture, reserving the remaining mint for garnish. Season this mixture with the fish sauce and transfer to a platter. Mound attractively with your hands or a mold. Garnish with the remainder of the mint leaves.

*Presentation*

For a luncheon buffet, this dish may be garnished "Thai-style" in the following way: flowerets cut from fresh green and red chillies on top, a ring of cucumber slices with serrated edges, lime wedges. (See Chapter 4, Fruit and Vegetable Carving.)

•

## PORK AND SHRIMP MINCE · NEUA TANG

*4 Servings*

A delicate dish with subtle flavor, *Neua Tang* is quickly and easily prepared. It makes an excellent entrée for a light lunch.

- ½ *pound small, cooked shrimp, finely chopped*
- ½ *pound ground pork*
- 1 *cup "Thin" coconut milk*
- 1 *teaspoon salt*
- ½ *teaspoon ground black pepper*
- 1 *teaspoon granulated sugar*
- 2 *fresh green Serrano chillies, seeded and sliced cross-wise*
- 1 *tablespoon coriander leaves*

Combine the shrimp and pork in a bowl. Heat the coconut milk in a saucepan over medium heat until it is just simmering. Stir in the shrimp/pork mixture. Bring to a boiling point and reduce heat to simmer. Cook uncovered for 3 minutes. Stir in the salt, pepper and sugar. Add the chilli slices. Pour into a serving dish and sprinkle with coriander leaves. Serve with plain rice.

## RAMA-A-BATHING · PRA RAM LONG SONG

*6 Servings*

The origins of this dish are unclear, but the name suggests that it was probably created in honor of a Thai king (Rama) by a palace cook. The "bathing" describes the way the meat is presented, floating over a sea of greens and sauce. The Thai use *pak bung* in this dish; a lush creeper growing in or near the water. Young leaves of spinach or any tender leaf vegetable will substitute beautifully.

- 1 *pound young spinach, washed, drained and cut into small pieces*
- 4 *cups "Thick" coconut milk*
- 2 *pounds round steak, cut across the grain into thin slices*
- 3 *tablespoons fish sauce* (Nam Pla)
- 2 *tablespoons palm sugar, or brown sugar*
- 2 *tablespoons all-purpose flour, mixed with 4 tablespoons water*
- 5 *dried red chillies, seeded and finely chopped*
- 1 *teaspoon Laos powder* (Ka)
- 7 *shallots, chopped*
- 8 *cloves garlic, chopped*
- 1 *stalk lemon grass, minced*
- 1 *teaspoon salt*
- ½ *cup chunky peanut butter*
- ½ *cup coconut "Cream"*

Blanch the spinach in boiling water and drain. Set aside. In a large saucepan bring the "Thick" coconut milk to the boil. Add the beef slices, fish sauce and palm sugar. Reduce heat and simmer until beef is cooked to your taste. Remove the beef with a slotted spoon and set aside. Simmer the remaining liquid in the saucepan until it is reduced by one half. Add the flour/water mixture and stir until the mixture thickens. Set the pan aside. In a mortar or food processor, pound or grind the chillies, Laos, shallots, garlic, lemon grass and salt to a paste. Stir in the peanut butter and mix well. Reserving 2 tablespoons of the coconut "Cream," heat the remainder in a wok until thick and oily. Introduce the peanut/spice paste and stir-fry until it changes in color (about 2 minutes). Add the beef slices and stir until coated. Now add the coconut beef sauce and simmer, stirring for 5 minutes. Arrange the spinach on a platter. Lift the beef slices from the sauce and arrange on the sea of greens. Pour the sauce from the wok over and around the beef slices. Spoon little dollops of the reserved coconut "Cream" on the beef slices and serve immediately.

•

## CHILLI BEEF · NEUA PAD PRIK

*4 to 6 Servings*

I wish that the tiny, sweet corn featured in this dish were available, fresh, in the markets here as they are in Thailand. They must be the sweetest and most succulent of vegetables, and play a starring role in many stir-fried dishes. As an attractive alternative to serving *Neua Pad Prik* with a side dish of plain rice, try the following presentation: rinse any convenient kitchen mold or bowl with cold water, forceably press freshly boiled (steamed) rice into it, invert the mold over a platter, gently unmold. The completed Chilli Beef may then be poured over and around the rice mold.

1 *pound lean round beef, very thinly sliced,* cut into 1" wide × 2" long pieces*
1" *piece ginger, crushed and minced*
1 *tablespoon palm sugar*
2 *tablespoons soy sauce*
2 *cloves garlic, crushed and chopped*

* If you do not wish to use your microtome (an instrument for cutting thin slices of tissue, etc., for study under the microscope), try placing the beef in your freezer until almost frozen, or, better, the converse; remove the already frozen beef from the freezer and, when it is almost thawed, proceed to slice with a sharp knife.

4 *tablespoons vegetable oil*
1¾ *cups (approximately) or 1 can miniature corn, drained*
2 *green peppers, cored, seeded and cut into ½" squares*
5 *dried Chinese mushrooms, soaked in hot water, stemmed and sliced*
1 *white onion, cut pole-to-pole into slivers*
4 *Serrano chillies, seeded and sliced into strips*
¾ *cup beef stock*
1 *tablespoon cornstarch mixed with 2 tablespoons water*
2 *tablespoons oyster sauce*
2 *tablespoons fish sauce* (Nam Pla)

In a mixing bowl, combine the beef slices with the ginger, palm sugar, soy sauce and garlic. Mix until the beef is thoroughly coated and let marinate for at least 30 minutes.

In a wok, heat the oil. Drain the beef, reserving the marinade. Fry the beef over high heat, stirring, until brown. Add the corn, peppers, mushroom slices, onion and chillies and stir-fry for 1 minute. Add the marinade and beef stock. Reduce heat to medium and cook for 3 minutes. Stir in the cornstarch liquid and season with the oyster and fish sauce. Serve with plain rice.

•

## SWEET AND SOUR BEEF · NEUA BRIO WAN

*4 Servings*

4 *tablespoons vegetable oil*
5 *cloves garlic, finely chopped*
2 *cups top round beef, thinly sliced, ½" × 2"*
1 *large onion, chopped*

- 1 *cup cucumber, peeled, seeded and cut into 1" cubes*
- 1 *large tomato, chopped*
- 5 *fresh red or green Serrano chillies, sliced diagonally*
- 1½ *tablespoons granulated sugar*
- 1 *tablespoon soy sauce*
- 1 *tablespoon white vinegar*
- 1 *tablespoon cornstarch mixed with 3 tablespoons water*
- 5 *green onions, white parts only, cut into 1" pieces*
- ½ *teaspoon ground black pepper*
- 2 *tablespoons coriander leaves, chopped*

In a wok, heat the oil and fry garlic until golden. Add the beef and fry until medium rare. Remove the beef slices and set aside. Add the onion, cucumber, tomato and chillies to the wok, stir-frying between each addition. Return the beef to the wok and heat through. Add sugar, soy sauce and white vinegar, stirring until sugar dissolves. Stir in the cornstarch, green onions and black pepper. Cook until the sauce thickens. Sprinkle with coriander leaves, transfer to a dish and serve.

•

## ROAST RED PORK · MOO DAENG

*6 Servings*

- 1 *loin of pork (approximately 2 pounds)*
- ½ *teaspoon red food coloring dissolved in 2 tablespoons water*
- 1 *tablespoon fish sauce* (Nam Pla)
- 1 *tablespoon soy sauce*
- 2 *tablespoons Hoi Sin sauce*
- 1 *tablespoon cooking sherry*

*1 tablespoon palm sugar*
*2 cloves garlic, crushed and finely chopped*
*1 tablespoon fresh ginger, minced*
*½ teaspoon Five Spice Powder*
*1 tablespoon sesame oil*
*Sprigs of coriander for garnish*

Pat the loin dry and rub all over with the diluted food coloring. Combine all the remaining ingredients except the coriander in a blender or food processor and blend on high for about 30 seconds. In a shallow dish, marinate the "red" pork with the mixture from the blender for at least 2 hours, turning occasionally.

Preheat your oven to 450° F. Line a medium (approximately 12") baking dish with aluminum foil. Place a rack in the dish to elevate the roast during cooking. Now lay the pork on this rack and place in the oven. Reserve the marinade for basting, preferably using a bulb baster (your hands are now permanently discolored from the food coloring, no sense burning them as well attempting to brush or pour the marinade).

After 15 minutes, reduce the oven to 350° F. Cook the roast for about 1 hour (30 minutes per pound) or until a meat thermometer reaches 185° F. Baste at intervals, ultimately using all the marinade. When the loin is properly cooked, remove from heat and let it "set-up" for about 15 minutes or until it is cool enough to handle.

*Presentation*

Thinly slice (¼") the roast into disks and layer around a platter. Garnish with coriander leaves and serve with plain rice.

**N.B.** Pork cooked in this fashion, sliced into strips or cubed, is a savory and decorative addition to many stir-fried and soup dishes.

•

## SWEET PORK · MOO WAN

*6 Servings*

•

*Moo Wan* is the traditional Thai equivalent of ham, although in recent years ham and sausages are produced commercially. Because of the paucity of refrigeration in the villages, the Thai prepare the sweet pork and reboil it daily. Refrigerated, it will keep for at least a week. The pork is sliced, cold, and used in fried rice and other stir-fried dishes. It can also be served in its own gravy, garnished with crisp-fried onions and eaten over plain rice.

- 2 *pounds pork loin or butt, untrimmed*
- 1 *cup palm sugar or ½ cup brown sugar and ½ cup molasses*
- 1 *cup fish sauce*, (Nam Pla)
- 3 *cups water*
- ½ *cup crisp-fried onion flakes**

Place all the ingredients except the onion flakes in a large saucepan. Bring to a boil then cover and reduce heat to a simmer. Cook for 30 minutes. Uncover and skim off any fat that has risen to the surface. Bring back to the boil and cook, uncovered, until the meat is very tender and any fat adhering is transparent. The sauce should reduce by at least one-half and have become thick and syrupy. Lift the pork onto a serving dish and pour the sauce over. Refrigerate or, if serving immediately, sprinkle with the onion flakes and serve hot with plain rice.

**N.B.** *Siracha* sauce, or any similar Thai hot sauce, is the perfect accompaniment to *Moo Wan*.

•

*See Chapter 3, Fundamentals.

## FRIED PORK AND LONG BEANS · MOO PAD TUA FAK YAW

*4 to 6 Servings*

A substantial stir-fried main dish, *Moo Pad Tua Fak Yaw* was introduced to me by one of my household cooks, Lad Da.

Lad Da would occasionally disappear "up country" for a week at a time when some special family occasion would call. (Any place over a few kilometers from the perimeter of Bangkok is referred to, regardless of direction, as "up country.") Lad Da's uncle, whom she visited frequently during her absences, owned a general store which was the commerce and social hub of her village. She never used the dilapidated country buses, preferring instead the swift "*klong* boats," as the rivers and canals serve the outlying communities far better than the sparse road system.

The "Long Beans" in her recipe are actually long-podded cowpeas; a skinny bean-type vegetable growing sometimes over 12" in length. These can be found in the Thai food stores in the United States. If they are not available, fresh, crisp green beans (or frozen) may be substituted.

- 2 *tablespoons vegetable oil*
- 8 *cloves garlic, chopped*
- ½ *pound pork loin, cut into 2" long × 1" wide strips*
- ½ *pound raw shrimp, shelled, cleaned and deveined*
- 1 *pound long beans, cut into about 2" lengths* *
- 3 *tablespoons fish sauce* (Nam Pla)
- 2 *teaspoons granulated sugar*
- 1 *teaspoon ground black pepper*

In a wok, heat the oil over high heat. Add the chopped garlic and quickly stir-fry until light brown. Immediately add the pork and toss with the garlic until pork is light brown. Add the shrimp and continue frying for

* For an interesting variation, consistent with the Thai approach, use zucchini, celery or cabbage instead of beans.

1 minute. Add the long beans and cook for an additional 2 minutes. Stir in the fish sauce, sugar and black pepper. Toss everything together and remove to a serving dish.

•

## PORK AND CHICKEN STEW · DOM KEM

*4 to 6 Servings*

- 1 *teaspoon salt*
- 1 *teaspoon whole black peppercorns*
- 1 *teaspoon garlic, chopped*
- 1 *teaspoon coriander roots*
- 1 *tablespoon vegetable oil*
- 1 *cup water*
- ½ *cup dark, sweet soy sauce*
- 1 *tablespoon palm sugar*
- 2 *whole chicken breasts, boned, skinned and quartered*
- ½ *pound salt pork, sliced (3/8" thick) and crisp-fried*
- ½ *packet bean curd, juice expressed and crisp-fried*
- 6 *dried Chinese mushrooms, soaked in warm water and stemmed*
- 3 *whole Serrano chillies*
- 1 *bunch spinach, washed and sliced*
- 5 *hardcooked eggs, peeled and halved**

In a mortar or food processor, pound or grind the salt, peppercorns, garlic and coriander roots to an even paste. In a wok, heat the oil and fry this paste for about 1

*For decoration, cut the eggs as flowers: pierce the eggs around their "equators" with a sharp, small paring knife, forming continuous, successive *V*'s. The knife should penetrate the egg exactly to the center so the eggs will divide smoothly.

minute or until fragrant. Add the water, soy sauce and palm sugar. Stir over heat until sugar is dissolved. Add the chicken and pork pieces and additional water, if necessary, to just cover. Bring to a boil and add the bean curd, mushrooms and chillies. Now add the spinach, reduce heat to simmer and cook until chicken is tender (about 15 minutes). Pour this mixture into a warm ovenproof dish, geometrically arranging the meats. Place in the egg halves decoratively. Serve with plain rice.

•

## CHICKEN IN COCONUT MILK AND LAOS · DOM KA GAI

*6 to 8 Servings*

A small coterie of enthusiastic students cooked this dish at my first Thai cooking class in California in May 1977. The recipe is authentic and introduces the unfamiliar and exotic spice Laos (*Ka*).

- 3 *pounds chicken pieces (breast split in two, drumsticks, thighs, etc.)*
- 8 *pieces dried Laos* (Ka), *soaked in hot water for 10 minutes*
- 2½ *cups "Thin" coconut milk*
- ½ *teaspoon cracked black pepper*
- 6 *coriander roots, crushed*
- 1 *lime zest, sliced*
- ¼ *teaspoon Kaffir lime powder* (Pew Makrut)
- 3 *green Serrano chillies*
- 1 *teaspoon salt*
- 4 *young citrus leaves*
- 1½ *cups "Thick" coconut milk*
- 2 *tablespoons fish sauce* (Nam Pla)
- *Juice of 1 lime*

*3 tablespoons coriander leaves, chopped*

In a wok or large saucepan, place the chicken pieces, Laos, "Thin" coconut milk, black pepper, coriander roots, lime zest, Kaffir lime powder, chillies, salt and citrus leaves. Bring to a boil, reduce heat to medium and simmer, stirring occasionally, until chicken is tender and sauce reduced by almost one half (approximately 30 minutes). Add the "Thick" coconut milk and turn heat to high. Stir constantly until mixture returns to the boil. Remove from heat and stir in the fish sauce and lime juice. Serve in a bowl sprinkled with coriander leaves.

•

## HEAVENLY CHICKEN · GAI SAWAN

*8 to 10 Servings*

The "heavenly," *Sawan,* in the title must refer to the flavor as these delicate chicken and fish squares are food for the gods!

*Chicken Squares*

*1 medium (2½ pound, approximately) boiling chicken, washed and patted dry*
*1½ cups green (raw) shrimp meat*
*1 cup white fish fillets (cod, haddock, sole, etc.)*
*1 teaspoon salt*
*2" piece ginger, chopped*
*½ cup water (for paste)*
*Water for stock*

*Sauce*

*2 tablespoons cornstarch, dissolved in ½ cup water*
*2 cups chicken stock (from above)*

*1" piece ginger, minced*
*2 tablespoons soy sauce*
*½ teaspoon ground black pepper*

*Garnish*

*Coriander leaves*
*5 red Serrano chillies, cut into flowers*
*4 green onions (white only), cut into tassels*

Carefully skin the chicken, keeping the sheets as intact and large as possible and set aside. Place the whole, skinned chicken into a large saucepan and almost cover with water. Bring to a boil, reduce heat and simmer for 45 minutes to produce a rich, concentrated stock. Strain the stock, reserving 2 cups, and keep the chicken meat and bones for some other use. In a food processor or with two cleavers, mince the shrimp and fish together, finely. Add salt, ginger and enough water to form a smooth paste. Spread this paste on the chicken skin to a thickness of ½". Heat water in a steamer and, when boiling, steam the chicken skin with paste for 30 minutes. In a medium saucepan, mix the cornstarch liquid with the 2 cups chicken stock (from above) and cook over low heat, stirring, for 3 minutes or until a smooth, thickened sauce is formed. Stir in the minced ginger, soy sauce and black pepper. Cook, stirring for a further minute. Remove from heat, cover and keep warm. Remove the chicken skin from the steamer and let it cool enough to be handled. With a sharp knife, cut into 2" squares or diamonds. Arrange these on a deep platter and pour the cornstarch/chicken sauce over the top. Sprinkle with the coriander leaves and garnish with the chilli flowers and green onion tassels.

•

## CHICKEN WITH CHESTNUTS · GAI GUP KAO LAD

*4 to 6 Servings*

Water chestnuts can be substituted for (but not confused with) chestnuts when the latter are out of season.

- 4 *cloves garlic, chopped*
- 2 *tablespoons coriander roots*
- 1 *teaspoon peppercorns*
- 2 *tablespoons vegetable oil*
- 1 *pound boned chicken meat, cut into bite-sized pieces*
- 1½ *cups chicken stock (canned or fresh)*
- 4 *chicken livers, diced*
- 16 *(approximately) chestnuts, shelled, boiled and halved or 1 8-ounce can water chestnuts, drained and halved*
- 1 *teaspoon salt*
- 1 *tablespoon palm sugar*

In a mortar, pound the garlic, coriander roots and black peppercorns to a paste. In a wok, heat the oil and fry the paste, stirring, for 2 to 3 minutes. Add the chicken pieces (not the livers) and stir-fry until they are just brown. Pour in the chicken stock and now add the chicken livers. Adjust heat and simmer for 5 minutes. Stir in the chestnuts, season with salt and sprinkle with palm sugar. Cover and simmer until the chicken is tender, about 5 minutes.

•

## CHILLI CHICKEN · PANAENG KRUANG DON

*4 Servings*

Another dish from the Thai countryside, this chilli-spiced chicken is presented in an unusual and attractive style.

- 8 *dried red chillies, seeded, soaked in warm water and finely chopped*
- 2 *cloves garlic, chopped*
- 2 *shallots, chopped*
- 1 *stalk lemon grass, minced*
- 1 *teaspoon coriander roots*
- 1 *teaspoon shrimp paste*
- 3 *pieces Laos* (Ka), *chopped*
- 1 *teaspoon black peppercorns*
- 2 *cups "Thick" coconut milk, reduced by about ½ until thick and oily*
- 1 *tablespoon granulated sugar*
- 2 *tablespoons fish sauce* (Nam Pla)
- 1 *pound chicken meat, cooked and cut into bite-sized pieces*
- 4 *fresh red chillies, cut into flowers*
- 2 *tablespoons coriander leaves*

Place chillies, garlic, shallots, lemon grass, coriander roots and shrimp paste in a food processor and process to a coarse paste. Put Laos and peppercorns in an electric spice grinder and grind to a powder. Add the powder to the paste and process once more to mix thoroughly.

Pour *one half* the reduced "Thick" coconut milk into a wok and bring to a boil. Stir in the curry paste from the processor and cook over medium heat until the mixture is almost dry. Stir in the sugar and fish sauce and remove from heat. Arrange the chicken pieces on a large, heated platter. Carefully drop a spoonful of the curry mixture onto each piece. Top this with a spoonful of the remaining "Thick" coconut milk. Decorate with red chilli flowers and sprinkle with coriander leaves. Serve warm.

•

## SIAMESE FRIED CHICKEN · GAI TORD

*2 to 3 Servings*

8 *cloves garlic*
2 *tablespoons peppercorns, freshly ground*
2 *tablespoons coriander roots*
6 *chicken pieces*
*Oil for deep frying*

Grind or pound the garlic, peppercorns and coriander roots to a paste. Wash and thoroughly pat dry the chicken. Rub the paste all over the chicken and let stand to marinate for at least 30 minutes. Heat oil in a wok to 375° F. and deep-fry the chicken until golden and tender. Drain the chicken on paper towels. Serve hot with rice and Sweet and Hot Chilli Sauce.*

•

## CHICKEN AND CABBAGE · GAI GALUMBLEE

*4 to 6 Servings*

8 *peppercorns*
1 *teaspoon coriander roots*
¼ *teaspoon salt*
3 *whole chicken breasts, boned, skinned and sliced into 2" pieces*
3 *cups "Thick" coconut milk*
½ *teaspoon powdered Laos* (Ka)
3 *cups cabbage, coarsely chopped*
1 *tablespoon roasted curry paste* (Nam Prik Pao)
1 *tablespoon fish sauce* (Nam Pla)
1 *teaspoon granulated sugar*
1 *tablespoon lime juice*

*See Chapter 15, Sauces.

With a mortar and pestle, pound together the peppercorns, coriander roots and salt into a paste. Place the paste in a wok, together with chicken pieces, coconut milk and Laos powder. Over moderate heat, bring to a boil and cook, stirring, until chicken is tender. Add the cabbage and continue to boil, stirring, until the cabbage is cooked but crisp. In a bowl, combine the roasted curry paste, fish sauce, sugar and lime juice into a smooth sauce. Pour the contents of the wok into a serving dish, sprinkle the sauce over, and serve.

•

## BRAISED CHICKEN IN SPICES · GAI TUNG

*6 to 8 Servings*

The first time I ate *Gai Tung* was in a little street restaurant in the Yao Rat area of Bangkok. I had been to the Sam Peng market (bazaar) with some friends and, after several hours well spent—looking at Thai bronze utensils (mortars, pestles and the like), and impulsively buying such splendors as meters of Thai silk to be run up by the local dressmaker—we were all hungry. Tired from shopping, we found a close corner restaurant where one of my friends ordered *Gai Tung,* a marvelous, savory chicken-in-gravy poured over large helpings of rice. We devoured this new concoction with relish and were almost elevated to a higher plane of existence (Satori). Fueled with exciting food and exhilarated with one another's companionship, we decided to make a day of it. We finished the afternoon with a visit to a local movie theater where the American film was almost obscured with both Thai and Chinese subtitles. I am sure we breathed garlic fumes over the Thai around us, but they were happily unaware, having lunched on some equally garlicky dish!

5 *dried red chillies, seeded and minced*
5 *shallots, chopped*
1 *teaspoon shrimp paste* (Kapee)
1 *stalk lemon grass, minced*

5 *cloves garlic, sliced*
5 *coriander roots, chopped*
½ *teaspoon salt*
1 *teaspoon Laos powder* (Ka)
½ *teaspoon ground cinnamon*
5 *tablespoons vegetable oil*
2½ to 3 *pounds frying chicken, jointed*
1 *cup water*
1 *teaspoon tamarind concentrate, dissolved in 2 tablespoons hot water*
2 *tablespoons fish sauce* (Nam Pla)

In a mortar or food processor, pound or grind the chillies, shallots, shrimp paste, lemon grass, garlic, coriander roots, salt, Laos powder and cinnamon to a fine paste. Heat the oil in a wok over medium heat and fry the paste until it is light brown and the aroma has mellowed. Add the chicken parts and stir until they are coated. Turn the heat to high and add the water and bring to a boil. Cover, reduce heat to medium and continue to boil the mixture, stirring occasionally, until the chicken is cooked and tender. Lower heat, uncover and add the tamarind liquid and fish sauce. Correct the seasoning adding more salt if necessary. Leave on low heat until the chicken meat is almost falling from the bone. Serve with plain rice.

•

## CHICKEN WITH GINGER · GAI KING

*6 to 8 Servings*

I have eaten *Gai King* with variations in restaurants both here and overseas, however, previous to my classes, I never personally prepared it. When I began teaching in Los Angeles, my students, already in love with this savory combination of chicken, ginger and mint, gave me no peace until I researched the recipe so they could cook it in class. You may use whole or boned chicken; I prefer the eating convenience of the latter.

| | |
|---|---|
| *3* | *tablespoons vegetable oil* |
| *1* | *onion, thinly sliced, pole-to-pole into slivers* |
| *5* | *cloves garlic, chopped* |
| *2½ to 3* | *pound chicken (including giblets), skinned, boned and cut into bite-sized pieces* |
| *2* | *tablespoons soy sauce* |
| *2* | *tablespoons ginger, finely chopped* |
| *2* | *tablespoons mint leaves* |
| *8* | *dried Chinese mushrooms, soaked in hot water, stemmed and sliced* |
| *5* | *green onions (including some green), cut into 1" long pieces* |
| *2* | *fresh red Serrano chillies, seeded and slivered, or 1 teaspoon dried red chilli flakes* |
| *2* | *tablespoons Chinese rice vinegar* |
| *1* | *teaspoon granulated sugar* |
| *2* | *tablespoons fish sauce* (Nam Pla) |

Heat the oil in a wok and fry the onions until limp. Add the garlic and fry, stirring, for 2 additional minutes. With a slotted spoon, remove onions and garlic and set aside. Now, to the same wok, add the chicken and stir-fry for 2 minutes. Add the soy sauce, ginger and *two-thirds* of the mint leaves and mix together. Add the mushrooms, green onions, chillies, return the onions and garlic and continue cooking until the chicken is tender, stirring and turning the bird pieces. After a few minutes, when the chicken is just cooked, quickly season with rice vinegar, sugar and fish sauce and remove from heat. Decorate with the remaining *one-third* of the mint leaves and serve hot with rice.

•

## FRESH PORK SAUSAGE · MOO YAW

*3 to 4 Servings*

This *Moo Yaw* is freely adapted and considerably changed from a recipe that comes from Udon in Northeast Thailand. The original was written down for me by a young Thai student who remarked, disarmingly, that it tasted like Spam! My version is more highly spiced, and I hope the young student of so long ago would now approve.

Just a few comments about sausage-making. In Thailand the sausage is formed in large (3″+ diameter) logs and wrapped in banana leaves or muslin before steaming or boiling. I think commercial casings are esthetically more appealing and easier to handle, serve and freeze.

You may embark on a sausage-making adventure armed with muslin or cheesecloth and a food processor, but I find a meat grinder *cum* sausage-maker* and commercial casings indispensable. In either case you will need imagination and patience. However, the experience will be fun, sensuous and guaranteed to require substantial kitchen cleanup.

Serve *Moo Yaw* sliced with stir-fried vegetables, in sandwiches or dipped in beaten egg before frying.

- 2 *teaspoons salt*
- 1 *teaspoon ground black pepper*
- 4 *cloves garlic, sliced*
- 12 *coriander roots, sliced*
- 1 *teaspoon dried red chilli flakes*
- 1¼ *pounds fresh ground pork*
- 2 *tablespoons all-purpose flour*
- *Sausage casings*

With a mortar and pestle, pound the salt, black pepper, garlic, coriander roots and chilli flakes to a coarse

* Of the several advantages of having a meat grinder, the most important to me is the ability to select my own cut of pork, grind it to the exact consistency I choose and control the fat content. (To clear the remaining meat from the grinder, try inserting torn pieces of stale bread.)

paste. In a large mixing bowl, with your hands, knead thoroughly the paste, pork and flour. Now, according to the instructions with your meat grinder/sausage maker, stuff the sausage into one long casing. This recipe, with standard casings, should make one 2" diameter, 1½' long sausage. Tie off both ends. Fill a saucepan with water and bring to a boil. Prick the casing several times and drop into the water, reduce heat to simmer and cook for about one-half hour. Remove and let drain. In a large fry pan, over medium high heat, fry the sausage until its sides are browned. (This will require repeated turning, balancing and, inevitably, spattering grease over your front.) Serve hot or cold, whole or sliced.

**N.B.** Either before boiling or frying you can freeze the sausage. In fact, the Thai seldom fry theirs, preferring to eat it just after it is boiled.

•

## CHICKEN IN PEANUT SAUCE · GAI TUA

*4 to 6 Servings*

The original version of this dish uses whole, roasted peanuts that are pounded to a paste in a mortar. It is much easier to use peanut butter. I suggest the "chunky" kind; the peanut pieces add textural variety to the sauce.

- 1" *piece ginger, chopped*
- 3 *cloves garlic, chopped*
- 1 *teaspoon curry paste (use Thai fresh or ready-made, flavor of your preference)*
- ¼ *cup coconut "Cream"*
- 3 *whole chicken breasts (6 halves), boned and cut into 2" pieces*
- ½ *pound broccoli or 1 pound spinach, cleaned*

*and drained (equivalent amounts by weight of frozen may be substituted), chopped*

8 *green onions (including tops), cut into 2" lengths*
2 *tablespoons vegetable or peanut oil*
½ *red onion, minced*
½ *teaspoon dried red chilli powder (Cayenne)*
3 *tablespoons chunky peanut butter*
1 *tablespoon granulated sugar*
1 *teaspoon fish sauce* (Nam Pla)
¾ *cup "Thick" coconut milk*

In a food processor, process the ginger, garlic and curry paste until smooth. Add the coconut "Cream" and give the blade another few turns. Place the chicken in a bowl. Pour over the curry/cream mixture and marinate for 30 minutes. In a saucepan, boil the broccoli and green onions in just enough water to cover for 3 minutes. Drain well and place on a heated platter. In a wok, heat the oil and fry the onion until golden. Add the marinated chicken with its marinade and stir-fry to just brown the chicken. Add the remaining ingredients, stir to coat the chicken well and continue until a thick sauce has formed and the chicken is tender. Lift the chicken pieces and lay on the warmed bed of greens. Pour the sauce over and serve.

*In the swift stream*
*You washed the fish,*
*Rubbed them with ocean*
*salt.*

NOTO

TWELVE

# Fish and Seafood

## PLA LAE AHARN TA LAY

The Gulf of Siam is enclosed on three sides by the sprawling coastline of Thailand. Rarely more than fifty meters deep, this warm, rich sea teems with plankton, which provide food for the vast abundance of fish, both variety and quantity.

The arteries of Thailand are inland waterways, nearly two thousand miles of superb fishing. If all this plentitude were not enough, fish are found in every flooded rice paddy, swamp, ditch, canal and pond. Bangkok itself is a spider's web of canals or *klongs* and, being at sea level or slightly lower, the city floods during the rainy season when the tides are high. The quiet, little *soi,* or lane, where we lived would become a rushing river six inches deep when the rains came; with the flood would come the fish, wiggling down the roadbed and playing tag with the vehicles.

It is easy to understand why fish are the principal addition to the main diet of rice. Over sixty percent of the country-Thai catch their own fish for their meals. They catch the freshwater species with anything at hand: rods, traps, baskets, square nets, and even fences built across the streams. One of the main varieties of freshwater fish is carp, and it proliferates in about seventy species.

The fishermen in the Gulf of Siam usually resort to fish traps in the shallow waters and use boats for seining in the open seas. The boats are between eighteen and forty-five feet long and are frail-looking affairs without the refinement of cabins. They link up in clusters for net-fishing, frequently at night. An unforgettable experience is to stand on the still-warm sands of Pattaya beach at dusk and look out at the Gulf. The dark sea is lighted like a carnival with strings of lights connecting the fishermen.

At daybreak, the market in Pattaya village on the Gulf is already bustling. The stalls are heavily laden with gleaming fish of every size and shape; gills pumping frantically for life as they flop over each other on the slabs, and even leap to the floor in their attempt to get back to water. Each stall has sections of shellfish: shrimp, prawns, crab and lobster, whiskers waving gently at the passersby. Sea bass, pomfret, tuna, mackerel, squid, oysters, herring and eels are all to be found in their appointed pens. The vendors deftly behead and fillet the fish with a few strokes of the knife, while their juvenile helpers chase away the dogs which slink around the stalls prepared to devour anything proffered or purloined.

All the small seaside towns lining the Gulf have rows of beachfront kiosks which sell plates of freshly steamed or sautéed fish to hungry visitors and residents. On the coast, a few miles east of Bangkok, stands a long pier, reaching out into the sea. On the end is a high, rambling building, reminiscent of the old Victorian amusement palaces. This is *Ban Poo,* literally translated, the House of the Crab. A visit is an experience not to be missed. You drive your car out along the pier and park at the end. Walking through the entrance, you enter a vast dance hall and restaurant filled with Thai families out for the day. A Thai band plays loudly and enthusiastically, if a little off-key. The dance floor is jumping with couples, rocking and whirling to the latest American disco beat. The Western numbers are interspersed with the occasional *Ram Wong*. You stop and watch, then you gradually realize that this is not the main attraction. The dancing is only to work off the effects of the eating—and what a glorious feast! Waiters, bearing trays piled high with steamed crab claws, bowls of pink shrimp swimming in coconut milk, barbecued whole fish decorated with ginger and coriander and mountains of steamed rice, hurry between the tables. This banquet is washed down with copious quantities of Thai beer and iced tea. When the food and noise become too much, couples will break away and stroll out and back along the two seaward arms of the pier. A leisurely sojourn to rekindle the appetite and then back to the table for more dishes of curried crab, spicy, lemony, prawn soup, *Dom Yam Gung*, and fried, stuffed herring. No, the Thai do not take their pleasures sadly, and fish is the perfect appeasement to an appetite sharpened by the brisk sea breeze.

Certain areas of Bangkok are renowned for seafood restaurants, heavily patronized by visitors and natives alike. One of these areas is New Petburi Road, which is lined with lavish eateries, set in their own large gardens and all devoted to the art of preparing every imaginable fish in the finest Thai and Oriental style. It is conceivable that one could dine for a year along the Road and never repeat a specialty. Most of the restaurants feature enormous tanks from which the diner's choice is plucked, still wriggling, to be summarily dispatched in the kitchens and returned in culinary glory; poached, steamed, sautéed, barbecued or curried.

Tropical clawless lobsters proliferate in the warm waters of the Gulf of Thailand and freshwater crayfish are also plentiful in the country. The Thai serve them in simple style; sauced with chilli sauce or, for the foreigner, merely with butter and a flourish of lime.

Following are some of the Thai names for fish which are found both in Thai waters and in seas closer to us. Unless ordering from a Thai, these names will confuse your fish merchant, but may be helpful in deciphering a menu in a Thai restaurant.

| | |
|---|---|
| Shrimp | *Gung Narng* |
| Prawns | *Gung Foi* |
| Crab | *Poo* |
| Lobster | *Gung Ta Lay* |
| Sea Bass | *Pla Kapong* |
| Pomfret | *Pla Chalamet* |
| Tuna | *Pla O* |
| Mackerel | *Pla In See* |
| Squid | *Pla Muek* |
| Oysters | *Hoy Narng Rom* |
| Cat Fish | *Pla Duk* |
| Eel | *Pla Lai* |
| Shark | *Pla Chalarm* |
| Shark's Fin | *Hoo Pla Chalarm* |

The recipes that follow are just a sampling of this bounty of seafood. I only wish that some enterprising expatriate Thai would open a fish restaurant, Thai-style, here in the United States.

## SELECTION AND PREPARATION

When choosing any species, ask several questions: Does it appear approximately as it does in its natural habitat? When a whole bony fish (class Osteichthyes) is purchased, red snapper for instance, does the skin glisten, are the gills pink and moist and, especially, do the eyes appear clear and liquid? With mollusks (oysters, clams, mussels) are all but a few shells tightly closed and unbroken? (A few may be open but should close with pressure or other stimuli—do not stick your finger inside.) Do fresh crab, crayfish and, particularly, lobster (all crustaceans) appear ambulatory, albeit lethargic, clean and whole with no major limbs missing? Are the shells of fresh shrimp clear and is the flesh dull gray or white with most of the tails intact? Is the squid (also a mollusk, class Cephalopoda) milky and speckled? The most important question concerning the above should be "have they been properly stored, either fresh-caught and refrigerated or frozen?" And is there an unusual odor or the normal smell of the sea from where they came? If the answer to any of the above is negative, cook watermelon! But, if you are fortunate enough to have a fisherman in the family, a "fisherfriend" or a good fishmonger, rejoice and use your catch immediately.

When cleaning any of the whole, fresh, bony fish (Osteichthyes), make a slit about halfway down the underneath (ventral) side starting behind the head and continue to the anal fin in order to remove the intestines and other internal organs. If you wish the fish to remain whole (with head), remove the gills and trim the edges of the fins with scissors. If you are removing the head and/or filleting use a sharp blow with a cleaver just behind the pectoral fins. Scale it with a knife or scaler and wash thoroughly in cold, fresh water. These steps will normally be taken by your fisherman or at the fish market.

With fresh clams, mussels and oysters, I scrub the shells under running water, using a vegetable brush. In the case of clams, I soak them for several hours, preferably overnight, in cold water laced with liberal doses of cornmeal. The clams will ingest some of the cornmeal (water soluble), mistaking it for sand, and disgorge most of their residual sand. With any of the above, do not open with a knife unless you are a professional shucker (you risk slicing your fingers and hands severely). I prefer to spread these bivalves on a cookie sheet and place them in a 300° F. oven for several minutes until they peek open. You may also accomplish this partial opening by pouring boiling water over the collected, closed shells in a pan. Now, you must use a paring knife to further open the shells and remove the meat. The knife must also be used to scrape the shell clean and separate the meat from the tendon that attaches it near the hinge. If you have an overweening desire for these mollusks raw, on the half-shell, visit your nearest oyster bar—my favorites are in New Orleans and on the beach front in Pattaya.

Live lobsters, crabs and crayfish are most humanely killed and cooked by immersing in boiling, salted water for several minutes; size of the crustacean and amount of water dictating the time.

Just a word here about the confusion surrounding the types of lobster and crayfish and their distinguishing features. Of all the crustaceans that belong to the order Decapoda, the term "lobster" usually refers to the large-clawed, cold-water species of the North Atlantic (genus *Homarus)*, while the term "spiny lobster" refers to the many species of tropical, clawless lobsters (genus *Panulirus)*. Crayfish are freshwater species of the genus *Astacus* and *Cambarus* and are clawed. They are closely related to the lobster *(Homarus)* for which they are sometimes mistaken by the uninitiated.

Successful cracking of the shell of large lobster demands force. Use a hammer to strike the cleaver home. Dungeness and Alaskan King Crab shells can be shattered by a cleaver alone.

I make frequent references to the use of Bay shrimp. It is an inexact term and merely refers to those tiny species that exceed forty count per pound. These are caught, beheaded and cooked (almost immediately) by Japanese fisherman in Arctic waters. To devein the larger green, or raw, shrimp is almost a misnomer. What is essentially implied is the removal of the alimentary canal along the back (dorsal) side with a sharp knife, patience and good fingernails. This process is primarily indicated for esthetics and differs from shrimp to shrimp depending on how well they digested their last meal. The Thai seldom devein shrimp.

The pen, chitin backbone, of fresh squid may be removed with a very strong pull on it to bring it through the anterior of the mantle (abdominal covering). Carefully, without breaking it, remove the ink sac through the same end, the head. (Orientals and Mexicans use the ink for color and flavoring.) Incidentally, the tentacles may be removed, again for esthetic reasons, but I prefer them for texture and authenticity. Good frozen and thawed squid are available (already cleaned) from better fish markets. Unfortunately, when frozen, they only come in three and five pound bricks—be prepared to use a lot.

## WHOLE FRIED FISH WITH GINGER SAUCE · PLA BRIO WAN

*6 to 8 Servings*

Buy a glisteningly *fresh* fish of about 3 pounds or two 1½ pounders. No larger, or the head and tail will hang over the edge of your wok and it will not cook uniformly. Have your fish merchant clean and scale the fish. Traditionally it should still have its head, but if you buy a beheaded fish, you may cook it in the same fashion with good results. Prepare and simmer the sauce before you cook the fish.

The diner should be confronted with the newly-wedded combination of crisp fish and silky sauce.

*Sauce*

- 10 *dried Chinese mushrooms, soaked in hot water for 10 minutes, stemmed and sliced*
- 4 *tablespoons rice vinegar*
- 6 *tablespoons palm sugar*
- ¾ *cup water*
- 3 *tablespoons dark, sweet soy sauce*
- 2 *green onions, finely sliced*
- 3″ *piece of fresh ginger, peeled and finely chopped*
- *Juice of 1 lime*
- 1 *tablespoon cornstarch blended with ¼ cup cold water*

*Fish*

- 1 *whole fresh fish (approximately 3 pounds), cleaned and scaled*
- *Salt*
- ½ *cup seasoned flour (½ cup flour sifted with ½ teaspoon salt and ¼ teaspoon black pepper)*
- 3 *cups vegetable oil*

*Garnish*

- 4 *fresh red chillies, cut into flowers*
- ¼ *cup picked coriander leaves*

*Sauce*

Put the mushrooms, vinegar, sugar, water and soy sauce all together in a medium saucepan and bring to a boil over medium heat. Boil, stirring, for 5 minutes. Add the green onions and ginger and stir until onions are limp. Pour in the lime juice and stir once or twice. Introduce the cornstarch and water mixture, a dash at a time, stirring rapidly until it blends in and is uniform. This sauce will then thicken and become shiny and syrupy. Remove from heat and hold at room temperature.

*Fish*

Trim any ragged edges on the fins and tail with kitchen scissors. Wash under cold, running water and pat dry. Wipe out the cavity, and salt. Now place the fish on a sheet of waxed paper and fill a sifter with the seasoned flour. Veil both sides of it with a fine dusting.

Heat the oil in your largest wok or frying pan until a thin haze of smoke begins to appear. Carefully introduce the fish to the wok and fry until crisp golden on the first side (approximately 3 minutes). Using 2 spatulas, turn the fish carefully and fry the other side until it also is golden. Immediately remove to a large platter, letting the excess oil drain. Pour the sauce over the top, masking the fish completely. Garnish this arrangement with the chilli flowers and sprinkle with coriander leaves. Serve at once.

*Serving*

Make a shallow incision along the dorsal edge from just below the head to the beginning of the tail. Separate the cut on either side of the dorsal fin(s). Allow the diners to help themselves from the flesh on one side. When most of the flesh is removed and the vertebrae are exposed, turn and repeat on the other side. When completed, if the diners are not jackhammer operators, the complete fish skeleton, head and tail attached, should be left on the plate.

## THAI FRIED FISH · PLA TOO TORD

*4 Servings*

*Pla Too* is the name of a fish indigenous to Thailand and found only in the Gulf of Siam. Trout, herring or mackerel are good substitutes.

- 4 *fresh whole trout or 8 herrings*
- 1 *teaspoon salt (preferably rock or sea salt)*
- ½ *teaspoon turmeric*
- 6 *tablespoons vegetable oil*

Gut and clean each fish well under running water (see "Fish and Seafood," selection and preparation, in this chapter). Dry thoroughly with paper towels. In a mortar, pound the salt together with the turmeric and rub the mixture well onto the surface of the fish(es). Heat the oil in a wok and fry the fish, one or two at a time, until golden crisp on both sides. Do not overcook—no more than a minute or so on each side. Drain well and serve at once with *Nam Prik,* Thai Hot Sauce (chapter 14).

•

## FRIED FILLETS IN TAMARIND SAUCE · PLA CHIEN

*4 to 6 Servings*

- 2 *pounds fish fillets (sole, halibut, snapper, etc.)*
- ½ *cup peanut oil*
- 6 *cloves garlic, crushed and chopped*
- 3 *tablespoons soy sauce*
- 2 *tablespoons palm sugar or unrefined brown sugar*
- 1½ *tablespoons fish sauce* (Nam Pla)
- 1 *teaspoon tamarind concentrate, dissolved in 6 tablespoons hot water*
- 2" *piece ginger, minced*

6 *green onions (including green), cut into 1" lengths*
2 *tablespoons crisp-fried onion flakes (see Onion Flakes, "Fundamentals," chapter 3)*
*Coriander leaves for garnish*

Wash the fish, trim if necessary and dry thoroughly. In a wok, heat the oil on a high setting and briefly fry the fillets, one at a time, on both sides until golden. Drain on paper towels. Pour off all but 2 tablespoons of the oil remaining in the wok and reheat over medium heat. Fry the garlic until light brown, stirring, and add the soy sauce, palm sugar, fish sauce and tamarind liquid. Cook for 1 minute, stirring. Carefully return the fish to this sauce. Sprinkle with ginger and green onions and cook for 2 more minutes, spooning the sauce over the fish. Lift the fillets carefully to a serving dish and pour the sauce over them. Sprinkle with fried onion flakes and garnish with coriander leaves.

•

## STEAMED FISH CURRY · HAW MOK

*6 Servings*

In Thailand *Haw Mok* is steamed in banana leaves. Artichokes, with the centers removed, make delightfully ornamental containers, although the substitution is not quite authentic. Allow one stuffed artichoke per person.

6 *artichokes*
*Boiling salted water*
½ *tablespoon vegetable oil*
2 *tablespoons green curry paste (*Krung Gaeng Keo Wan)
2 *tablespoons fish sauce* (Nam Pla)
2 *cups "Thick" coconut milk*
1 *tablespoon rice flour*

1 *egg, beaten*
2 *green onions, finely sliced*
4 *citrus leaves, shredded*
2 *pounds fresh fish fillets (any firm, white fish), thinly sliced*
12 *fresh basil leaves*
2 *fresh red Serrano chillies, seeded and slivered*

Wash the artichokes. With a cleaver or large knife, lop off about 1" of the artichoke tops. With kitchen scissors, clip off the ends of all the leaves on each artichoke. Place these edible plants in a very large saucepan of boiling, salted water. Cover and continue cooking over high heat for 20 minutes, or until a fork can be inserted easily into the base. Remove from heat, drain and let stand until cool. With a spoon, core out the fibrous inner leaves and choke. Set aside.

In a wok, heat the oil and stir-fry the curry paste for one minute. Add the fish sauce, "Thick" coconut milk, rice flour, egg, green onions and citrus leaves. Stir until the mixture thickens slightly and immediately remove from heat. Place the fish fillets in a mixing bowl and pour the mixture from the wok over them.

Place 2 basil leaves in the bottom of each artichoke. Pour an equal amount of fish/cream mixture into each artichoke. Decorate the tops with chilli slivers. Place the stuffed artichokes in a steamer (water boiling) for 20 minutes or until the filling is firm. Serve hot or cold.

•

## STEAMED YELLOW FILLETS · PLA NERNG LEUNG

*3 to 4 Servings*

½ *teaspoon dried red chilli flakes*
4 *cloves garlic, chopped*
1 *small onion, chopped*

3 *stalks coriander (including roots), chopped*
¼ *teaspoon ground turmeric*
¼ *teaspoon ground black pepper*
2 *tablespoons fish sauce* (Nam Pla)
½ *cup "Thick" coconut milk*
1 *egg, beaten*
1 *pound firm fish fillets (sole, flounder, red snapper, etc.), patted dry, lightly salted and sliced cross-wise into 1" wide strips*
3 *teaspoons rice flour*

In a mortar or food processor, pound or grind together the chilli, garlic, onion and coriander to a juicy paste. Scrape the paste into a mixing bowl and stir in the turmeric, pepper, fish sauce, coconut milk and the beaten egg. Mix together thoroughly. Carefully add the fish pieces and coat each with the milk/egg mixture. Separately drain each fish piece, dust with rice flour and place on the rack of a steamer (the steamer should be up to temperature, water boiling, and you may choose to line the rack with aluminum foil for cleaning ease). Steam for about 15 minutes until the pieces are tender but firm. Serve hot, accompanied by plain rice.

•

## FLIM-FLAN FISH · PLA SAMPANTAMIT

*4 Servings*

*Sampantamit* means friendship in Thai, and this dish comes from a restaurant on the "Friendship Highway," north out of Bangkok. The road is so named because it was built by American engineers and was the first major highway in the country.

In fun, I have called the dish "Flim-Flan" because it is an elaborate and delicious deception; a fake fish composed of layers of pounded fish stuffed with a mixture of pork, crab and chicken.

*Fish Mold*

12 *peppercorns*
6 *coriander roots*
2 *pounds firm white fish fillets (cod, haddock, halibut, etc.), washed and dried*

*Filling*

1 *tablespoon lard or vegetable oil*
2 *cloves garlic, chopped*
½ *pound ground pork*
1 *whole (both halves) chicken breast, boned and chopped*
9 *ounce packet frozen crabmeat, defrosted*
6 *dried Chinese mushrooms, soaked, stemmed and sliced*
3 *green onions, chopped*
2 *tablespoons fish sauce (*Nam Pla*)*
1 *tablespoon soy sauce*
1 *teaspoon granulated sugar*
4 *half sections banana leaf* (approximately 10″ × 6″), washed and patted dry*
*Peppercorns and green onions for decoration*
*Coriander leaves for garnish*

*Fish Mold*

In a mortar, pound the peppercorns and coriander roots together until thoroughly pulverized. Place the fish in a food processor, add the mixture from the mortar and process to a smooth paste. With a rubber spatula, remove the paste to a bowl and wash and arrange the processor for future use.

*Filling*

In a wok, heat the lard and fry the garlic until

*Dried banana leaves, obtainable in Oriental stores, can be used or, failing all, cooking parchment is a satisfactory substitute.

golden brown. Add the pork and stir-fry until it changes color. Now drop in the chicken and continue frying until pieces are firm. Add crabmeat and mushrooms and cook, stirring, for 3 more minutes. Fold in the green onions, fish sauce, soy sauce and sugar. Remove from heat and place mixture in the food processor. Roughly chop for a few seconds and set aside to cool.

*Mold Form*

On a piece of paper, draw the rudimentary outline of a fat fish, approximately 4″ wide × 6½″ long. Cut around this outline to form a paper "fish." Placing this "fish" template or pattern on each of the banana-leaf segments, cut out 4 "fish" from the leaves.

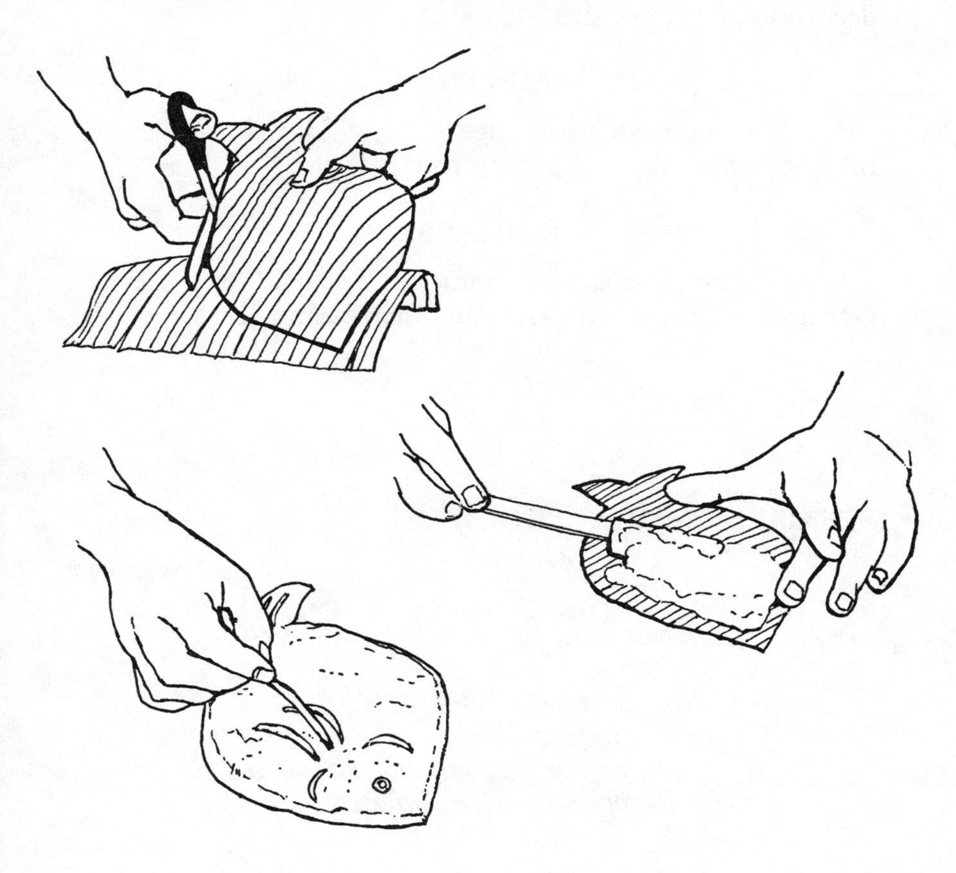

*Assembly*

Place a cut banana-leaf "fish" on a plate. Using an oiled spatula or table knife, evenly mold ⅛ of the fish paste over the surface of the banana leaf, taking care that the edges are smooth. Mound ¼ of the filling in the middle of the "fish," spreading out toward the edges, leaving a margin of uncovered paste mold. This arrangement should now be in the shape of a three-dimensional fish. Using a further ⅛ of the fish-mold paste, carefully spread an even top layer over the form, filling the entire fish outline. Seal and taper the edges to simulate a fish. Repeat these steps until four fish are formed.

Whimsically decorate the mock fish with peppercorns for eyes, green-onion strips for fins, tails, etc., pressing the decorations gently onto the fish mold.

*Cooking*

In a steamer, steam the "fish" for about 30 minutes or until paste is very firm.

*Presentation*

With a spatula, remove the "fish" to a platter. Garnish the edges with coriander leaves and serve.

•

## STEAMED CRAB · POO DOON

*2 to 3 Servings*

*1 piece white bread, crusts removed*
*¼ cup milk*
*½ cup cooked crabmeat*
*½ cup ground pork*
*1 clove garlic, crushed and chopped*
*1 tablespoon chopped onion*

*1 egg, beaten*
*½ teaspoon ground black pepper*
*Salt to taste*
*1 tablespoon coriander, chopped*
*2 fresh red chillies, seeded and cut into strips*
*Coriander sprigs for decoration*

Soak the bread in milk. In a bowl, mix together the crabmeat, ground pork, garlic, onion, egg, bread and milk. Add the black pepper, salt and chopped coriander. Mix thoroughly until smooth and uniform. The mixture can be stuffed into one or more crab-shell bodies, placed in patty shells or small, individually made pans formed from aluminum foil. Decorate the top of each with chilli strips and a sprig of coriander. Heat the water in the steamer and when it is boiling, steam the crab for about 15 minutes or until firm. (The steaming time will vary with the number of cakes and the volume of mixture per serving.) Serve warm with *Siracha* sauce.

•

## STEAMED AND FRIED CRAB CAKES · POO CHA

*3 to 4 Servings*

These "Dearest Crab" (literal translation) are popular snacks in Thailand but also may be served as an accompaniment to a meal. The native version of *Poo Cha* is steamed in small containers fashioned from banana leaves. If your banana tree is not flourishing, either buy small aluminum foil (approximately 3" diameter) containers or, easier, mold your own from foil. Of course the ideal, hassle-free, Western arrangement is the ramekin.

*1 teaspoon coriander roots*
*1 teaspoon ground black pepper*
*3 cloves garlic, chopped*
*3 eggs, separated*

½ *pound cooked crabmeat, flaked*
4 *tablespoons coconut "Cream"*
2 *tablespoons fish sauce (*Nam Pla*)*
½ *cup coriander leaves, chopped*
*Oil for deep frying*

In a mortar or food processor pound or grind the coriander roots, black pepper and garlic to a smooth paste. In one medium mixing bowl whisk the egg whites until firm and in another beat the yolks. In yet another bowl thoroughly mix the crabmeat, paste and coconut "Cream." Fold this into the egg whites and season with fish sauce.

Heat the water in a steamer to a rolling boil, then reduce to simmer. Grease the individual containers and fill with the crab/paste mixture. Brush the tops with egg yolk and sprinkle with coriander leaves. Place the containers in the steamer, cover and cook until set and firm, about 15 minutes. Remove from the steamer and drain off any excess liquid. Upend the containers to remove the crab cakes and set aside to drain.

Heat the oil in a wok or deep-fryer and fry the crab cakes until just crisp and light brown on the outside.

*Poo Cha* may be served hot or cold accompanied by chilli sauce.

•

## KORAT MARINATED SHRIMP · KOI GUNG

*4 Servings*

The marinating of the seafood in this recipe resembles the Peruvian Cerviche, which tends to show that it is a technique which has crossed the Pacific, as it is also employed in the cuisines of the South Sea Islands.

1 *cup large, green shrimp (20 count), shelled, cleaned, deveined and chopped*
*Juice of 2 limes*

½ *teaspoon salt*
3 *eggs, beaten*
½ *cup ground pork, cooked*
1 *sprig citrus leaves, chopped*
1 *stalk lemon grass, finely minced*
20 *or more mint leaves*
1 *lettuce, separated into leaves*
1 *cucumber, peeled and sliced*
*The young leaves from the center of a head of celery, chopped*

*Sauce*

*Juice of the marinated shrimp or prawns*
*Juice of 1 lime*
1 *tablespoon palm sugar*
½ *teaspoon tamarind concentrate, dissolved in 2 tablespoons water*
1 *tablespoon fish sauce* (Nam Pla)
1 *teaspoon mung beans, dry-roasted and pounded*
1 *teaspoon roasted curry paste* (Nam Prik Pao)
4 *tablespoons coconut "Cream"*

In a bowl, mix together the chopped prawns or shrimp, lime juice and salt, squeezing together again and again until the meat becomes whitened. Squeeze out the juice, reserving it, and place the meat in a dish. In a greased frying pan over low heat, fry the beaten eggs slowly until they set firmly into an omelet. Remove to a plate, cool and cut into short, thin strips.

In a bowl, mix together the cooked pork, citrus leaves, lemon grass and 10 mint leaves. Stir in the prawn or shrimp meat and the egg strips. Line a platter with lettuce leaves, mound the prawn mixture in the center and surround it with cucumber slices and young celery leaves. Sprinkle the remaining mint leaves over the top.

Combine all the sauce ingredients together in a saucepan, stirring over low heat for 3 minutes, then pour into a small bowl and use as dressing over the *Koi Gung*.

## FRIED MUSSEL PANCAKES · HOY MAN POO TORD

*4 to 6 Servings*

This chewy pancake can be filled and rolled or merely sliced and sauced—either way a fun snack to be eaten with your hands. Several restaurants in Bangkok are renowned for their *Hoy Man Poo Tord.* It can also be found wherever fresh mussels and seafood are available. Equivalent amounts of medium shrimp may be substituted for these flavorful mollusks.

- 2 ½ *pounds whole, fresh mussels (which should yield just under 4 ounces of mussel meat)*
- 5 *tablespoons all-purpose flour*
- 1 ½ *tablespoons cornstarch*
- 1 *teaspoon salt*
- ½ *cup water*
- 2 *eggs, beaten*
- 2 *green onions, finely sliced*
- 3 *teaspoons coriander leaves, chopped*
- ¼ *teaspoon ground black pepper*
- 1 *teaspoon (approximately) vegetable oil*
- 2 *limes, quartered into wedges*
- *Sprigs of coriander to garnish*

### *Mussels*

Preheat oven to 350° F. Wash the mussels under cold running water. Spread the mussels onto a cookie sheet and put in the oven for about 5 minutes or until the shells peek open. Remove from oven and set aside to cool. When the shells return to a comfortable temperature, pry open the shells and cut out the meat. Place the meat in a colander and wash and drain. Halve the individual mussel bodies lengthwise.

### *Batter*

In a bowl, sift together the flour, cornstarch and salt. Add the water, eggs and beat well until smooth and the texture of heavy cream. Now add the mussel meat, green onions, chopped coriander leaves and black pepper and stir thoroughly.

*Pancakes*

Wipe a large (10″+) frying pan with a paper towel moistened with the oil. Heat the pan over medium high heat. Pour ½ the mussel batter into the frying pan and cook for about 2 minutes (shaking and rotating the pan to cook evenly) or until the bottom of the pancake has brown veins and the top is set. Remove from heat and place the obverse side of a plate over the pan. Quickly rotate the frying pan/plate to drop the pancake on the plate. Return the pan to heat and slide the pancake back onto it. Cook for an additional 1 minute until it is firm. When cooked, flip the pancake again onto a serving platter and garnish with lime wedges and coriander leaves. Repeat with the remaining ½ of the batter. Serve with *Siracha* sauce.

•

## FISH CURRY SOUP · NAM YAR PA

*6 Servings*

*Nam Yar Pa* is usually served as a thin, spiced fish soup; however, this recipe calls for a more substantial version. This is one of the many Thai dishes that can either be served as an ample soup or as a curried main dish over rice.

- 8 *cups "Thick" coconut milk*
- 10 *cloves garlic, cut into thin slices, lengthwise*
- 6 *shallots, cut into thin slices, lengthwise*
- 2 *stalks lemon grass, white only, minced*
- 6 *slivers dried lesser ginger* (Krachai), *chopped and ground*
- 4 *pieces dried, whole Laos* (Ka), *ground*
- 1 *teaspoon shrimp paste (*Kapee*)*

2 *boned kipper (or other smoked whitefish) fillets, flaked (approximately 4 ounces)*
1 *pound cooked Bay shrimp*
1 *cup coconut "Cream"*
4 *green Serrano chillies, seeded and finely sliced cross-wise*
½ *cup bean sprouts*
2 *hardcooked eggs, quartered*
10 *sweet basil leaves (optional)*

In a large saucepan or wok, bring the coconut milk to a boil. Add the garlic, shallots, lemon grass, lesser ginger, Laos, shrimp paste, and kipper fillets. Bring back to a boil and cook, stirring, until the fish has completely disintegrated. Add the shrimp and cook for 2 more minutes. Turn off heat, add the coconut "Cream" and all the remaining ingredients. Stir and cover for 2 to 3 minutes and pour into a serving dish. Serve hot over rice or on its own in soup bowls.

•

## FRIED OYSTERS IN RED CURRY PASTE · HOY NARNG ROM PAD PRIK

*4 Servings*

2 *tablespoons vegetable oil*
2 *cloves garlic, finely chopped*
1 *teaspoon fresh ginger, finely chopped*
1 *pound fresh oyster meat,* drained and patted dry*
1 *tablespoon red curry paste* (Krung Gaeng Ped)
2 *tablespoons granulated sugar*
2 *tablespoons fish sauce (*Nam Pla*)*
1 *teaspoon dried shrimp powder*
*Juice of 2 limes*

*Pacific (Olympia) oysters may be used whole, but the larger (Galveston, Carolina, Maine) varieties must be halved. For fresh oyster preparation, see Chapter 12, Selection and Preparation.

*Garnish*

2 *green onions, cut into fine slivers*
2 *red Serrano chillies, seeded and cut into fine slivers*
2 *limes, thinly sliced*

Heat the oil over medium high heat in a wok and fry the garlic and ginger until the garlic is golden. Add the oysters and stir-fry for about 2 minutes. Remove the oysters with a slotted spoon to a serving dish. Turn heat to low and fry the curry paste for 2 minutes. Season the paste with sugar and fish sauce and stir in the shrimp powder and lime juice. Continue frying and stirring for 1 more minute. Spoon the seasoned paste attractively over the oysters. Decorate with the green onions and red chillies. Ring the platter with lime slices. Serve accompanied with plain white rice.

•

## FRIED STUFFED PRAWNS (SHRIMP) · GUNG TIPAROT

*4 Servings*

This delicious and unexpected treatment of prawns, *Gung Tiparot*, is the specialty of certain seafood restaurants on the Gulf of Siam and on New Petburi Road in Bangkok. The large prawns are split, stuffed with a savory filling and batter-fried. When you bite into the crisp, juicy prawn, the filling comes as a pleasant surprise.

8 *peppercorns, dry roasted and pounded or ground to powder*
1 *large clove garlic, chopped*
1 *teaspoon coriander roots, chopped*
¼ *cup ground pork*
1 *tablespoon fish sauce* (Nam Pla)

1 *teaspoon granulated sugar*
8 *green prawns (15 count or less per pound),* cleaned, shelled and split down the back to remove the alimentary canal and allow for stuffing*
4 *tablespoons lard or vegetable oil*
3 *tablespoons rice flour*
2 *eggs, beaten*
Siracha *or Sweet and Hot Chilli Sauce*

In a mortar or food processor, pound or grind the peppercorns, garlic, coriander roots, pork, fish sauce and sugar to an even paste. Holding the prawn open, taking care not to separate into half, spread the split with pork paste using the blade of a table knife (approximately 1 teaspoon per prawn).† Heat the lard in a wok to 375° F. for frying. Dust the stuffed prawns with the rice flour. Holding them by their tail, dip them in the eggs and quickly drop them into the hot lard. Fry the prawns, turning as necessary, until crisp, about 5 minutes each. Serve with *Siracha* sauce or Sweet and Hot Chilli Sauce for dipping.

* Allow more than 1 prawn per person if *Gung Tiparot* is a principal dish for the meal.

† If the stuffing is too bulky or the prawns separate, you may secure the body with broken toothpicks before battering and frying.

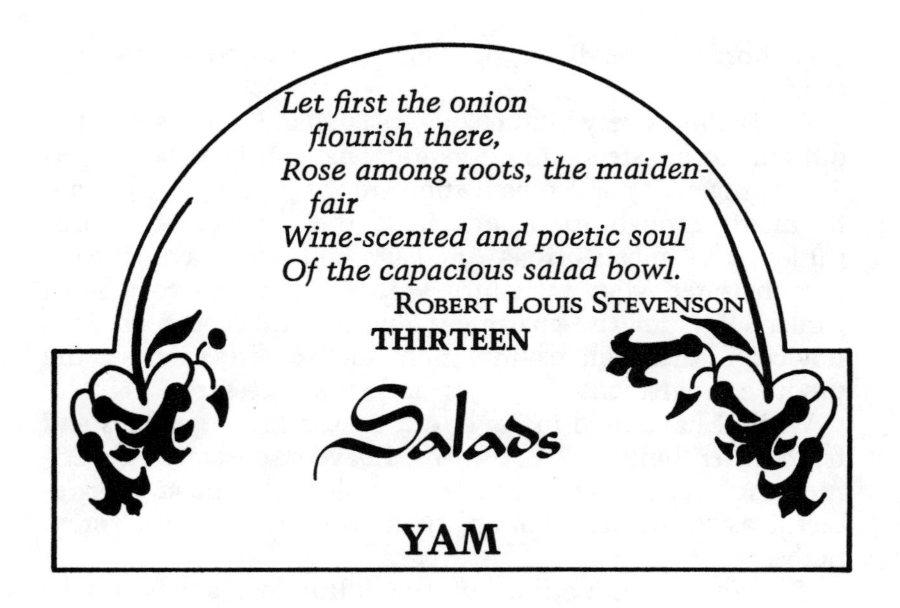

*Let first the onion*
*flourish there,*
*Rose among roots, the maiden-*
*fair*
*Wine-scented and poetic soul*
*Of the capacious salad bowl.*

ROBERT LOUIS STEVENSON

# THIRTEEN

# Salads

## YAM

You are standing in a sunny lane in Thailand, lined with shady trees and thick, luxuriant vegetation. Walking slowly down in front of you is a Thai woman in flowered *pasin* and a loose, cool, white blouse. Every so often she stops and pulls at the trees then bends down and plucks plants from the roadside. If it were another country, you might suppose she was gathering the components of a centerpiece for the table to save the cost of buying flowers. But, if you could follow her in your imagination, you would see her enter the kitchen, carefully wash all the leaves and plants and, then, use them to compose a salad for the next meal.

The trees and shrubs in Thailand produce myriad succulent, edible flowers and leaves. For instance, sprigs of flowers and young leaves from the mango tree become salad ingredients; likewise the leafy shoots and fruit of the roseapple tree, or *chompoo.* There are many vines growing in and along the banks of the multitudinous rivers and canals which produce tender, young tendrils and leaves for salads. More than half the culinary vegetables and herbs described in a

Thai horticultural book are from uncultivated shrubs and trees.

While this is very picturesque in Thailand, it does make it difficult to construct an authentic Thai salad in the United States; ingenuity and substitution are the passkeys. If you are fortunate enough to benefit from the harvest of a large garden, the substitutions are easy and you have already demonstrated your ingenuity with your access to a large garden. But, for the apartment dweller and/or the produce novice, a thorough examination and investigation of the produce department in a supermarket is necessary.

While I have used many of our customary vegetables and fruits when building Thai salads, I have also enjoyed experimenting with, what might be considered, unusual ingredients as substitutions or approximations for Thai hedgerow herbs.

Try any combinations of the following, a few might spark your imagination and ingenuity: watercress; young carrot tops; young celery leaves; Chinese cabbage; mustard greens; the leaves and root of fennel; raw broccoli flowerets; raw zucchini; green, tart apples; thinly sliced *Daikon,* Japanese white radish; imported cucumber with skin; strips of bamboo shoots; beansprouts; raw, green beans, thinly sliced; celery stalks, shaved into curls; fresh mint; fresh sweet basil leaves; fresh citrus leaves; green onions; chives; red onion rings; blanched asparagus; spinach leaves; red radishes; slices of hard, unripe pears; green peppers; raw brussels sprouts; cauliflower flowerets; endive; chicory; mustard; escarole and any variety of head or leaf lettuce.

After you have selected the ingredients for your "Thai" salad, mindful of the balance of colors, textures and flavors, decoratively cut or carve them (see chapter 4, "Fruit and Vegetable Carving"). The Thai generally assemble their salads with combinations of cooked meat strips and fish or shellfish. The salad is always presented on a platter where the full effect of skillful arrangement can be appreciated. A variety of thin, spiced dressings are sprinkled over the ingredients. Further ornamentation is effected by toppings of crushed peanuts, dried, red chilli flakes, crisp-fried onion or garlic flakes, chopped mint or coriander leaves, powdered, dried shrimp and dried, unsweetened coconut flakes. Garnish the creation with lime or lemon wedges, pickled garlic or ginger and red or green fresh chillies, cut into flowers.

A well-conceived and carefully presented "Thai" salad will make a superb centerpiece and talking point at your buffet table, winning the hearts of both Thai and Occidental friends alike. They will know that you have gone to the trouble of creating something which is unique and which shows the Thai appreciation for good food and beauty.

●

## THAI BEEF SALAD · YAM NEUA

*3 to 4 Servings*

*Salad*

- 6 *(approximately) lettuce leaves (e.g., Bibb, Boston, leaf, etc.)*
- 8 *mint leaves, torn*
- 8 *coriander leaves*
- 1 *stalk lemon grass, minced (only the tender bottom ⅔)*
- ½ *pound lean beef (tenderloin), barbecued or roasted rare, sliced into thin strips 2" long × ½" wide*
- 1 *red onion, finely sliced into rings*
- 6 *citrus leaves, torn*

*Dressing*

- 5 *cloves garlic, chopped*
- 5 *green Serrano chillies, seeded*
- 1 *tablespoon fish sauce* (Nam Pla)
- 2 *tablespoons lime juice*
- 2 *teaspoons granulated sugar*

*Garnish*

2 *tablespoons dried onion flakes, fried**
1 *teaspoon dried red chilli flakes, crushed*

Arrange the lettuce to cover a platter. Sprinkle with the mint and coriander. Top this with the lemon grass. Now, evenly lay on the cooked beef pieces. Cover with onion slices and citrus leaves. Pound the garlic and chillies together with a mortar and pestle. Add the fish sauce, lime juice, sugar and stir in the mortar until evenly mixed. Pour this dressing over the beef. Sprinkle with the onion and chilli Garnish. Refrigerate and serve.

•

**BAMBOO SALAD WITH PORK · YAM NO MAI GUP MOO**

*4 to 6 Servings*

In Thailand, fresh bamboo, cooked and shredded, is used for this dish. In the United States, we use canned bamboo shoots, which require no preparation.

2 *shallots, finely chopped*
2 *cloves garlic, finely chopped*
2 *cups canned bamboo shoots, drained and sliced the size of matchsticks*
3 *tablespoons fish sauce* (Nam Pla)
*Juice of 2 limes*
1 *teaspoon granulated sugar*
2 *green onions, chopped to include tops*
¾ *cup cooked pork, cut into matchsticks*
8 *(approximately) lettuce leaves (red Romaine, Butter, leaf, etc.)*

*See chapter 3, Fundamentals.

*Garnish*

¼ *teaspoon dried red chilli flakes*
3 *sprigs mint leaves*

In a mortar, pound the shallots and garlic to a paste. Wrap the paste in a small packet of aluminum foil and place directly onto a burner or under a broiler. Broil on each side for 1 minute. Remove and place the paste in a mixing bowl. Add the bamboo shoots, fish sauce, lime juice, sugar, green onions and pork strips. Mix together gently. Line a plate with the lettuce leaves. Mound the bamboo mixture in the center of the lettuce. Sprinkle with chilli flakes and decorate with sprigs of mint. Serve at room temperature or chilled, if preferred.

•

## SHRIMP AND ORANGE CHILLI SALAD • PLA GUNGSOD GUP SOM KEO WAN

*3 to 4 Servings*

6 *ounces cooked Bay shrimp*
3 *oranges, peeled, seeded and sliced (Mandarin oranges may be substituted)*
½ *teaspoon dried red chilli flakes*
3 *cloves garlic, crushed and finely minced*
½ *teaspoon salt*
6 to 12 *mint leaves, coarsely chopped*
*Juice of 1 lime*
½ *tablespoon fish sauce* (Nam Pla)

In a bowl, combine the shrimp and orange slices. Add the chilli flakes, garlic, salt and mint leaves and mix thoroughly. Dress with lime juice and fish sauce. Toss again, refrigerate and serve.

## PAPAYA AND SHRIMP SALAD · SOM TAM

*6 to 8 Servings*

In Thailand, *Som Tam* is made with green (unripe) papaya, which is not available in America; but ripe, firm papaya makes a very attractive and flavorful alternative.

- 1 *head leaf lettuce, washed and separated*
- ½ *white cabbage, finely shredded*
- 2 *papayas, peeled, seeded and thinly sliced*
- 2 *firm medium tomatoes, sliced*
- ½ *pound cooked Bay shrimp*
- 2 *tablespoons roasted peanuts, coarsely crushed*
- 2 *green Serrano chillies, seeded and cut into slivers*
- *Juice of 3 limes*
- 2 *tablespoons fish sauce* (Nam Pla)
- 2 *tablespoons palm sugar*
- 2 *green onions, finely chopped*

Arrange the lettuce leaves on a platter. In a bowl, combine the shredded cabbage with the papaya slices and tomatoes, reserving a few slices for garnish. Place this mixture on the platter and sprinkle with shrimp and peanuts. Decorate with the remaining tomato slices and chillies. Mix the lime juice, fish sauce, palm sugar and green onions together in a bowl until the sugar has dissolved. Pour this dressing over the salad and refrigerate until served.

**N.B.** An equal amount of cooked pork cubes makes an interesting substitution for the shrimp.

•

## SPICY SHRIMP SALAD · YAM GUNG

*4 Servings*

This salad, *Yam Gung,* has quite a sharp, citrus flavor, plus the bite of ground red chillies. A mound of plain rice on the side of your plate is a nice way to balance the tartness.

- 1 *pound medium green shrimp (approximately 20 count), peeled, halved, deveined and briefly cooked**
- 3 *tablespoons fish sauce* (Nam Pla)
- 3 *tablespoons lime juice*
- 2 *cloves garlic, finely chopped*
- ½ *teaspoon ground red chilli powder (Cayenne)*
- 2 *stalks lemon grass, minced*
- ¼ *red onion, thinly sliced*
- 2 *whole green onions, finely chopped (including some green)*
- 1 *tablespoon coriander leaves, chopped*
- 1 *head of lettuce (Red Romaine, Bibb, etc.), washed and separated*
- 1 *lime, thinly sliced*
- 10 to 20 *mint leaves*

Place the cooked shrimp in a mixing bowl. Season with fish sauce, lime juice, garlic and powdered chilli. Mix well. Add the lemon grass, red onion, green onions and coriander leaves. Toss lightly and refrigerate. Chill a large platter. Rim it with alternating batches of lettuce leaves and lime slices. Sprinkle one half the mint leaves in the center. Mound the shrimp salad attractively in the center and decorate with the remaining mint leaves.

*Pack the cleaned, raw shrimp in a strainer and place them in a saucepan of boiling, salted water (enough to cover the shrimp) and cook for about 30 seconds. These crustaceans will change color, gray to pink, and curl.

## SIAMESE WATERCRESS SALAD · PAK SIAM

*4 Servings*

- 2 *tablespoons oil*
- 2 *tablespoons shallots, minced*
- 2 *tablespoons garlic, minced*
- 4 *tablespoons cooked shrimp*
- 4 *tablespoons cooked* loin of pork, cut into small pieces*
- 4 *tablespoons cooked* pork skin, cut into fine shreds or strips*
- 3 *tablespoons roasted peanuts, roughly chopped*
- 1 *cup watercress, chopped*
- 2 *tablespoons fish sauce* (Nam Pla)
- 2 *tablespoons lime juice*
- 1 *tablespoon granulated sugar*
- 2 *fresh red chillies, cut into fine strips*

In a frying pan or wok, heat the oil and fry the shallots and garlic until golden. Remove and drain.

In a large bowl, mix together the cooked shrimp, pork and pork skin. Add the chopped peanuts and toss together. Add the watercress and mix lightly. In another bowl, combine the fish sauce, lime juice and sugar. At the point of serving, pour this fish sauce dressing over the meats and cress mixture and toss lightly. Decorate with the red chilli strips, sprinkle with fried shallots and garlic, and serve.

*The pork meat should be blanched in a small amount of water and remain tender. The pork skin should be boiled until very tender and almost jelly-like.

## PORK AND CELERY SALAD · YAM MOO CEUN CHAI

*6 Servings*

The Thai celery is a miniature cousin to our large, hearty bunches. To approximate the Thai celery, remove the large, outside stalks of domestic celery, and use only the heart including the young green leaves.

- 1 *cup cooked pork (loin or butt), fat removed, thinly sliced and cut into slivers*
- 2 *cups young celery stalks and leaves, chopped*
- 1 *medium red onion, thinly sliced into rings*
- *Juice of 2 limes*
- 1 *tablespoon fish sauce* (Nam Pla)
- 1 *teaspoon granulated sugar*
- ¼ *teaspoon dried red chilli flakes*
- 2 *tablespoons dried onion flakes, crisp-fried in oil and drained**

Place the pork, celery and onion in a bowl. Toss together with the lime juice and fish sauce. Stir in the sugar and toss again. Place the mixture on a platter and sprinkle with dried chilli flakes and onion flakes. Chill and serve.

•

## CUCUMBER SALAD · YAM TAENG KWA

*3 to 4 Servings*

The Thai cucumber is a fat little vegetable measuring between 3" and 4" in length and bursting with seeds. When adapting this recipe, I have made allowances for our longer cucumbers.

* See Chapter 3, Fundamentals.

*2 cups cucumber, peeled, seeded and chopped*
*1 tablespoon onion, minced*
*2 tablespoons dried, salted shrimp, pounded into pieces*
*1 teaspoon granulated sugar*
*3 tablespoons lime juice*
*2 tablespoons fish sauce* (Nam Pla)
*8 lettuce leaves (Bibb, Boston, etc.)*
*2 tablespoons roasted peanuts, coarsely crushed*
*¼ teaspoon dried red chilli flakes*

Line a bowl with paper towels. Place the chopped cucumbers in the bowl and gently squeeze out the moisture. Remove the towels and mix the cucumbers with onion, dried shrimp and sugar. Sprinkle with lime juice and fish sauce. Toss gently. Line a platter with lettuce leaves and mound the cucumber mixture in the center. Sprinkle with peanuts and chilli flakes. Chill and serve.

•

## CUCUMBER BOATS · YAM NEUA LAE TAENG KWA

*4 Servings*

*2 short cucumbers, peeled, halved and quartered, with the seeds scooped out so they resemble boats*
*1 clove garlic, crushed and minced*
*4 tablespoons mint leaves, finely chopped*
*1 tablespoon fish sauce* (Nam Pla)
*2 tablespoons lime juice*
*1 teaspoon granulated sugar*
*¼ teaspoon ground black pepper*
*1 cup cooked (medium rare) roast beef, thinly sliced and shredded*

½ *cup dried onion flakes, crisp-fried in oil, drained**
8 *lettuce leaves*
*Coriander sprigs for decoration*
4 *red Serrano chillies, seeded and cut into flowers*

Using paper towels, mop the cucumber "boats" to remove any moisture. In a bowl, combine the garlic, mint, fish sauce, lime juice, sugar and pepper, stirring until sugar dissolves. Stir in the shredded beef and onion flakes. Spoon this mixture into the cucumber "boats" until they resemble fully loaded barges. Line a platter with lettuce leaves and arrange the "boats" on the sea of leaves. Garnish with coriander sprigs and chilli flowers. Chill and serve.

•

## OYSTER AND CHILLI SALAD · PLA HOY NARNG ROM

*4 to 6 Servings*

Fresh oysters have a limited season in Thailand. The Thai incorporate them in this delicious and unusual salad. Oyster lovers may like to try it when tired of merely slipping the bivalves down their throats.

1 *pound fresh oyster meat (Olympia, etc.)*
½ *teaspoon salt*
4 *cloves garlic, chopped*
2 *fresh green Serrano chillies, stemmed*
1 *cucumber, peeled, serrated with the tines of a fork and thinly sliced*
½ *red onion, cut into slivers*
1 *teaspoon white vinegar*

* See Chapter 3, Fundamentals.

| | |
|---|---|
| | *Juice of 2 limes* |
| | *Half a honeydew melon, flesh scooped out and reserved for another purpose* |
| *10 to 15* | *mint leaves* |
| *1* | *red Serrano chilli, seeded and sliced* |

Wash the oyster meat thoroughly and drain well in a colander. In a mortar pound the salt, garlic and green chillies to a paste. In a bowl, blend this paste together with the oyster meat. Stir in the cucumber slices and onion. Season with vinegar and lime juice. Spoon the oyster mixture into the melon half, decorate with mint and red chilli slices. Chill and serve.

•

## GALA SALAD · PAK SOD

*8 to 10 Servings*

*Pak Sod* is a selection of as many different, colored vegetables as possible made into an attractive salad dish. The vegetables must be as crisp and fresh as possible. The selection and amount will depend on seasonal availability and your artistic judgment.

| | |
|---|---|
| *8 to 12* | *radishes* |
| *4 to 8* | *green onions* |
| *4 to 6* | *carrots, peeled* |
| *2 to 4* | *zucchini, peeled* |
| *3 to 4* | *celery stalks* |
| *1* | *cucumber, peeled* |
| *1* | *jicama, peeled* |
| | *Large bowl of water filled with ice* |
| *1* | *head lettuce (leaf or head)* |
| *½* | *red cabbage, sliced* |
| *¼* | *white cabbage, sliced* |

*2 to 4 Jalapeño chillies, sliced into strips*
*1 ½ cups cherry tomatoes*

Using a small, sharp knife, decoratively cut and carve the radishes, green onions, carrots, zucchini, celery, cucumber and jicama into flowers, tassels, etc., as your imagination dictates.* Place them all into the ice water.

Using an attractive platter, preferably one with a pedestal, arrange the lettuce leaves on the face as if to begin a flower arrangement or bouquet. On top of the lettuce place the red and white cabbage slices radiating outward to join the next layer. Now mound the carved vegetables, interspersing Jalapeño chillies and cherry tomatoes, and alternating colors and textures, on the cabbage to form a cone.

Serve accompanied with bowls of *Nam Prik* or *Lon* sauces.

•

## CABBAGE SALAD · YAM GALUMBLEE

*6 Servings*

This salad bears a resemblance to Indonesian and Malay cabbage dishes particularly in the use of coconut milk in the dressing.

*2 tablespoons peanut oil*
*5 cloves garlic, finely chopped*
*½ red onion, finely chopped*
*½ cup cooked pork, finely chopped*
*3 cups white cabbage, blanched and finely chopped*
*1 teaspoon salt*
*1 ½ tablespoons fish sauce* (Nam Pla)
*Juice of 1 lime*

* See Chapter 4, Fruit and Vegetable Carving.

1 *tablespoon roasted peanuts, coarsely crushed*
½ *cup "Thick" coconut milk*
10 *medium cooked shrimp, halved lengthwise*

Heat peanut oil in a frying pan and fry the garlic and onion until brown. Drain with a slotted spoon and set aside. In a large bowl, combine the pork, cabbage, salt, fish sauce, lime juice, peanuts and "Thick" coconut milk. Mix well and mound on a platter. Decorate with cooked shrimp halves and sprinkle with fried garlic and onion. Serve immediately.

•

## PORK SKIN SALAD · YAM NANG MOO

*6 Servings*

Although Westerners are used to eating crisp-fried pork rind as snacks *(Chicharrones)*, the idea of eating boiled pork skin may seem strange and unappetizing. However, after cooking the pork until tender and marinating in herbs, spices and cream, *Yam Nang Moo* makes a surprisingly delicious salad. The texture is reminiscent of cooked baby squid, but the flavor is definitely pork. Pork skin can be bought in sheaths in the larger, more comprehensive Oriental markets that have meat counters.

1 *piece pork skin, 8" × 8" (approximately), boiled until tender and cut into matchstick sized slivers*
½ *cup lean, cooked pork, thinly sliced and cut into matchstick sized slivers*
½ *cup mint leaves*
1 *stalk lemon grass, finely minced*
3 *tablespoons dried shrimp powder*
8 *citrus leaves, shredded*

1 *tablespoon coriander leaves, chopped*
2 *shallots, finely chopped*
2 *tablespoons coconut "Cream"*
1 *tablespoon* Siracha *sauce*
*Juice of 1 lime*
2 *tablespoons fish sauce* (Nam Pla)
2 *teaspoons granuated sugar*
*Sprigs of sweet basil or mint leaves to garnish*

In a large bowl, mix together all the ingredients except the garnish. Place the bowl in the refrigerator for at least 30 minutes. Remove and mound the salad on a decorative platter. Garnish with the sprigs of sweet basil or mint.

•

## WATER CHESTNUT SALAD · YAM KRACHUP

*6 Servings*

1 *tablespoon peanut oil*
1 *medium white onion, finely chopped*
5 *cloves garlic, finely chopped*
2 *tablespoons fish sauce* (Nam Pla)
*Juice of 2 limes*
1 *tablespoon granulated sugar*
2 *cups canned water chestnuts, drained and sliced*
½ *cup cooked, ground pork*
½ *cup cooked (Bay) shrimp, chopped*
2 *tablespoons coriander leaves, chopped*
6 *citrus leaves, cut into strips*
3 *red Serrano chillies, seeded and sliced into strips*

Heat the peanut oil in a small frying pan and fry the onion and garlic until crisp. Remove from heat. In a bowl, combine the garlic and onion with any remaining oil, together with the fish sauce, lime juice and sugar to form a dressing. Stir well until sugar dissolves. Add the water chestnuts, ground pork and shrimp pieces. Toss together lightly. Place on a serving dish and sprinkle with coriander, citrus leaves and chilli strips.

•

## ROSE PETAL SALAD · YAM DOK GULAB

*6 to 8 Servings*

As well as leaves from wayside shrubs and trees, the Thai use flower petals in their salads as this charming *Yam Dok Gulab* testifies. Having no garden, when I first made this salad in the United States, I bought the roses from a florist. To ensure there was no insecticide on the petals I told the girl behind the counter that I wanted the flowers for a salad. She showed no surprise. With a deadpan expression she said, "When you buy a dozen, you get a dozen free. Do you want to eat them here or take them 'to go?'"

- 6 *large lettuce leaves (e.g., Red Romaine, Bibb, Boston, etc.)*
- 5 *tablespoons fish sauce* (Nam Pla)
- *Juice of 3 limes*
- 2 *teaspoons superfine granulated sugar*
- 1 *whole breast of chicken, cooked, boned and cut into matchstick sized pieces*
- ½ *pound Bay shrimp, cooked and chopped*
- ½ *pound ground pork, cooked*
- 2 *tablespoons roasted peanuts, coarsely crushed*
- 6 *cloves garlic, minced, fried until brown and drained*
- 6 *shallots, minced, fried until brown and drained*

*The petals from 12 roses, rinsed and patted dry*
2 *tablespoons coriander leaves*
3 *red Serrano chillies, seeded and cut into slivers*

Arrange the lettuce leaves to cover a platter and chill. In a large mixing bowl, blend together the fish sauce, lime juice and sugar, stirring until sugar has dissolved. Add the chicken, shrimp, pork and peanuts and toss until all the ingredients are well mixed. Stir in half of the garlic and shallots. Then add the rose petals. Toss lightly to minimize bruising the petals. Transfer this salad mixture to the platter, mounding it attractively over the lettuce leaves. Sprinkle the remaining shallots and garlic on top. Decorate with coriander leaves and complete the color-scheme contrast with a scattering of scarlet chilli slivers.

•

## GREEN MANGO SALAD · YAM MAMUANG

*6 to 8 Servings*

Green mangoes are seldom available in this country, but this salad is equally effective if made with tart, green cooking apples. Jicama, while not absolutely authentic, is a delicious addition.

4 *green mangoes or cooking apples, peeled, cored and thinly sliced*
½ *pound jicama, peeled and thinly sliced*
1 *teaspoon salt*
*Juice of 2 limes*
1 *tablespoon peanut oil*
5 *cloves garlic, crushed and thinly sliced*
6 *green onions (including some of the green), thinly sliced*
½ *pound ground pork*

1 *tablespoon shrimp powder*
4 *tablespoons fish sauce* (Nam Pla)
4 *tablespoons chunky peanut butter*
2 *tablespoons palm or brown sugar*
¼ *teaspoon ground black pepper*
½ *teaspoon dried red chilli flakes*

Put the mango or green apple and jicama slices into a mixing bowl and sprinkle with salt and lime juice. In a frying pan, heat the peanut oil and fry the garlic and green onions until garlic is just cooked. Remove with a slotted spoon and set aside to drain. In the same oil, while still on heat, fry the ground pork until the pink disappears. Add the powdered shrimp, fish sauce, peanut butter and sugar. Stir well and remove from heat. Combine the cooked ingredients from the saucepan to the marinating fruits/tubers in the mixing bowl adding the pepper and chilli flakes. Mix thoroughly. Chill in the refrigerator and serve cold.

•

## SQUID SALAD · YAM PLA MUEK

*6 to 8 Servings*

1 *pound squid, cleaned and cut into diamonds (tentacles may be removed), pounded and boiled in acidulated (add vinegar or lemon) water for 45 minutes to 2 hours (depending on size and desired tenderness)**
3 *tablespoons fish sauce* (Nam Pla)
3 *tablespoons lime juice*
3 *cloves garlic, minced*
½ *teaspoon red chilli powder (Cayenne)*
1 *stalk lemon grass, minced*

*Frozen squid of the highest quality is available from your local fish merchant, cleaned and frozen in layers. For cleaning fresh squid, see page 179.

3 *whole green onions, finely sliced (including some green)*
1 *stalk celery sliced lengthwise into several strips and cut 2" long*
10 *mint leaves, finely chopped*
1 *head lettuce (Red Romaine, Bibb, etc.), washed and separated*
*Sprigs of coriander for garnish*

Place the cooked squid into a mixing bowl. Season with fish sauce, lime juice, garlic and chilli powder. Mix thoroughly. Add lemon grass, green onions, celery and mint leaves. Toss lightly and refrigerate. Cover a platter with a layer of lettuce leaves. Mound the squid salad in the center and garnish with coriander sprigs.

*Epicurean cooks*
*Sharpen with cloyless*
*sauce his appetite*
WILLIAM SHAKESPEARE

FOURTEEN

# Sauces

## NAM PRIK, LON

*Nam Prik* sauce is the universal favorite of the Thai people through all strata of society. It is one of the ancient, traditional dishes of the country, records indicating that it was probably eaten in the twelfth and thirteenth centuries during the Sukhothai period. At that time it was likely that *Nam Prik* was made with peppercorns, not chillies.

M. R. Kukrit Pramoj, a former Prime Minister of Thailand; and for several years, my next door neighbor, and a leading culinary expert, avers that chillies were introduced to Thailand around the sixteenth century. It is probable, therefore, that the Thai depended on the indigenous black peppercorns for "bite" in their sauce.

At that time also, *Nam Pla,* the fish sauce which is the present-day basis for most sauces, was only eaten by the coastal Thai. Internal transportation systems were almost nonexistent so the people of the inland Kingdom of Sukhothai seasoned their food with *Pla Ra,* a condiment made from fermented freshwater fish and rice. Similarly, another seafood-based condiment added to *Nam Prik,*

*Kapee* (or shrimp paste) was antedated by *Tua Naw,* a fermented, soybean preparation.

The present-day *Nam Prik* sauces are basically composed of: dried shrimp or fish, shrimp paste, garlic and chillies, pounded together with *Nam Pla,* sugar and lime juice. Chopped, raw eggplant, *Makeua,* are also added. There are as many variations as there are good cooks who pride themselves on its preparation; a good sauce is the hallmark of an accomplished housewife.

The cooked sauces, *Lon,* are also produced with infinite variations. These sauces are often based on coconut milk. They are usually served with roasted or fried fish and raw vegetables.

Every meal will be accompanied by at least one or two sauces and they play as important a part within the cuisine as the French sauces do within their cuisine. In similar fashion, the Thai tend to regard their sauces with equal fervor, creativity and pride.

•

## THAI HOT SAUCE · NAM PRIK

*6 to 8 Servings*

This basic Thai hot sauce is on the table at every meal. There are as many versions of *Nam Prik* as there are cooks to prepare it. *Makeua Puong,* the tiny pea eggplant, is often chopped and added as are some other miniature eggplant varieties. If not available, *Makeua Puong* may be omitted, but the sauce characteristically contains small fragments of chillies and other ingredients.

2 *tablespoons whole, dried shrimp, chopped*
6 *cloves garlic, chopped*
4 *dried red chillies (including seeds), chopped*
1 *teaspoon granulated sugar*
3 *tablespoons fish sauce* (Nam Pla)

3 *tablespoons lime juice*
2 *fresh red or green Serrano chillies, seeded and finely chopped*
3 *pea eggplants (*Makeua Puong*), chopped (optional)*

In a mortar or food processor, pound or grind the shrimp, garlic, *dried* chillies and sugar until the mixture is fragmented and well blended. Gradually add the fish sauce and lime juice, spoonful by spoonful, until you have a consistent mixture. Pour in a serving bowl and stir in the *fresh* chillies and pea eggplant (if available). This sauce keeps well for several weeks, refrigerated, and even tastes better after a day or so of storage.

•

## ROASTED HOT SAUCE · NAM PRIK PAO

*Yields ¾ cup, approximately*

This is the basic recipe. Other ingredients such as roasted peanuts and dried shrimp powder may be added. *Nam Prik Pao* commonly accompanies plain rice, cooked vegetables and salads. Try it spread on toast rounds for cocktail canapés. The traditional method of preparation calls for the garlic and onions to be roasted, unpeeled, in the hot ashes of a wood or charcoal fire until the skins are black. With a nod to kitchen air pollution, I prefer to dry-fry these bulbs in a heavy frying pan. The quantities of the basic recipe can be increased if it is to be made ahead and stored. When preparing in advance, fry the finished paste in oil, then place in tightly capped jars in the refrigerator.

6 *cloves garlic*
2 *small onions, or 6 shallots*
1 *tablespoon shrimp paste* (Kapee)
1 *tablespoon brown sugar*

- 1 *teaspoon tamarind concentrate, dissolved in 1 ½ tablespoons hot water*
- 5 *large dried red chillies, chopped*

In a heavy, iron pan, dry-fry the unpeeled garlic and onions over high heat until skins are crisp and dark brown. Cool, peel and chop. Wrap the shrimp paste in a square of aluminum foil into a small, neat packet and dry-fry in the same pan over high heat for 2 minutes on either side. Cool and unwrap. Place all the ingredients in a mortar or food processor and pound or grind into a thick paste.

•

## SWEET NAM PLA · NAM PLA WAN

*8 to 10 Servings*

- 1 *tablespoon vegetable oil*
- 6 *shallots, finely minced*
- 8 *cloves garlic, finely minced*
- 1 *tablespoon dried red chilli flakes*
- ¼ *cup fish sauce* (Nam Pla)
- 1 *tablespoon palm sugar*
- 1 *teaspoon tamarind concentrate, dissolved in 3 tablespoons water*
- 2 *green onions, finely chopped*
- 1 *tablespoon coriander leaves, finely chopped*

Heat the oil in a small frying pan and fry the minced shallots and garlic until golden. Add the dried chilli flakes and fry until everything is crisp. (Take the pan off the heat just before the flakes are browned, as they will continue to fry after removal.) Set aside.

In a small saucepan, heat the fish sauce, palm sugar and tamarind water until sugar has dissolved and the mixture is almost at the boil. Stir in the chopped green onions and coriander and immediately remove from the heat. Combine the contents of both the pans and pour into a serving bowl. Serve at room temperature.

•

## SALTED EGG SAUCE · NAM PRIK KAI KEM

*4 to 6 Servings*

Another of the wide palette of Thai sauces, *Nam Prik Kai Kem,* is eaten in Thailand with plain, steamed rice. It is also served as an accompaniment to fried or steamed fish, garnished with fresh green onions.

2 *cloves garlic, finely chopped*
2 *green Serrano chillies, seeded and chopped*
2 *shallots, finely chopped*
4 *hardcooked egg yolks of salted eggs* (Kai Kem) *(plain hardcooked yolks may be substituted)*
1 *teaspoon shrimp paste* (Kapee)
1 *tablespoon palm sugar*
2 *tablespoons fish sauce* (Nam Pla)
*Juice of 2 limes*

In a mortar or food processor, pound or grind the garlic, chillies and shallots into a juicy paste. Blend in the egg yolks. Follow with the shrimp paste and palm sugar, pounding well or giving the food processor a few turns between each addition. Remove the paste to a bowl and stir in the fish sauce and lime juice. Correct the seasoning (you may wish to dilute slightly with 1 or 2 tablespoons of water). The sauce may be refrigerated in an airtight jar for a week, no longer. A label would be helpful so as not to confuse it with marmalade!

•

## HOT SAUCE DIP · NAM PRIK ONG

*6 to 8 Servings*

*Nam Prik Ong* is a quickly made dipping sauce for vegetables, fried pork rinds, etc. It also does wonders with plain rice or noodles; with the latter, becoming a Thai equivalent of spaghetti sauce.

- 2 *tablespoons vegetable oil*
- 4 *cloves garlic, finely chopped*
- 2 *shallots, finely chopped*
- 1 *teaspoon shrimp paste* (Kapee)
- 1 *tablespoon prepared chilli paste (e.g., Tadang, etc.)*
- ¾ *pound lean ground pork*
- 4 *fresh, peeled or 6 whole canned tomatoes*
- ¼ *teaspoon salt*

Heat the oil in a wok and fry the garlic and shallots until lightly browned. Add the shrimp and chilli pastes and pork and stir-fry until pork browns and the odor of the dish becomes less pungent. In a food processor or blender, purée the tomatoes quickly, about 10 seconds. Drain the tomatoes, reserving the liquid. Stir the purée into the pork and add the salt. Cover and bring to a boil. Uncover and cook for 5 minutes. The mixture should be the consistency of spaghetti sauce. If it is too dry, add a little of the reserved tomato juice. Serve hot or let cool and refrigerate for future use.

•

## CURRIED PORK DIP WITH VEGETABLES · LON GAENG SOM NAR MOO

*4 to 6 Servings*

2 *tomatoes, halved, seeds and pulp removed, chopped*
*Rind (green zest) of 1 lime*
1 *tablespoon orange curry paste* (Krung Gaeng Som)
1 *tablespoon vegetable oil*
5 *cloves garlic, crushed and minced*
½ *pound lean ground pork*
1 *teaspoon granulated sugar*
3 *tablespoons fish sauce* (Nam Pla)
1 *large grapefruit (melon may be used instead)*
2 *large cucumbers, peeled and cut into flowers or decorative shapes*
½ *small cabbage, cut into wedges*
1 *small white* Daikon *turnip, cut into sticks*
2 *zucchini, cut decoratively*
2 *carrots, peeled and cut into decorative shapes*
3 *fresh red chillies, seeded and cut into flowers*
1 *small packet crisp-fried pork rinds*

In a mortar or food processor, pound or grind the tomatoes, lime rind and *Krung Gaeng Som* paste together, until the mixture becomes smooth and sloppy. Heat the vegetable oil in a wok and fry the garlic until pale brown. Add the tomato mixture from the mortar or food processor and stir-fry for 3 minutes until the mixture thickens. Stir in the ground pork, sugar and fish sauce and continue to stir over medium high heat until the pork is cooked and a thick sauce is formed. Set aside. Form a decorative cup from the grapefruit by inserting a knife through to the center, one-third from the top and cutting round the circumference in a series of *V*-shaped serrations until the top is severed from the bottom two-thirds. Discard the top and scrape out the flesh, reserving it for some other use. Set the grapefruit in the center of a large platter and arrange the cut vegetables decoratively around it. The display should look as attractive as possible. Spoon the pork dip into the grapefruit bowl and serve, accompanied by the pork rinds in a separate dish.

•

## CRAB SAUCE OR DIP · POO LON

*4 to 6 Servings*

*Lon* are boiled sauces, as opposed to the uncooked sauces of *Nam Prik*. Boiled sauces are commonly served with fresh vegetables and small dried and fried fish of the herring family called *pla too*. This combination of vegetables, fish and sauce eaten with rice provides the basic meal of the Thai, eaten universally throughout Thailand.

- 6 *ounces crabmeat, cooked and flaked*
- 1 ½ *cups "Thick" coconut milk*
- ½ *teaspoon salt*
- 3 *shallots, finely chopped*
- 1 *teaspoon granulated sugar*
- ¼ *teaspoon tamarind concentrate, dissolved in 1 tablespoon hot water*
- 2 *green Serrano chillies, thinly sliced into disks*
- 1 *tablespoon coriander leaves, chopped*

In a medium saucepan, mix the crabmeat, coconut milk and salt. Bring to a boil, stirring. Reduce heat and simmer for 5 minutes, stirring occasionally. Add the shallots, sugar, tamarind liquid and chillies and continue to cook, stirring, for another 5 minutes until a thick, homogeneous sauce is formed. Transfer to a serving bowl, sprinkle with coriander and serve to accompany fried fish, any raw vegetable assortment or plain over steamed rice.

## SWEET AND HOT CHILLI SAUCE · SAUS PRIK

*Yields 3½ cups, approximately*

*Saus Prik* is my attempt to re-create the marvelous, hot sauce served in so many Thai restaurants, particularly Chai Talay on Rama IV in Bangkok. Similar sauces may be purchased bottled and labeled "All Purpose Sauce." They are also sweet/hot and garlicky but lack the personality of homemade. *Saus Prik* is the traditional, zesty accompaniment to shrimp rolls *(Hae Koon),* Thai-style fried chicken *(Gai Tord)* and cold meats. It is interesting to experiment and find your own application. This recipe yields 3 ½ cups and will noticeably become more spicy with age.

*1 ½ cups seedless golden raisins*
*5 tablespoons white vinegar*
*3 teaspoons red chilli flakes*
*8 cloves garlic*
*1 teaspoon salt*
*2 fresh red chilli peppers, seeded and sliced*
*1 cup whole canned tomatoes, with juice*
*12 ounces Red Plum jam*
*9 ounces pineapple juice*
*4 tablespoons brown sugar*

Place the first seven ingredients in a food processor or blender and blend to an even consistency. This will take several minutes and require stopping occasionally to scrape down the sides. Place the remaining ingredients in a saucepan over medium heat. Pour the blended ingredients in the saucepan. While stirring, let this mixture come to a boil. Reduce heat to simmer and cook for 20 more minutes. Store in airtight, sterilized jars. It will keep for at least 2 months, refrigerated.

*Put on the pot,*
*Says Greedy-gut,*
*We'll sup before we go.*
ANONYMOUS

FIFTEEN

# Noodles

## MEE

*"Gwaytio! Gwaytio!"* The noodle vendor's call rings out in the early-morning calm of the sleepy lanes. The three-wheeled bicycle cart creaks slowly up the road as gates open and slam and the housewives, gardeners and servants hurry out to buy the first meal of the day. *Gwaytio* is a wide, fresh rice noodle, purchased ready-made from the market. The *Gwaytio* vendor plunges the noodles briefly into his large pot of boiling water and puts a generous portion into each bowl. A ladleful of boiling meat stock follows and then a few pieces of pork or chicken. The customers indicate which condiments they prefer—dried chilli flakes, crushed peanuts, sugar—and the bowls are then topped with a shake of *Nam Pla* and a final hot shot of *Nam Prik Som* (fresh chillies chopped and soaked in vinegar).

If the breakfaster wishes privacy, he supplies his own bowls, which are then filled and taken back to the house for solitary consumption. But the noodle vendor's arrival is generally an occasion for the first gossip of the day. The little three-wheeled kitchen is surrounded by eaters, talking and joking until the bowls are emptied and washed, and the *Gwaytio* man pedals slowly away to the next lane.

Noodles play an important part in Thai cuisine, being served frequently as a snack. I imagine the Thai tribes who migrated from Southern China brought their noodle-eating habits with them. The prevalence of noodle consumption has further expanded with repeated immigrations of Chinese.

Noodles are available in Thailand in many shapes, forms and substances. Egg noodles, rice noodles and mung-bean noodles are the main categories. Egg noodles are locally made or imported from China. The Thai produce mainly rice noodles; either ribbon shaped or the thin, rice vermicelli noodles, as well as the aforementioned *Gwaytio.* The mung-bean noodles are also locally made. All these noodles plus a few others are available in the markets, food shops and noodle kitchens.

The rice vermicelli or rice stick noodles, *Sen Mee,* are available both in Thailand and in the United States, in eight- and sixteen-ounce bags, each containing two or four flat hanks of noodles. The rice sticks are white and brittle in their dried form and have to be soaked before use. After soaking, they are combined with meats and vegetables in stir-fried dishes and soups. One of the few instances in which they are deep-fried directly from the packet is for the famous *Mee Krob.* For this dish, the dried noodles puff up to twice-size when they come in contact with the hot oil. They are then drained and combined with a tangy sweet/sour sauce and contrasting textures of meat and vegetables to become a masterpiece. The dried rice vermicelli noodles will keep indefinitely if stored in an airtight container in a cool, dry cupboard.

*Gwaytio* noodles are produced commercially in wide, flat limp pancakes. These disks are folded and refolded into small squares which are then sealed in airtight, plastic packets. In this form, they can be purchased, refrigerated, from Thai stores here and in Thailand. To use, merely take off the wrapper, cut through the layers in strips and incorporate directly in wok dishes. The strips open out into wide ribbons during the stir-fry process.

Mung-bean noodles, called *Woon Sen,* are referred to as cellophane noodles. They are made from a puree of mung beans and water which is strained to produce a clear liquid. This liquid is then dried into sheets, or extruded to form noodles. In their dried form, these thin noodles (called bean-thread noodles) are extremely tough and can cut your hands if you try to break them. They must be soaked before using. Cooked in stir-fried dishes or soups, they have no discernible flavor of their own and absorb the dominant flavors of the dish. Bean-thread noodles may also be crisp-fried directly from the packet. They then form a crisp bed for other ingredients and a good contrast in textures. They can be bought in two-ounce hanks and are stored in the same manner as rice sticks.

When a Thai diner orders noodles, he will specify the type of noodle wanted for a particular dish and whether he wants the dish as a soup, with gravy, or dry. Thus: *Ba Mee Nam* means egg noodles in soup; *Gwaytio Haeng* means a dry stir-fried dish of wide rice noodles with meat, vegetables and seasonings. Sometimes the name and description of the dish will merely indicate the contents, such as: *Gwaytio Rad Nar,* a popular platter of stir-fried wide noodles combined with pork, broccoli and oyster sauce.

•

## THAI FRIED NOODLES · PAD THAI

*4 Servings*

*Pad Thai* are usually served as part of a luncheon meal or as a midday snack, as opposed to other "centerpiece" noodle dishes, around or on which other portions are served.

½ *cup vegetable oil*
6 *cloves garlic, finely chopped*

1 *cup small cooked shrimp*
1 *tablespoon granulated sugar*
3 *tablespoons fish sauce* (Nam Pla)
1 ½ *tablespoons tomato ketchup*
2 *eggs, beaten*
¾ *pound (approximately 3 hanks) rice vermicelli* (Sen Mee) *soaked in hot water for 15 minutes and drained*
1 *cup bean sprouts*

*Garnish*

1 *tablespoon dried shrimp powder*
2 *tablespoons peanuts, coarsely ground*
½ *teaspoon dried red chilli flakes*
2 *green onions, finely chopped*
2 *tablespoons coriander leaves, chopped*
2 *limes, sliced into ⅛" circles*

Heat the oil in a wok and fry the garlic until golden. Quickly add the shrimp and stir-fry until heated through. Add the sugar, fish sauce and ketchup and stir until sugar dissolves. Add the beaten eggs, letting them set slightly, then stir to scramble. Add the noodles and toss and stir for about 2 minutes. Reserving about 4 tablespoons of the bean sprouts, add the remainder to the wok. Stir over heat until the bean sprouts are barely cooked. Turn the *Pad Thai* onto a platter, placing the reserved, raw bean sprouts on one side.

*Presentation*

Sprinkle the noodles with the garnish ingredients in the following order: shrimp powder, peanuts, chilli flakes, green onions, coriander leaves. Ring the platter with the lime slices and serve.

•

## BANGKOK NOODLES · SEN MEE KRUNG TEP

*4 to 6 Servings*

*Sauce*

- 1 ½ *cups "Thick" coconut milk*
- ½ *cup ground pork*
- ¾ *cup bean curd, cut into ½" cubes*
- 2 *tablespoons dried shrimp*
- 2 *tablespoons bean sauce*
- 2 *tablespoons granulated sugar*
- ½ *cup small cooked shrimp*

*Noodles*

- 3 *tablespoons vegetable oil*
- 1 *red onion, cut pole-to-pole into slivers*
- 1 *pound packet rice vermicelli* (Sen Mee) *noodles soaked in water and red food coloring for about 5 minutes, or until soft*
- 1 *cup bean sprouts*
- 1 *tablespoon fish sauce* (Nam Pla)
- 2 *eggs beaten, with 1 tablespoon water, fried into an omelet and cut into strips*
- 6 *(approximately) lettuce leaves (e.g., Bibb, Boston, leaf, etc.)*
- 1 *lime, cut into wedges*
- *Sprigs of coriander leaves*
- 3 or 4 *green or red Serrano chillies, seeded and cut decoratively*
- Nam Prik, *or any other chilli sauce for accompaniment (optional)*

*Sauce*

In a heavy saucepan, bring the coconut milk to a boil. Add the remaining sauce ingredients except the cooked shrimp and cook until pork is tender. Add the cooked shrimp until they are warmed through. Pour the mixture in a serving bowl and reserve for accompanying the Noodles.

*Noodles*

Heat the oil in a wok. Stir-fry the onion until light brown. Drain the noodles and add to the onions, tossing and continuing frying for 5 minutes. Stir in bean sprouts and sprinkle with fish sauce. Remove from heat.

*Presentation*

Line a platter with the lettuce leaves. Mound the noodle mixture in the center of the lettuce. Arrange the omelet strips on top of the noodles. Place the lime wedges around the perimeter of the noodles. Garnish the top with coriander and chillies. Spoon the sauce over individual portions of noodles accompanied by optional small bowls of *Nam Prik* or other chilli sauce.

•

## EGG NOODLES AND PORK SOUP · BA MEE NAM

*6 to 8 Servings*

More of a complete lunch than a soup, *Ba Mee Nam* originated in China but has been modified by the Thai. It is purveyed by the soup vendors and served in the little "soup kitchens." I have even had a bowl handed to me from a "soup boat" or floating kitchen on a *klong.*

The vegetables for the soup should be blanched before you start to cook the recipe. The Thai bamboo-handled, deep, wire strainer is recommended for immersing the bean sprouts and noodles in boiling water. If you do not possess one, use a handled sieve to precook both ingredients.

1 *cup bean sprouts, blanched and drained*
1 *8-ounce package noodles* (Ba Mee) *boiled for 5 minutes and drained*
6 *cloves garlic, chopped and crisp-fried in 1 tablespoon vegetable oil*
6 *cups chicken stock*

4 *tablespoons ground pork*
2 *tablespoons dried shrimp*
2 *tablespoons fish sauce* (Nam Pla)
3 *lettuce leaves, torn into strips*
8 *thin slices cooked pork, approximately 1 ½" × 3" long*
2 *green onions, thinly sliced*
1 *tablespoon coriander leaves, chopped*
1 *teaspoon granulated sugar*
2 *tablespoons roasted peanuts, coarsely crushed*
1 *tablespoon dried red chilli flakes*

Place the cooked bean sprouts in a large serving bowl or tureen. Top with the cooked noodles. Pour the fried garlic with its oil over the noodles. In a saucepan, heat the chicken stock, ground pork, dried shrimp and fish sauce until it comes to the boil. Drop in the torn lettuce leaves and immediately pour this soup over the noodles in the tureen. Garnish with pork slices, green onions and coriander leaves. Sprinkle with sugar, peanuts and chilli flakes and serve immediately.

**N.B.** Instead of completing the dish in one tureen, you may portion out the solid ingredients (bean sprouts, noodles, garlic) into individual bowls and pour over each pork soup mixture and decorate.

•

## FRIED CELLOPHANE NOODLES · PAD WOON SEN

*4 Servings*

- 3 *tablespoons vegetable oil*
- 6 *cloves garlic, chopped*
- 1 ½ *cups pork, chicken, or shrimp, sliced*
- 8 *ounces (approximately) cellophane noodles, soaked in hot water, drained and cut into 3" lengths*
- 2 *eggs*
- 2 *tablespoons fish sauce* (Nam Pla)
- 1 *teaspoon ground black pepper*
- 4 *tablespoons roasted peanuts, coarsely pounded*
- 1 *cup bean sprouts*
- *Heart (including leaves) of 1 head of celery, finely chopped*
- 1 *tablespoon coriander leaves, chopped*

In a wok, heat the oil and fry the garlic until golden. Add the meat and cook until tender. Place in the noodles, stirring and tossing. Make a hole in the center of the mixture and break the eggs into it. Slowly stir the eggs until set and then break and mix them with the noodles. Season with fish sauce and pepper. Stir in the peanuts, bean sprouts and celery and cook until heated through. Garnish with coriander leaves and serve.

•

## THAI CRISP-FRIED NOODLES · MEE KROB

*6 to 8 Servings*

Crisp-fried noodles come to us from the Chinese, but the Thai have elaborated on it and, with additions, made it peculiarly their own *Mee Krob.* The noodles are always the thin, thread-like, rice noodles, or vermicelli, as they are sometimes called. The additions to the noodles vary greatly with what is available in the market or family larder, but there is always a combination of seafood and meat or poultry mingling with the noodles and the sweet/sour sauce. *Particular* care must be taken with frying the noodles, as the success of the dish depends on the perfection with which they puff up when fried.

- 2 *bunches rice vermicelli (approximately 8 ounces)*
- *Oil for deep frying*
- 1 *large onion, finely chopped*
- 5 *cloves garlic, finely chopped*
- ½ *pound pork fillet, sliced and cut into 1" long pieces*
- 1 *whole chicken breast, boned and sliced, cut into 1" long pieces*
- 6 *dried Chinese mushrooms, soaked and finely sliced*
- 2 *small fresh chillies, seeded and finely sliced*
- 3 *tablespoons soy sauce*
- *Juice of 2 limes*
- 2 *tablespoons rice vinegar*
- 4 to 5 *tablespoons granulated sugar, white or brown*
- 3 *tablespoons fish sauce* (Nam Pla)
- 3 *tablespoons small shrimp, cooked or raw*
- 4 *eggs, beaten*
- *Handful bean sprouts*
- 6 *green onions, finely chopped*
- 4 *tablespoons fresh coriander, chopped*
- 2 *green onions, cut for decoration*
- Optional Additions: *crab meat, bean curd, dried shrimp*

Tear the noodles into handful bunches in a large shopping bag. This will contain the noodles and keep them from decorating your kitchen. Set aside the torn noodles and save the bag. Heat the oil in a large wok and fry the noodles in individual bunches until they puff up. (Oil must be very hot or noodles will be tough. Turn noodles and briefly fry on the other side. Noodles should be crisp and pale gold.) Repeat the frying with each bunch and drain them in the paper bag with paper towels. Continue until all the noodles are cooked and drained and set aside. Pour off oil leaving approximately 6 tablespoons in the wok. Lightly fry onions and garlic. Add the pork and cook it through. Add chicken and fry for 3 more minutes. Add the mushrooms and chillies. Reduce heat. In a separate bowl mix the soy sauce, lime juice, vinegar, sugar and fish sauce. Add this mixture to the wok and simmer until liquid has reduced by half and is becoming syrupy. Add shrimp and cook for 1 minute. Make a hole in the center of the ingredients and pour in the beaten eggs. Let the eggs set and then stir to distribute. Add the bean sprouts and drained noodles, turning and tossing lightly to coat with the sauce and allow the meats to mix. Do not allow the noodles to break up too much—they are very brittle. Heat the combination through.

*Presentation*

Transfer to a serving platter and sprinkle with chopped green onions and coriander. Decorate with cut green onions.

**N.B.** The eggs may also be fried separately into a thin omelet, which is then cut into strips and used for garnish.

•

## NOODLES AND BROCCOLI · GWAYTIO RAD NAR

*4 Servings*

1 *packet (approximately 1 pound)* Gwaytio *noodles (wet rice noodles)*
2 *tablespoons vegetable oil*
3 *cloves garlic, finely chopped*
½ *pound pork, chicken or beef, cut into thin strips and briefly cooked in ¾ cup stock*

1 *cup blanched broccoli, cut on the diagonal into 2" lengths*
3 *tablespoons oyster sauce*
1 *tablespoon fish sauce* (Nam Pla)
½ *teaspoon granulated sugar*
*Dash each of salt, pepper and monosodium glutamate (the latter, optional)*
1 *teaspoon cornstarch dissolved in 1 tablespoon water*

Remove the wrapping from the noodles and, while still wet and folded, cut them in wide (approximately ½") strips. Heat the oil in a wok on high, and lightly fry and toss the garlic and noodles for 2 minutes. Add the meat and its stock. While stirring, let this mixture come to a boil. Now add the broccoli and all the remaining ingredients while tossing and stirring. Serve immediately with rice.

*I have come to ask you*
*for seeds of melon,*
*marrow and gourd, so*
*that I may plant my fields.*
PREM CHAYA, TRANSLATOR

SIXTEEN

# Accompaniments

## KREUNG KIEM, PAD PAK

This category of recipes corresponds more closely to the side dishes and vegetable dishes of Western cuisines than it does to any similar category in Thai meals. In Thai menus, vegetable dishes are not generally grouped together under one heading, but will fall into various subcategories. These depend on whether they are cooked or raw; stir-fried or steamed. To illustrate this: A dish of carved, raw vegetables to be dipped into a particular specified sauce and eaten would be grouped under the category of Sauces; the sauce being considered the more important item.

Egg dishes can be regarded as main dishes, or as snacks. This depends on the time of day and meal structure within which they are eaten. The main definition used to separate egg dishes in this chapter from the egg dishes in the initial chapter on Appetizers and Snacks, is that these egg dishes must be eaten with a utensil, and are not finger food: a qualification shared by all the dishes in this chapter. The majority of these recipes share another common denominator: they contain meat or seafood, but not in large enough quantities to justify placing them under those chapter headings.

All this tends to make this chapter somewhat of a catchall. These dishes are of subsidiary importance to the meal, being chosen to balance the menu after the main dishes are selected. However, in their suitability to the Western framework of eating, the majority will make very pleasant, light lunch dishes. These fit very happily into our new concepts of *Cuisine Minceur,* and should produce a relatively low calorie count. As an added bonus, because of the low ratio of meats to vegetables, they are most suitable for those on tight budgets.

•

## FRIED BEAN SPROUTS · PAD TUA NGORK

*4 to 6 Servings*

2 *tablespoons vegetable oil*
4 *cloves garlic, crushed and chopped*
½ *pound pork loin, thinly sliced and cut into strips, ½" × 2"*
6 *ounces cooked Bay shrimp*
1 *tablespoon fish sauce* (Nam Pla)
1 *teaspoon granulated sugar*
¼ *teaspoon ground black pepper*
½ *pound bean sprouts, washed and drained*

In a wok, heat the oil and fry the garlic until golden. Quickly add the pork and stir-fry for 1 minute. Add the shrimp and warm through. Sprinkle with fish sauce, sugar and pepper. Stir in the bean sprouts and stir-fry for 1 to 2 minutes, or until sprouts are tender but still crisp. Serve immediately.

•

## STUFFED ZUCCHINI OR CUCUMBER · FAN TIENG

*4 Servings*

A decorative and delicious lunch dish for the diet-conscious.

- 3 *large (diameter) zucchini, about 6" long or 2 medium cucumbers, ends trimmed and sliced into 1 ½" long columns*
- ¾ *pound ground pork*
- 3 *cloves garlic, crushed and chopped*
- ½ *teaspoon ground black pepper*
- 1 *tablespoon fish sauce* (Nam Pla)
- 12 *(approximately) cooked Bay shrimp*
- 2 *tablespoons crisp-fried onion flakes**
- *Coriander sprigs for garnish*

Heat the water in a steamer. With a spoon, carefully scoop out most of the zucchini seeds and some of the flesh to form a dish in each column. Set aside. In a bowl, combine the pork, garlic and black pepper until well mixed, then season with fish sauce. Stuff each vegetable dish with the pork mixture, packing well down into the cavity. When the steamer is on the boil, steam the stuffed vegetables for about 10 minutes; until the vegetable is firm and the pork cooked and firm. Remove the *Fan Tieng* to a platter and decorate each with a cooked shrimp, pressing it firmly into the center of the filling. Sprinkle with onion flakes and garnish the platter with coriander sprigs.

•

* See Chapter 3, Fundamentals.

## SAUTÉED GREENS · BAI GUP KAO

*4 Servings*

In Thailand, *pak bung*, an aquatic water creeper resembling spinach, is often used for this side dish, as are young leaves freshly picked from trees and shrubs. We can use fresh greens from the produce department. (Turnip greens, mustard greens, spinach, lettuce, etc.)

- 2 *tablespoons vegetable oil*
- 7 *cloves garlic, minced*
- 1 *cup cooked chicken or crab meat, chopped*
- 1 to 2 *pounds fresh greens, washed and torn into large pieces, together with any water remaining on the leaves*
- 2 *tablespoons fish sauce* (Nam Pla)
- ¼ *teaspoon ground black pepper*

In a wok, heat the oil and fry the garlic briefly until barely gold. Add the chicken or crab pieces and stir-fry until warmed through. Add all the greens at once. The oil should be hot enough that there will be a resounding hiss of steam as the wet leaves are introduced. Turn the greens over once or twice so that they are coated with the oil, chicken and garlic and begin to reduce in volume. Sprinkle with fish sauce and black pepper and, covering the wok, reduce the heat and simmer for 2 to 5 minutes. (The length of time will depend on which variety of greens are used.) Uncover, transfer the contents to a serving dish and serve at once.

•

## STEAMED STUFFED ONIONS · HỪA HOM SOD SAI

*6 Servings*

6 *large onions, peeled, and parboiled or steamed for 5 minutes*
10 *peppercorns, browned in the oven, or dry-roasted in a frying pan*
4 *cloves garlic, chopped*
1 *teaspoon coriander roots, chopped*
1 *pound ground pork*
1 *cup cooked crabmeat*
2 *tablespoons vegetable oil*
1 *tablespoon fish sauce* (Nam Pla)
1 *teaspoon granulated sugar*
6 *green onions, green tops only, cut into tassels*
6 *fresh, red Serrano chillies, seeded, cut into flowers*

Cut the bases off the onions so they sit upright. Core out the middles, leaving outer shells of 3 to 4 layers. Reserve the middles for some other use. Place the onion shells in a bowl of cold water until needed. In a mortar, pound the peppercorns, garlic and coriander roots together into a juicy paste. Place the pork and crab meat in a bowl and add the contents of the mortar, mixing everything together thoroughly. Heat the oil in a wok and stir-fry the mixture until light brown. Sprinkle with fish sauce and sugar. Stir, remove from heat and let cool. Remove the onion shells from the water, drain and pat dry. Stuff them firmly with the pork/crab mixture. Heat the water in a steamer and when it is boiling, place the onion shells inside and steam for 10 minutes, or until onions are tender and filling is firm to the touch. Remove and place on a platter, decorating each with a green onion tassel and a chilli flower. Serve with a side bowl of soy sauce or any *Nam Prik*.

•

## FRIED BROCCOLI WITH SHRIMP · PAK PAD GUP GUNG

*4 to 6 Servings*

This dish is widely available in restaurants and food shops throughout Thailand; probably because of the ease and speed of preparation. Suggested substitutes for broccoli are mustard greens, Swiss chard, *Bok Choy*, or any dark green, leaf vegetable. The use of oyster sauce marks it as originally Chinese; the garlic is a typical Thai touch.

- 3 *cups broccoli, cut on the diagonal into 1" lengths*
- 3 *tablespoons vegetable oil*
- 5 *cloves garlic, minced*
- 1 *tablespoon fish sauce* (Nam Pla)
- 1 *tablespoon oyster sauce*
- 1 *teaspoon granulated sugar*
- ½ *pound cooked Bay shrimp*

Soak cut broccoli in iced water for 15 minutes. (This preserves the crispness throughout the cooking.) In a wok, heat the oil and fry the garlic until it just changes color. Quickly add the broccoli from the bowl, without draining, and stir-fry for 3 minutes. Cover the wok and turn heat to low. Simmer for 5 minutes, or until broccoli is tender but still crisp. Uncover, stir in fish sauce, oyster sauce, sugar and shrimp. Stir until shrimp are heated through and sugar has dissolved. Serve with plain rice.

•

## PORK STUFFED BELL PEPPERS · PRIK YAI SAI MOO

*4 to 6 Servings*

- 1 *cup ground pork*
- ½ *red onion, minced*

2 *teaspoons coriander roots, finely chopped*
½ *teaspoon ground black pepper*
4 *cloves garlic, finely chopped*
1 *egg, beaten (for stuffing)*
½ *teaspoon salt*
4 *medium peppers or 6 small, topped, seeded and cored*
2 *tablespoons vegetable oil*
2 *eggs, beaten (for nets)*
*Coriander leaves for garnish*

In a bowl, mix together the pork, onion, coriander roots, black pepper, garlic and *1* egg and salt. Stuff the peppers with this mixture and, with the water boiling, place in a steamer. Steam for 8 to 10 minutes and remove the peppers to cool. Heat the oil in a wok. Dip fingers in the *2* eggs and trail back and forth across the wok to form a net (see Chapter 3, Fundamentals). Wrap each of the steamed peppers with an egg net, place on a serving dish and sprinkle with coriander leaves. Serve hot.

•

## PORK STUFFED OMELETS · KAI YAT SAI

*4 to 6 Servings*

*Kai Yat Sai* is commonly served as a lunch dish at the brief, midday break of the Thai worker. After one particularly long and frustrating morning spent in a government office, trying to obtain permits, I remember lunch in a little wooden, food shop, set in the middle of an adjacent field. Three Thai members of our office staff were with me, and we all ordered *Kai Yat Sai*. The owner made the omelets right before us, and I marveled at the deft way in which he set and folded them. The speed and efficiency of his service contrasted sharply with the slow motion of officialdom we had just left.

3 *cloves garlic, chopped*
8 *peppercorns*
8 *coriander roots, chopped*
4 *tablespoons vegetable oil*
½ *cup ground pork*
1 *medium onion, chopped*
½ *cup Chinese snow peas, chopped*
1 *medium tomato, chopped*
1 *teaspoon granulated sugar*
8 *eggs, beaten*
1 *tablespoon fish sauce* (Nam Pla)
2 *tablespoons coriander leaves, chopped*

In a mortar, pound together the garlic, peppercorns and coriander roots into a juicy paste. In a wok, heat *half* the oil and fry the paste for 2 minutes. Add the pork and stir-fry until brown. Now put in the onion, snow peas and tomato, stir-frying for 1 minute between each addition. Stir in the sugar and set the wok aside. Beat the eggs and fish sauce together. Heat *half* the remaining oil in a frying pan over medium heat. Pour in *half* the eggs and rock the pan until it is evenly coated. Set the eggs, then spoon half the pork mixture down the center of the omelet. Fold both sides over the filling then slide the omelet onto a plate. Keep warm. Repeat the process with the remaining ingredients to make a second omelet. Cut both omelets into serving portions and sprinkle the top with coriander leaves.

•

## STEAMED EGGS · KAI DOON

*4 to 6 Servings*

8 *eggs, beaten*
½ *red onion, minced*
1 *shallot, minced*
3 *tablespoons fish sauce* (Nam Pla)

¼ *pound (approximately) ground pork*
½ *teaspoon ground black pepper*
4 *dried red chillies, seeded, soaked and cut into strips*
1 *green onion (including green), thinly sliced*
½ *cup "Thin" coconut milk, stock or water*
1 *tablespoon coriander, chopped*

In a mixing bowl combine all the ingredients. Mix well and pour into a greased, ovenproof baking dish. Heat the water in a steamer to a boil. Place the baking dish in the steamer, replace the top and steam for 15 to 20 minutes or until the eggs are well set. Serve *Kai Doon,* hot (preferably) or cold in its own baking dish.

•

## GROUND PORK OMELET · KAI TORD GUP MOO

*2 to 4 Servings*

With the conventional (9") frying pan, the amount of these ingredients yields two omelets. You may adjust the size of the pan and/or the amount of ingredients to produce more or less omelets of varying sizes.

8 *eggs, beaten with 2 tablespoons fish sauce* (Nam Pla)
½ *pound ground pork*
2 *cloves garlic, crushed and minced*
3 *shallots, minced*
1 *tablespoon fresh coriander, finely chopped*
*Vegetable oil for frying*

Place all the ingredients, except the oil, in a mixing bowl and thoroughly stir. Heat the greased pan over medium high heat until the oil just begins to vaporize. Pour in *half* the egg mixture and rotate the pan to coat the bottom evenly. Fry until the underside of the eggs are golden. Turn and fry the other side until it also is golden; less than half the time required for the first side. Transfer to a warm platter. Swab out the pan, removing any remnants, and repeat the frying process with the remaining egg mixture. Stack the omelets together on the platter and serve whole or sliced. If the omelets appear too oily, pat them dry with a paper towel before serving.

•

## SWEET AND SOUR FRESH CUCUMBER · TAENG KWA BRIO WAN

*6 to 8 Servings*

This fresh relish is usually served in Thailand as an accompaniment to chicken Satay with peanut sauce. *Taeng Kwa Brio Wan* is also a delightful side dish to meat balls, fish dishes or cold meats. Freshly made in larger amounts it can be refrigerated in jars for a week—no longer. To increase the amounts, multiply the ingredients in proportion.

- 2 *large cucumbers, peeled, halved lengthwise and sliced thinly*
- 1 *small red onion, peeled, halved and sliced thinly*
- ½ *teaspoon dried red chilli flakes*
- 4 *tablespoons granulated sugar*
- ½ *cup water*
- 5 *tablespoons white vinegar*
- ½ *teaspoon salt*

Place the cucumber, onion and chilli flakes in a mixing bowl. In a small saucepan, over low heat, dissolve the sugar in the water. Remove from heat and stir in the vinegar and salt. Pour this mixture over the vegetables in the bowl. Stir and refrigerate until served.

## PICKLED VEGETABLES · PAK DONG

*Yields 6 cups, approximately*

These pickled vegetables, freshly made, can be refrigerated in jars for one or two weeks. They are commonly served with fried meat or fish balls, shrimp or crab cakes or to accompany stuffed chicken wings. Other vegetables such as carrots, broccoli or *Bok Choy* may also be included.

- *2 cups white or rice vinegar*
- *1 tablespoon granulated sugar*
- *1 teaspoon salt*
- *1 cup cauliflower, cut into flowerets about 1 ½"*
- *1 cup cucumber, peeled, seeded and cubed*
- *1 cup Chinese cabbage, cut into 1" squares*
- *1 cup corn kernels, stripped off the cob*
- *6 cloves garlic, chopped*
- *6 shallots, chopped*
- *6 dried red chillies, seeded and finely chopped*
- *½ cup peanut oil*
- *1 tablespoon sesame seeds, dry-roasted pale brown*

In a saucepan, heat the vinegar, sugar and salt until boiling. Immerse the chopped vegetables and cook until tender but crisp. Remove from heat and set aside to cool.

In a mortar or food processor, pound or grind the garlic, shallots and chillies to a paste. In a wok, heat the peanut oil and fry the paste, stirring for 2 to 3 minutes. Add the vegetables and vinegar and continue to cook, stirring, for 2 more minutes. Pour into a serving dish and sprinkle with the roasted sesame seeds. Serve warm or leave to cool and pour into a jar; cover tightly and refrigerate for later use.

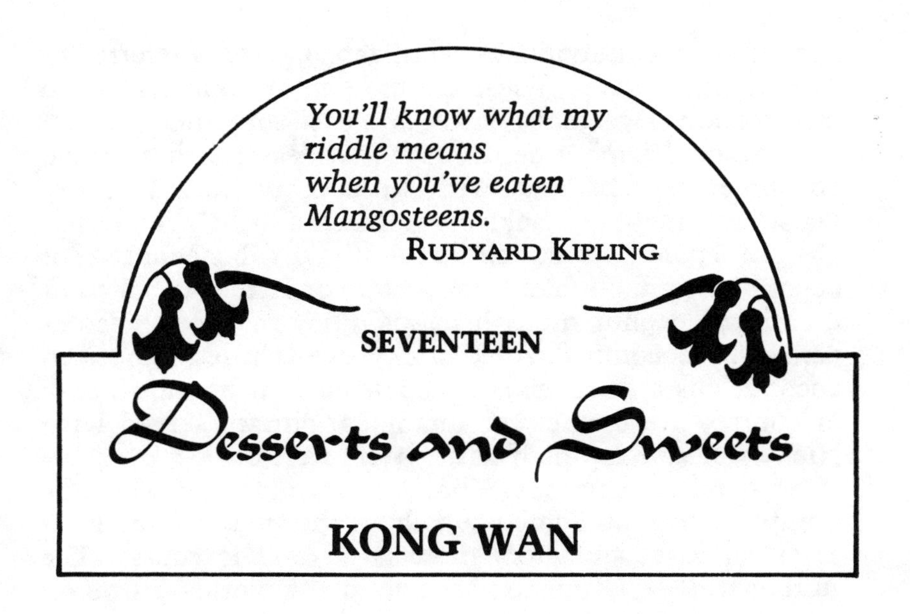


Thai desserts and sweets are almost a whole cuisine to themselves. As much care, skill and art goes into their confection as that applied to the best Continental patisseries. I have added the Dessert classification because it is satisfying to display one's skill at the conclusion of a meal, by presenting a dazzling and intricate masterpiece of a dessert. In Thailand, however, a fresh fruit platter is the normal finale; sweetmeats are reserved for special occasions and formal entertaining.

In the United States, Thai restaurants tend to confine their menus to a minimum of desserts. *Sungkaya,* the coconut-milk custard, or the ubiquitous coconut ice cream are two commonly served specialities. Both are delightful, but unfortunately, give the diner no idea of the vast array of delectable sweets available in Thailand.

Thai sweets fall into two main classifications. First are the liquid desserts, consisting of all manner of fruits and vegetables, raw or boiled, served in coconut milk blended with palm sugar, or in delicately scented sugar syrups.

Second are the individual sweetmeats, generally referred to as *Kanom,* or cakes. These are mere mouthfuls concocted from various sweetened pastes and coconut jellies.

Some of the more delicious liquid desserts that I have consumed in Thailand, with little or no regard to my waistline, include: jackfruit segments in thick syrup; custard apple, served chilled with the benediction of coconut cream; chunks of sweet taro or yam, soft-boiled in a bath of coconut milk; luscious, juicy mangoes, accompanied by coconut-flavored sticky rice; chilled lichees in coconut custard; bananas caramelized in palm sugar, and, of course, the famous, or infamous, durian, served with sticky rice and anointed with coconut cream.

No detailed account of Thai desserts and fruits would be complete without some word about the amazing durian. It is either loved or hated; there is no middle course. The durian fruit—the most expensive in the world—grows on glossy-leaved trees and is very large; about the size of a man's head. It has a thick, green rind covered with pyramidal prickles. The central seed is the size of an egg, and is surrounded by a creamy, yellowish pulp or flesh with the texture of blancmange and a superb cream-like flavor. The rind of the fruit, unfortunately, exudes a smell comparable to rotten onions and stale cheese. Durian lovers advise you to hold your nose while eating the fruit! Prized varieties of the fruit can cost as much as thirty U.S. dollars, and on the Thai economy, that sum will keep a farmworker for a month. The orchards are protected by electrified fences and guard dogs.

The fame of this fruit spread to Europe in the mid 1700's, and in 1892, Bayard Taylor, in his book on Siam, wrote,

Of all fruits, at first the most intolerable but said by those who have smothered their prejudices, to be of all fruits, at last, the most indispensable. When it is brought to you at first, you clamor till it is removed; if there are durians in the next room to you, you cannot sleep. Chloride of lime and disinfectants seem to be its necessary remedy. To eat it, seems to be the sacrifice of self-respect; but endure it for a while, with closed nostrils, taste it once or twice, and you will cry for durians thenceforth, even—I blush to write it—even before the glorious mongosteen.

A certain Thai prince, a very elevated member of the royal family, who is addicted to durian, recounted to me a certain occasion that he was flying to another country and had smuggled some durian on board. It was to be a gift and was secured in a tightly sealed container. (Durian is forbidden on planes!) He placed the can at his feet and fastened his seat belt. After takeoff, he was embarrassed to notice that there was an increasing odor of durian arising round his seat. Adjacent passengers were giving him sidelong glances and sniffing the air in a rather pointed manner. Looking down he noticed, to his horror, that the can was bulging and the lid lifting up. The durian, with the altitude, was exuding a gas which the can could not contain. He said that he jammed both his feet down on top of the lid in an attempt to hold it on, but the game was up. Nemesis, in the form of the Thai flight attendant, came down the aisle and politely, with due deference to his high station, asked him if he had durian in the container. It was nauseatingly obvious that he had, whereupon she even more politely asked him to give it to her and disappeared into the back galley with the offending object. What she did with it, he does not know, but he never got it back!

The little dessert sweets or cakes are made from a variety of ingredients including glutinous or sticky rice, rice and tapioca flours, yams, agar-agar (seaweed gelatin), mung-bean paste, egg yolks, palm sugar, and, of course, coconut milk and cream. The cakes are fashioned to represent miniature fruits, or glazed with a solution of agar-agar; frosted with coconut shreds, or festooned with egg threads. Fragrant flower essences are used for flavor and crushed leaves, flowers and cochineal for color. Some cakes are served in little cups fashioned from banana leaves, while others are cut into diamonds or squares. None are over-sweet. The Thai achieve a fine balance of sweet and salt, which pleases even palates which have tuned out sugar. Many cakes can be bought ready-made in the markets, for their confection requires a high degree of skill and patience. However, for the enthusiast with ambition to try something really different, I have included some of the more complicated recipes in this chapter as well as the simple, everyday desserts.

## MANGOES AND STICKY RICE

The mango season in Thailand is eagerly awaited; for to most people fortunate enough to have eaten tropical fruit, the luscious, juicy mango is the crown prince of fruit, if not the king. While many Thai revel in the taste of ripe mangoes, they are also partial to the green, unripe fruit, sliced and eaten with sugar, salt, and dried red chilli flakes. Thai partiality posed a big problem for me.

In Bangkok, the majority of houses in which I lived had mango trees in the garden, generally overhanging the hedges and road. I would wait, anxiously, as the blossoms turned to fruit and the pendulous clusters of green mangoes got bigger and bigger. Then came the overnight disaster and frustration—a swarm of locusts, in the shape of small boys, would descend (or should I say ascend?) and pick the trees bare before the mangoes were ripe. I would swear and curse, and stomp into the kitchen to complain to the cook. She would look at me and smile gently. "In Thailand, if the fruit is by the road, it belongs to everybody," she would tell me.

One year, having had enough of this wholesale thievery, I determined to outwit the rapacious hordes. We were living on Soi Dejo, in the center of Bangkok, in a large house which had several empty bedrooms. Intent on feasting on ripe mangoes, and with dim memories of English apples stored in attics, I told the gardener to pick all the ripening fruit. We then laid our harvest in neat rows, covering the entire, bare teak floor of one of the empty rooms. My cook grinned and shook her head. I heard the buzz of voices from the kitchen as she and the "wash amah" discussed the latest, crazy thing that their "madame" had thought up.

They knew best: I had not reckoned with the humid heat of Bangkok. Yes, the mangoes surely ripened; but in twenties and thirties a day, until the bounty reached four hundred a week! There is a limit to how often you can eat anything, even a mango.

The next year, I resigned myself to "the Thai way." The boys got my mangoes, and I bought mangoes and sticky rice from the street vendors, just like everyone else. After all, I was a *farang,* and even if I was not an American millionaire—every Thai knows that all *farang* are wealthy, and can well afford to give away mangoes!

•

## MANGOES AND STICKY RICE · MAMUANG KAO NIEO

*4 to 5 Servings*

- 1 ½ *cups glutinous rice (sticky or sweet rice), soaked overnight and drained*
- 1 *cup "Thick" coconut milk, boiled until reduced by ⅓*
- ½ *cup granulated sugar or palm sugar, whichever preferred*
- ½ *teaspoon salt*
- 5 *ripe mangoes, peeled, halved, stone removed, and each half cut into 4 transverse slices*
- 4 *tablespoons coconut "Cream"*

Cook rice according to rice instructions, Chapter 3, Fundamentals. Pour the "Thick" coconut milk into a bowl and stir in sugar and salt until dissolved. Add the warm sticky rice and let the mixture stand for 30 minutes.

Arrange the reassembled mango halves on a platter and spoon the sticky rice in heaps beside them. Spoon the coconut "Cream" over the sticky rice. Refrigerate, or serve immediately.

**N.B.** Before purchasing mangoes, read information in Appendixes, Glossary.

•

## BANANAS IN COCONUT MILK · KLUAY BUAT CHEE

*4 to 5 Servings*

This dish is not widely known to foreigners, even those in Thailand. Among the Thai it is seldom served to guests. Siamese Buddhist nuns dress in white, from whence comes the Thai name for the dish, *Kluay Buat Chee;* exactly translated: Nun Bananas.

5 *ripe bananas, peeled and quartered*
1 ½ *cups perfumed "Thick" coconut milk* *
½ *teaspoon salt*
2 *tablespoons granulated sugar*
2 *tablespoons roasted mung beans, crushed*

In a 2-quart coated saucepan, place all the ingredients except the mung beans. Bring to a boil, then simmer for 2 minutes. Pour into a serving dish and sprinkle with mung beans. Serve warm or chilled.

•

* Add 2 to 3 drops jasmine essence *(Yod Nam Malee)*

## BANANAS AND CORN IN COCONUT CREAM · KLUAY LAE KAOPOT BUAT

*4 to 6 Servings*

A variation of the last recipe, *Kluay Lae Kaopot Buat* is a dessert for the adventurous to try. Some people cannot get used to the idea of corn incorporated into the dish, but to those used to Thai combinations of vegetables and fruit, this is delightful.

- 4 *firm bananas, peeled and cut into 1" pieces*
- 1 *medium can whole corn kernels, drained*
- 2 *tablespoons palm sugar*
- 1 *cup "Thick" coconut milk and "Cream"*
- ½ *teaspoon salt*
- 2 to 4 *drops jasmine essence* (Yod Nam Malee)
- 2 *tablespoons sesame seeds, dry-roasted pale brown in a frying pan*

Place the banana chunks and corn in a medium saucepan. In a bowl, dissolve the palm sugar in the coconut milk. Add to the saucepan and stir in the salt. Bring to a boil, reduce heat and simmer for 2 minutes. Remove from heat and stir in the jasmine essence. Pour into a serving bowl, sprinkle with sesame seeds and refrigerate.

•

## CHILLED LICHEES IN CUSTARD · LEENCHEE LOI MEK

*4 Servings*

If fresh lichees are not available, canned may be substituted. Melon balls also make an attractive substitute.

- 5 *eggs, separated*
- 5 *tablespoons granuated sugar*

| | |
|---|---|
| *1 ½* | *cups unsweetened, evaporated milk* |
| *15 to 20* | *fresh lichees, peeled, or equivalent of canned, or melon balls, drained* |

Whisk egg whites until soft peaks are formed. Place in a sieve and steam over a pan of boiling water until firm. Set aside. In a saucepan, beat the egg yolks and stir in sugar and evaporated milk. Stir over low heat until it becomes a smooth custard. Remove from heat. Place lichees in a serving bowl. Pour the custard over them. Spoon the egg-white foam over the custard. Refrigerate and serve.

•

## STEAMED COCONUT CUSTARD · SUNGKAYA

*2 to 4 Servings*

*Sungkaya* is popular both in Thailand and the United States. The Thai normally steam the custard inside young, green immature coconuts. Unfortunately, they are not readily available here. Mature coconut shells can only be used if all the meat is first removed. (When the mature meat is steamed, it has a pronounced, soapy flavor.) Pumpkins make an attractive substitute and are used as an alternative container in Thailand.

| | |
|---|---|
| *1* | *cup "Thick" coconut milk* |
| *3* | *eggs, beaten* |
| *½* | *cup palm sugar* |
| *¼* | *teaspoon salt* |
| *1* | *coconut shell, top cut off and meat scraped out, or 1 pumpkin, about 9" in diameter, treated in similar fashion* |

In a bowl, combine coconut milk, eggs, sugar and salt, until well blended. Pour into prepared coconut or pumpkin shell. In a steamer, heat water until boiling and place coconut or pumpkin inside. Reduce heat to low, or until water is simmering, and simmer until custard is firm (approximately 30 minutes). Remove and chill in refrigerator. To serve: Custard is scooped out in portions. Alternatively, if a pumpkin is used, it may be sliced and served with the custard.

•

## BAKED CUSTARD SQUARES · KANOM MO KAENG

*6 to 8 Servings*

*Kanom Mo Kaeng* is a popular dessert in Thailand. As an alternative to baking the custard to set, it may be steamed and put under a broiler until browned.

- 1 ½ *cups "Thick" coconut milk with its cream*
- 6 *eggs, beaten*
- ¾ *cup palm sugar (brown sugar may be substituted)*
- ½ *teaspoon salt*

Preheat the oven to 350° F. Beat all the ingredients together thoroughly in a saucepan. In a double boiler* over high heat, stir this mixture until it thickens and resembles soft, scrambled eggs (approximately 10 minutes). Pour this into a greased, oven-proof dish and bake for 30 minutes. Now place under a broiler and broil until the top is golden brown, no more than a few minutes. Remove, cool and cut into small squares.

•

*Immersing a Pyrex bowl in a larger pan of boiling water is acceptable.

## TAPIOCA AND COCONUT CREAMS · TAKAW

*Yields 16 to 20 creams*

One of my favorite sweets, this delicate confection of tapioca flour, sugar and coconut milk literally slides down the throat almost without swallowing. Some versions are perfumed with *Bai Toey Hom,* the pounded leaves of Pandanus (screw pine leaf; see Appendixes, Glossary), while others are scented with jasmine or rosewater. *Takaw Haeo,* one version, is ornamented with chopped water chestnuts, while yet another version, *Takaw Kao Pot,* includes chopped corn kernels. None of them is oversweet as they contain a balance of both salt and sugar. In the markets, they can be bought in individual little containers fashioned from banana leaves, but when preparing the recipe here, I suggest you use the tiny, fluted paper cups which are sold for fondants and other sweets.

- ½ *cup tapioca (cassava) flour*
- 6 *tablespoons superfine granulated sugar*
- 1 ⅓ *cups water*
- 4 *drops jasmine essence* (Yod Nam Malee) *or 1 teaspoon rosewater*
- 2 *tablespoons rice flour*
- 1 *cup "Thick" coconut milk*
- ¼ *teaspoon salt*

In a bowl, mix together the tapioca flour, sugar and water until the sugar has dissolved and the mixture is smooth. Strain the mixture through damp muslin into a medium sized saucepan. Heat the mixture over medium flame, until it thickens and becomes clear. Remove from heat and stir in the jasmine essence or rosewater. Pour into little, fluted, paper cups, filling each about half full. Place the cups on a plate and refrigerate while you are preparing the next layer.

In another saucepan, blend the rice flour with the "Thick" coconut milk, stirring until the mixture is smooth. Add the salt, place the saucepan over low heat and stir constantly until the mixture thickens. If a skin forms over the top stir it back in. Remove the cups from the refrigerator and pour the coconut custard layer over the first. Refrigerate for 1 to 2 hours or until both layers are set firm. (Makes 16 to 20 little cups.)

•

## THAI SILK · FOI TONG

*4 to 6 Servings*

The name *Foi Tong* means literally "strings of gold." The little spools of egg threads are each piled into a *wai,* a narrow pyramid, resembling the hands put together for the traditional Thai greeting. Practice makes perfect with the egg-thread technique. I have seen a Thai cook deftly trickle the egg threads into perfect skeins, arranging them in smooth little cushions with the aid of chopsticks. The first time I tried it, mine looked like bird's nests assembled by an absentminded sparrow. Do not be discouraged. The dish will become progressively more artistic with practice. The *Foi Tong* maker, mentioned in chapter 2, "The Thai Kitchen," speeds the process. It is available in most Thai stores and by mail order.

- 8 *eggs, separated*
- 3 *cups granulated sugar*
- 1 *cup water*
- 8 *drops jasmine essence* (Yod Nam Malee)

Break up the egg yolks and strain them through a fine sieve. Sieve about 1 teaspoon of the egg white also and mix into the yolks. Slowly bring sugar, water and jasmine essence to a boil and simmer gently until the syrup thickens slightly. Using a pastry tube with a fine nozzle or a paper cone, pour the beaten yolks in a thread-like trickle into the syrup, and spiral them into separate little pyramids. As soon as each sets, remove carefully to a heated serving dish. Cook a few at a time and keep warm until all the egg yolk mixture has been used up.

•

## COCONUT PANCAKES · KANOM KLUK

*Yields 12 pancakes*

These delicate, colored pancakes can be bought freshly made in the markets in Thailand. This is one of the few dishes in which sweetened, flaked coconut can be used. One of my Thai maids was almost addicted to these pancakes and always returned from the market with a big paper bagful. She preferred these to another, stickier version, in which the pancakes are made, unsweetened, and then consumed with copious quantities of sweetened condensed milk poured over them prior to rolling up. This recipe yields approximately twelve 6″ pancakes.

2 *cups "Thin" coconut milk*
1 ½ *cups rice flour*
3 *eggs, beaten*
½ *cup granulated sugar*
½ *teaspoon salt*
½ *cup sweetened, flaked coconut*
6 *drops each, red and green food coloring*
*Vegetable oil for frying*
¼ *cup sweetened, flaked coconut for garnish*

In a bowl, beat coconut milk, rice flour, eggs, sugar and salt into a thin batter. Fold in the coconut, reserving a small amount. Divide the mixture equally into 3 bowls; tinting one batch pale green, one batch, pink and leaving one uncolored. Wipe a small, 6″ omelet or pancake pan with a paper towel soaked in oil, and heat the pan over moderate heat. Pour in just enough batter to coat the bottom of the pan when rotated. Cook until bottom is flecked with pale brown. Flip the pancake and cook briefly on the other side. With a spatula, roll up the pancake and slide onto a warm platter. Keep warm. Repeat until all the mixtures are used up, stacking the pancakes according to color. Sprinkle with the reserved coconut and serve while still warm.

•

## THREE CHUM CAKES · KANOM SAM KLOE

*6 to 8 Servings*

*Kanom Sam Kloe* is one of the many sweets served at marriage ceremonies in Thailand. The sweet, fritter-like balls are made in groups of three. The tradition goes that their continued attachment during cooking is used to predict the future of the newlywed couple. If the balls stick together well when fried, it augurs a happy and successful marriage. If one ball breaks away, the marriage will be childless. If all three balls separate, the marriage will be unsuccessful; presumably without children. A little covert cheating goes on though. If the batter is thick enough, the balls will surely stick together. Cleverly placed toothpicks have also been used to ensure a happy future! (They are removed prior to serving to preserve the deception.)

*Na Kachik* (Sweetmeats ingredients, following) is a cooked, sweetened mixture of grated coconut and palm sugar, boiled until thick and syrupy. It is used in fillings and as a component of Thai sweets. Sweetened, shredded coconut, store-bought in packets, is an effective and convenient substitute.

*Sweetmeats*

*6 tablespoons glutinous rice flour*
*4 tablespoons mung beans, dry-roasted until brown and finely ground to a powder (flour) in a mortar or electric grinder*
*Cold water*

1 *cup sweetened, shredded coconut* or Na Kachik
½ *cup sesame seeds, dry-roasted until light brown*
4 *tablespoons palm sugar*

*Batter*

¾ *cup rice flour (all-purpose flour may be substituted)*
¼ *cup "Thin" coconut milk*
1 *egg, beaten*
¼ *teaspoon salt*
*Vegetable oil for deep-frying*

*Sweetmeats*

In a saucepan, off heat, mix together the rice flour and mung-bean powder with enough water to form a paste the consistency of heavy cream. Stir in the sweetened coconut, sesame seeds and palm sugar. You may need to add a little more water at this stage, enough to maintain the sticky consistency. Place the pan over low heat, stir until the mixture becomes thick, the sugar melts and the mass is solid enough to be able to roll into balls. Remove the pan from heat and when the mixture cools enough to handle, roll into little balls, about ½" in diameter.

*Batter*

Place the rice flour in a bowl and stir in the "Thin" coconut milk. Beat into this the egg and salt until a smooth, thick batter is formed. Heat the oil in a wok to about 375° F. and, after dipping the balls in the Batter, deep-fry them in groups of three until crisp, golden brown. Drain and serve warm.

•

## THAI FRIED BANANAS · KLUAY TORD

*2 to 4 Servings*

*Kluay Tord* is a frequently eaten snack or dessert. It can be bought from street vendors' stalls, but is commonly served as an afterthought when the Thai housewife is too rushed to prepare anything more elaborate.

- *4 fresh, firm bananas*
- *2 tablespoons butter*
- *4 heaped tablespoons palm sugar or brown sugar*
- *Juice of 2 limes*

Peel bananas; slice lengthwise, then cross-cut slices in half (this quarters the bananas). Heat the butter in a wok until the butter bubbles. Add banana slices. Fry bananas on both sides over medium heat until golden and soft. Sprinkle in palm sugar and stir over heat until the sugar dissolves and thickens to a syrup. Immediately transfer to a shallow bowl, sprinkle with lime juice and serve.

•

## CANDIED SESAME BANANAS · KLUAY TORD LAD NAM CHUAM

*4 Servings*

*Kluay Tord Lad Nam Chuam* is a sensational combination of ice-cold, crackled candy around a hot, moist banana. This recipe gives good results for a variety of fresh fruits including apples, oranges, peaches, etc. The cooking method is slightly complicated and requires the use of a candy thermometer unless you are an experienced candy-maker, as the sugar/water mixture must be very near, not above, 290° F.

| | |
|---|---|
| 4 | *firm, fresh bananas, peeled and sliced on the diagonal (allow approximately 1 banana per person)* |
| | *Juice of 2 limes (omit with citrus fruits)* |
| | *Ice cubes and water* |
| | *Oil for deep-frying* |
| 1 ½ | *cups boiling water* |
| 2 | *cups granulated sugar* |
| ⅛ | *teaspoon cream of tartar* |
| | *Sesame seeds for decoration* |

Place the bananas in a mixing bowl and sprinkle with lime juice. Fill another mixing bowl with equal parts of ice cubes and water. Heat the oil in a wok and when it just begins to vaporize (not the wok, the oil), quickly fry the marinated banana slices, several at a time, until each starts to turn brown. Set aside.

Remove the boiling water from heat and add the sugar and cream of tartar, stirring until sugar dissolves. Return the sugar/water mixture to heat, cover and cook for 2 to 3 minutes (this allows the partially dissolved sugar crystals to wash down from the sides of the pan with the water vapor). Uncover and, stirring occasionally, place in the thermometer; near the center but not touching the bottom. Let the temperature increase to 290° F. (reading the temperature because of heat and juxtaposition may require some gymnastics); this will require at least 3 minutes over high heat. While waiting for the proper temperature, prepare (1) a double boiler, or a saucepan of hot water larger than the syrup saucepan, and (2) a large, greased serving platter. When the syrup reaches temperature, remove the pan and place it in the double boiler or larger pan filled with water. Maintain the water temperature by placing the pans on low heat, so that the syrup does not cool and thicken. In a production-line-like fashion, drop a banana piece into the syrup, remove with a long-handled fondue fork and roll in the sesame seeds. Dunk directly into the ice water and place on the platter. Repeat until all bananas are coated. Serve at once.

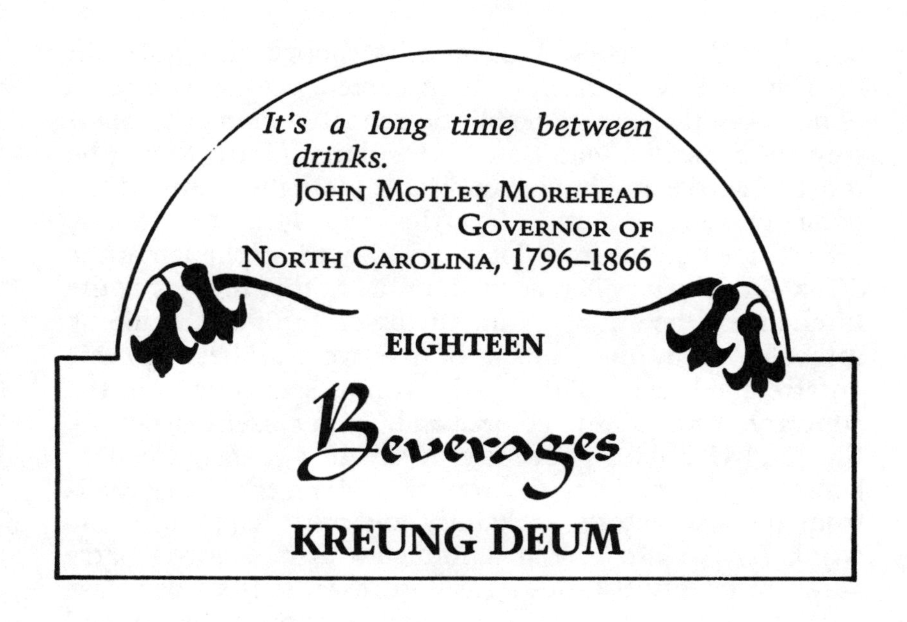

*It's a long time between drinks.*

JOHN MOTLEY MOREHEAD
GOVERNOR OF
NORTH CAROLINA, 1796–1866

EIGHTEEN

# Beverages

## KREUNG DEUM

Every little village store in Thailand has wide wooden shelves lined with an array of brightly colored pop bottles. "Coca-Cola" and "Pepsi" are household words; the Thai name being the same as the English. *"Coca-Cola! Dee Tee Soot!"* echoes over the airwaves, closely followed in frequency by another soft-drink commercial that begins with the magnified sound of a bottle being opened and the gurgle and fizz of the carbonated contents being poured into a glass. Garish billboards depicting smiling Thai faces and gigantic pop bottles loom over the major thoroughfares and speak eloquently of a national preoccupation with soda pop and burgeoning budgets for the local advertising agencies.

Iced tea and iced coffee are widely drunk, being poured into glasses stacked high with ice. When a meal is ordered "upcountry," a glass of water is put on the table. It will generally be a pale straw color, being tinted with a weak infusion of tea leaves to signify that the water has been boiled. A little aside about ice. Although the water in Bangkok is safe to drink (it is inspected weekly by a team of doctors), the foreign population mostly shuns it, preferring fresh bottled water such as Polaris, North Star. The most sensitive and hypochondriacal *farang* will attend the obligatory social round of parties, specifying religiously, "Bottled water, please!" They never focus on the ice in the drink—maybe it is just as well. In the nether regions of the kitchen will be a little man, sitting on the floor, chipping mightily at a huge block of ice wedged between his outstretched legs. The block is not sparkling; on the contrary, it looks mud-colored and, upon closer inspection, the mud is a dense covering of sawdust. Large, wooden-bodied, open trucks have brought it along the dusty roads from the ice factory, sackcloth coverings flapping in the wind. I have often seen a foreigner at a cocktail party absentmindedly fish out a fleck of sawdust from her glass with a finger, too deep in conversation to stop and speculate how it got there. I can only add, as a rider, that I have never been stricken with "Bangkok Belly" or whatever name the universal affliction goes under in Thailand.

Singha Beer and Amarit Lager, the two local brews, are universally popular in Thailand, being sold in a variety of bottle sizes. Large quantities of each accompany curry lunches and add conviviality to all sorts of social gatherings.

Wines are not produced in Thailand, as the tropics are conducive neither to the growing of grapes nor the manufacture and storage of wine. The Chinese rice spirits and local Thai whiskies are in demand all over the country.

I remember a long train journey down to the South of Thailand to visit some Danish friends in Ban Dong. (Their cook, trained to perfection by generations of homesick East Asiatic Company employees, made the best Smørrebrød I have eaten, outside of Denmark.) We spent most of the convivial evening in the restaurant car as the darkening plains sped by the window. There were large parties of Thai men at adjacent tables, and as the bottles stacked up on the tables so the parties became increasingly rowdy. We beat a hasty retreat to our compartment when a somewhat inebriated Thai at the next table pulled a gun from his belt and brandished it in the air, swigging whiskey from his glass as he did so. At breakfast the next morning, we asked the dining-car attendant whether there had been an incident. He shook his head and told us that it was only a farmer returning home from Bangkok. He had won money at the horse races and had become *"keemao"* or drunk, so his friends had hauled him off to bed.

Besides alcoholic drinks and soda pop, the Thai make a wide selection of fruit syrup drinks and some others made with coconut milk. My favorite has to be *Nam Manao,* the Thai version of limeade. We always had a freshly made jug of it in the refrigerator, and its tart, tangy flavor makes it the best thirst quencher there is.

•

## THAI COFFEE · CA FE

Here in America there has arisen a considerable mystique about Thai coffee. Because of the difference of ingredients (use of canned milks), people are persuaded that the beverage differs entirely from American coffee. In a sense it does; fresh milk is rarely used as dairy products were virtually unknown to Thailand until recently. The Thai have always substituted canned evaporated, or canned condensed milk. While in no sense recipes, I am listing the types of coffee drinks ordered in Thailand and their composition. In all cases, the basic brew is freshly ground Thai coffee or your favorite blend or brand. When ordering, use the following terms:

*Ca Fe Dam—Mai Sai Nam Tan:* Black Coffee without Sugar
Merely a good, strong brew of filtered or percolated coffee served hot in a glass.

*Ca Fe Dam Ron (Oh-Yuah):* Black Coffee with Sugar
The term *Oh-Yuah* is the familiar name for *Ca Fe*

*Dam Ron:* Sugar cubes or sugar syrup are added to taste and it is also served in a glass.

*Ca Fe Ron:* Hot Coffee with Milk
As this coffee is without sugar, canned, unsweetened, evaporated milk is added and it is served in a cup.

*Ca Fe Yen:* Iced Coffee with Milk (usually unsweetened)
A tall glass stacked with shaved ice and filled ⅔ full with a strong brew of coffee. A good measure of sweetened, condensed milk is poured in and swirled with a spoon. (If you do not wish sugar, merely say, *"Mai Sai Nam Tan,"* and unsweetened, evaporated milk will be substituted.)

*Ca Fe Dam Yen (Oliang):* Sweetened, Iced Black Coffee
A glass filled with shaved ice and a good, strong brew of black coffee poured in. The coffee is sweetened with a simple sugar syrup.

Some establishments will put a pinch of cinnamon or ground cardamom in the coffee. It makes for a touch of exoticism.

•

## THAI TEA · NAM CHA

Tea is grown in the north of Thailand, in the hills where the climate is cooler. There are two varieties: one where the leaves are black when dried and the other where they are as red as the red earth of eastern Thailand. Both are powdery and would do well in tea bags. If using either variety, I suggest you filter them similar to the method of filtering coffee, to prevent the powder floating on top of your brew.

In Thailand, tea is served in the same containers as coffee: transparent glass, rather than porcelain cups. With the paucity of fresh dairy products, canned milk is traditionally added and, when used in the red tea, a startlingly brick-red liquid results.

Thai tea is made stronger than we might prefer, hence the dilution with milk.

Chinese teas of all varieties are also available in Thailand and are, obviously, popular among the Chinese-Thai. They are served and consumed in the traditional Chinese manner.

•

## THAI LIMEADE · NAM MANAO

*Yields 12 to 16 glasses*

This cool, refreshing lime drink is popular with Thai and *farang* alike. The Thai tend to prefer it made with salt instead of sugar, but I find that the inclusion of both makes for a perfect effect. Strong potions of *Nam Manao* are to be found both at the exclusive Royal Bangkok Sports Club and at the British Club. Each of these venerable institutions has its coterie of devoted *Nam Manao* followers swearing that their club boasts the finest limeade. Having drunk both clubs' infusions, I believe them to be equally good. The following recipe should produce a drink of similar "limeheartedness" and yields about 4 cups concentrate.

- 6 *fresh limes*
- ½ *cup granulated sugar*
- 2 ½ *cups boiling water*
- ½ *teaspoon salt*
- 12 *ice cubes*

Roll the limes on a cutting board using hard pressure with the palm of your hand. This loosens the flesh and releases the juice more readily. Cut the limes in half and squeeze the juice, minus seeds and pith, into a jug. (They should yield approximately 1 cup juice.) Reserve the squeezed lime rinds, placing them into another jug, and cover them with the sugar. Pour the boiling water over the sugared lime rinds and allow it to steep for 15 minutes. This infusion draws the aromatic oil from the skin. Do not over-steep or the brew will become bitter. Add the salt and stir thoroughly. Strain the warm liquid into the jug containing the lime juice. Add the ice cubes and refrigerate. When serving, fill each glass with at least 4 additional ice cubes and pour in the limeade.

•

## THAI BEERS · BEER TRA SINGH, AMARIT

Although beer is historically a fairly universal drink, it was not common in Thailand until just less than eighty years ago.

In the center of Bangkok there is a large area taken up by the Boon Rawd Brewing Company. The Thai family who pioneered the brewing of Singha beer also imported German Brew Meisters to provide technical assistance. Latecomers in a competitive field, the Bhirompakdi family was determined to manufacture a beer that would hold its own in international ratings. They succeeded. Singha beer is a strong, rich brew, dark gold in color. It compares favorably with San Miguel of the Philippines, Tiger from Malaysia and the Japanese Kirin and Asahi. It is only recently available in the United States as an "ale," as the alcohol percentage (4.8 percent) is considered too high for categorization as "beer." It is imported in 11-ounce bottles.

Amarit is the name of Thailand's other indigenous brew. It is a delightful, pale amber lager, with a 3.8 percent alcohol content and the qualities of the best German beers. Again, German Brew Meisters supervised its inception in Thailand. A relative newcomer to the world beer scene, it has won several international awards. It was the first Thai beer available in America.

Both Singha and Amarit are widely distributed and drunk in Thailand and can be found in the battered refrigerators of the most remote village store.

•

## WHISKY AND KINDRED SPIRITS · WISAKEE, LAO

There is a curious fact of life and commerce in the Orient, unknown to outsiders save the grateful Scotch distillers. From Tokyo to Singapore, Bangkok to Borneo, Scotch whisky is the universal coinage of goodwill; highly regarded, especially in those countries that have large import taxes. From a welcoming gift for one's host, to the clincher in an elaborate deal involving thousands of tons of rice, teak or heavy machinery, a bottle or case of genuine Scotch is the token of esteem and obligatory "cumshaw." More particularly, Johnnie Walker Black Label takes the palm as the preferred brand.

In 1962, I started to design the first line of Thai-inspired furniture, furnishing fabrics and accessories to be produced in Thailand both for export and for local sale. As part of my research, it was necessary for me to make a trip to the northern capital of Chiengmai, the handcraft center of Thailand.

I was traveling by myself and knew virtually no one. Through Bangkok friends, I was given an introduction to the Thai manager of Berli-Jucker, a Swiss-Thai trading company. Any qualms I may have had about being alone in a strange town were dispelled the moment I arrived. Apart from a two-hour delay at Chiengmai airport—their Majesties, the King and Queen, were departing for Bangkok and all planes were held on the aprons—my visit was effortlessly smooth. With typical Thai hospitality, my host went to endless lengths to make sure I enjoyed myself and saw everything I needed. Nothing was too much trouble—no place too far. He insisted that the last night of my stay be crowned with a good dinner, and picked me up at my hotel at seven to take me to a large Chinese-Thai restaurant overlooking the river and the bridge at the edge of the walled city.

At our table were waiting several of his Chinese-Thai friends, all male; their faces wreathed in smiles. After a round of handshaking and exchanging *wai*, we all sat down. There was a rapid-fire exchange between my host and one of the gentlemen, who nodded and reached under his seat, and produced a bottle of Johnnie Walker with a flourish. (I subsequently discovered he had a large cardboard box of Scotch between the legs of his chair.) Glasses were poured and my health was toasted. I was then indoctrinated in the mysteries of *Yam Sing*, the Chinese equivalent of "Bottoms up."

The meal was lengthy, but great. A whole fish in sauce and red chillies was dispatched, followed by an enormous platter of fried chicken. A heaped dish of fried rice heralded the arrival of bowls of curries. Dishes of stir-fried noodles and pork were replaced by crisp-fried crab cakes. All this was punctuated by *Yam Sing* after *Yam Sing*, the empty bottle of Scotch being quickly replaced by a fresh one from the same box, and our waiter speedily answering calls for more ice. The Thai jokes were translated for me, the laughter level rose and, by the time the meal came to an end, I was viewing the world through rose-colored glasses, albeit out-of-focus.

We capped the evening in one of the two nightclubs of which Chiengmai then boasted, naturally bringing our whisky-carrying member with us. I remember little about the club except that it was dark as a tomb, predominantly red in color, pulsating with loud Thai music, and that protocol demanded that I, as the only female member in the party, dance with all of my dinner companions in turn. Having cemented Anglo-Thai friendship with the last toasts of the evening, we drove an erratic course back to the hotel through the deserted streets, where my host promised to collect me at eight sharp the next morning.

Punctually at eight, he arrived to escort me to the airport. He looked me over with a sympathetic eye, and grinned. "Suckotch wisakee is good for you—no hangover, you just tired. Lucky we don't drink *Mekong,* then you are too sick to go to Bangkok!"

The Mekong whisky to which he referred is the locally distilled Thai whisky. It relates more closely to bourbon than to Scotch and is relatively inexpensive as it does not bear the high tax burden of all imported spirits. It does, however, tend to produce hangovers. For those on a tight budget, it is possible to get accustomed to it and even regard it with affection. There are several other local spirits rejoicing in such names as "White Cock Whisky," etc. These make moonshine look good and are best left to the imagination and to the more hardy heads and stomachs of the Thai. They are really ferocious and can produce Armageddon the morning after.

# Appendixes

## PRONUNCIATION AND SPELLING GUIDE

This is not intended as a complete, definitive treatise on Thai pronunciation and phonetic spelling, but merely a guide to suggest the correct pronunciation and an explanation of the simple conventions I have chosen for spelling/pronunciation.

In fact, there is no standard convention for the transliteration of Thai to English. It is a matter of some debate among Southeast Asian scholars; if you ask five English-speaking Thai how to spell one of their words in English, they will offer five different versions and, probably, discuss it for hours. I theorize this lack of convention has to do with the fact that Thailand, contrary to some of its neighbors, has never been colonized by a Western power, unlike, for instance, Vietnam and Indonesia. Transliteration difficulties are further complicated by the obscure roots of contemporary Thai: predominantly Sanskrit, Pali and Chinese, with lesser etymological influences from its immediate neighbors, Ancient Cambodian, Laotian and Burmese. There are some Thai characters that have no approximate English sound; you must hear and imitate these to perfect them. Therefore, it is with some reluctance I offer my attempts at Romanization.

Spoken Thai is a tonal language in that the inflection enunciated with each word imparts a different meaning. There are five to seven tones, depending on your source, including rising, falling, middle, emphatic, staccato, etc. My language instructor in Bangkok gave me a couplet to demonstrate tonality. The word *mai* repeated five times in the proper tonal order can mean "the green wood does not burn."

Thai freely compound words, much as the Germans, to form new words and meanings. For instance the word *nam* means "water" and *kaeng*, "hard." Together, *namkaeng* is "ice."

The English- and Latinate-speaking people compose their own tones as they speak to alter the meaning of a phrase or sentence. We also have formal inflection (accent conventions) and capitalization for precise denotation. In Western writing there is also punctuation to indicate inflection. In contrast, the Thai have prescribed rules of tonal pronunciation for each word and their language is void of accents (´) and capitals. Their writing has no punctuation and is composed entirely of one-syl´ la • ble words, frequently combined.

Since most Thai words begin with consonants, I have chosen to separate the spelling and pronunciation of this initial letter into two categories, aspirated and unaspirated as in *kaeng*, "hard," and *gaeng*, "liquid." The former is an example of the aspirated, the latter the unaspirated. Whenever the consonants, *K, T, P* and *CH* are used followed by a vowel they are presumed aspirated, as in KILL, TEAR, POST and CHOOSE. The unaspirated, alliterative complements are *G, D, B* and *J*: GILL, DEAR, BOAST, JEWS.

| ASPIRATED | UNASPIRATED |
|---|---|
| K - KILL | G - GILL |
| T - TEAR | D - DEAR |

| ASPIRATED | | | UNASPIRATED | | |
|---|---|---|---|---|---|
| P | - | POST | B | - | BOAST |
| CH | - | CHOOSE | J | - | JEWS |

*NG* beginnings are pronounced as the ending in YOU*NG*. The Thai, as other Orientals, often interchange *L*'s and *R*'s as in *farang*, frequently *falang*, and endings with *T*'s and *D*'s, both in English spelling and pronunciation. Final consonants are almost swallowed, unaspirated, when spoken, hence the confusion with the ending *S*, *T* and *D*.

All my vowels are pronounced in the fashion listed below. Diphthongs conform to the standard *Webster*.

*A* as in BAR or the *U* sound in HUNG

*E* as in MET

*I* mostly as in HIT, occasionally as the *E* in FEED

*O* as in FOR and the shorter sound of FOB

*U* as in BRUTE and as the *OO* in FOOT

When you are in a restaurant or food store and attempting to speak Thai, say the words clearly, without hesitation, three or four times with an expectant smile. The friendly Thai will come to your aid; a worried frown of incomprehension will slowly change to a broad grin as the appropriate meaning is recognized: "Ah! You mean '_____.' You clever—speak our language!"

The Vocabulary that follows is a lexicon of commonly used words related to food, cooking and eating. It is indexed with the Thai equivalent first followed by its English translation. In parentheses, after the Thai, I have offered alternate spellings for numerous listings. The parenthetical additions show other common spellings and may help refine your own pronunciation.

The Glossary, following the Vocabulary, is tabulated by the common English name. Following is the scientific (Latin) species or variety to authenticate the citation and help those who may want to locate and grow their own ingredients; finally, their Thai/English equivalent with exact Thai characters for absolute identification.

## VOCABULARY: COMMON THAI WORDS

| THAI | ENGLISH |
|---|---|
| *AHARN* (ahaan) | Food, nourishment, provisions |
| *BAHT* (tical) | Unit of currency, about 5¢ |
| *BA MEE* (ba mi) | Egg noodles |
| *BAI GRAPAO* (bai krapow) | Sweet (holy) basil leaf |
| *BAI HORAPA* (bai horapha) | Sweet basil leaf |
| *BAI KAREE* (bai kari) | Curry leaf |
| *BAI MAKRUT* (bai makrood) | Kaffir lime leaf |
| *BAI MANGLUK* (bai manglook) | Sweet basil leaf |
| *BAI TOEY HOM* | Screw pine leaf |
| *BING* (ping) | To bake, toast, roast |
| *BRIO* (prio) | Sour |
| *CA FE* (cafay) | Coffee |
| *CEUN CHAI* (kern chai) | Celery |
| *CHEEN* (chin) | Chinese |

| THAI | ENGLISH |
|---|---|
| *CHOMPOO* (chumpoo) | Rose apple |
| *CHUD* (churt) | Clear soup, tasteless or insipid liquid |
| *DAM RAP* | Recipe |
| *DANG NOI* (tang noi) | Tapioca |
| *DAO* (tao) | Stove |
| *DEE LA* (ti la) | Sesame seed |
| *DEUM* (derm) | To drink |
| *DIP* | Raw, half-cooked |
| *DOK GULAB* (tok gulaab) | Rose |
| *DOK MAI* (tok mai) | Flower |
| *DOK MALEE* (tok mali) | Jasmine |
| *DOM* (tom) | To boil, cook in water |
| *DONG* (daung) | To pickle |
| *DOOANG* (duang) | To measure quantity, liquids or solids |
| *DOON* (toon, tun) | To steam |
| *DUM* (tum) | To pound, pulverize |
| *DURIAN* (turian) | Durian fruit |
| *FARANG* (falaang) | Foreigner, foreign, non-Thai |
| *GAENG* (kaeng, kaang, keng) | Liquid, as in curry or soup |
| *GAI* (kai) | Chicken |
| *GAI LAE PET* (kai lae pet) | Poultry |
| *GALUMBLEE* (kalampli) | Cabbage |
| *GRA DAT* (kra daat) | Taro root |
| *GRAM POO* | Cloves |
| *GUNG* (kung) | Prefix for shrimp, prawns, lobster |
| *GUNG FOI* | Prawns |
| *GUNG NARNG* | Shrimp |
| *GUNG TA LAY* | Lobster |
| *GWAYTIO* (quitio, gwitio) | Large wet, rice noodle; noodle soup |
| *HAENG* (haang, heng) | Dry (as opposed to wet) |

| THAI | ENGLISH |
|---|---|
| *HED HOM* (het hom) | Dried Chinese mushrooms |
| *HED HUNU* (het hoonoo) | Wood fungus |
| *HUA HOM* (wa hom) | Onion |
| *KA* (kha) | Galangal; Laos (Indonesian) |
| *KAENG* (kaang, keng) | Hard, solid, compact, dense |
| *KAI* (khai) | Egg |
| *KAMIN* (khameen) | Turmeric |
| *KAMMAM* (khamarn) | Elected headman |
| *KANOM* (khanom) | Cake, cookie |
| *KANOM PAN* (khanom pun) | Bread |
| *KANOON* (khanun) | Jackfruit |
| *KAO* (khow, kow) | Rice (generic), cereals or grain |
| *KAO NIEO* (khow nieo) | Glutinous or sticky rice |
| *KAPEE* (kapi) | Shrimp paste |
| *KAREE* (kari, kali) | Curry |
| *KIN* (gin) | To eat |
| *KING* (khing) | Ginger |
| *KLEM* (klam) | A group, mixed together |
| *KLONG* | Canal |
| *KLUAY* (gluay) | Banana |
| *KONG* (kaung) | Food eaten between meals, snack |
| *KRACHAI* | Lesser ginger |
| *KRATIEM* (katiem) | Garlic |
| *KRUNG THEP* (krung tep) | Bangkok (literal translation, City of Angels) |
| *LAMUT* (lamoot) | Sapodilla fruit |
| *LAM YAI* (lum yai) | Longan fruit |
| *LEENCHEE* (linchee) | Lichee fruit |
| *LON* (long) | To boil until tender or a jelly; a cooked sauce |
| *LUK GRAWAN* (look gravan) | Cardamom |

| THAI | ENGLISH |
|---|---|
| *MAFUENG* | Star apple, carambola |
| *MAKEUA PUONG* (makhua pong) | Pea eggplant |
| *MAKEUA TAET* (makhua tet) | Tomato |
| *MAK KAM* (makham) | Tamarind |
| *MAKRUT* (makrood) | Kaffir lime |
| *MALAKOR* (malakul, malakun) | Papaya |
| *MAMUANG* (mam muang) | Mango |
| *MAN FARANG* (mun falaang) | Potato |
| *MANAO* (menao, menow) | Lime |
| *MAPRAO* (maprow) | Coconut |
| *MEE* (mi) | Noodles |
| *MELLET PAK CHEE* (mellet pak chi) | Coriander seeds |
| *MELLET YIRA* (mellet jira) | Cumin, fennel, caraway seeds (no differentiation) |
| *MOO* (mu) | Pork |
| *MUNGKUT* (mongkut) | Mangosteen fruit |
| *NAM* (num) | Water |
| *NAM CHA* (num cha) | Tea |
| *NAM CHUAM* (num chuam) | Syrup |
| *NAM KAENG* (num keng) | Ice |
| *NAM KATEE* (num kathi) | Coconut milk |
| *NAM PLA* (num pla) | Fish sauce |
| *NAM PRIK* (num prick) | Pepper water |
| *NAM SOM* (num som) | Vinegar, orange juice; literally, sour water |
| *NAM SOM MAK KAM* (num som makham) | Tamarind water, tamarind juice |
| *NAM TAN* (num taan) | Sugar |
| *NAM TAN PEEP* (num taan pip) | Palm sugar |
| *NEM* | Spicy sausage |
| *NEUA* (nua, nuer) | Meat, flesh as in beef |

| THAI | ENGLISH |
|---|---|
| *NGOR* (ngaw) | Rambutan fruit |
| *NOI NAR* | Custard apple, sweet sop |
| *NOK* | Bird |
| *NOK KRA TA* (nok kra tah) | Quail |
| *NOM* | Milk |
| *OB CHEUY* (ob choy) | Cinnamon |
| *PAD* (phat) | Fried |
| *PAK* | Greens, green leafed vegetables |
| *PAK CHEE* (pak chi) | Coriander |
| *PAK CHEE FARANG* (pak chi falaang) | Parsley |
| *PAK KARD HOM* (pakard hom) | Lettuce |
| *PASIN* (paseen) | Sarong-like, traditional long skirt |
| *PED* (phet) | Pungent, peppery, spicy |
| *PEW MAKRUT* (pew makrood) | Kaffir lime powder |
| *PLA* (bla) | Fish |
| *POO* (pu) | Crab |
| *POY KAK BUA* | Star anise |
| *PRIK* | Chilli peppers (generic) |
| *PRIK THAI* | Black pepper |
| *PUAK* | Taro plant |
| *QUART* (kooat) | Bottle |
| *RAAN* (laan) | Shop |
| *RAAN AHARN* (laan ahaan) | Restaurant |
| *RAM WONG* (lam wong) | Traditional Thai circle dance |
| *RON* (rawn, lon) | Hot (thermal) |
| *SAKAY* (sakae) | Breadfruit |
| *SALEEM* (salim) | Liquid dessert with thin, tapioca noodles |
| *SAMLOR* (samlaw) | Three-wheeled, motorized pedicab |

| THAI | ENGLISH |
| --- | --- |
| *SANOOK* (snuk) | Amusing, interesting, fun, enjoyable |
| *SAUS PRIK* | Bottled chilli sauce |
| *SAWADEE* (sawaat di) | Thai greeting, "Hullo, good day." |
| *SEE* (si) | To grind or grate |
| *SEE CHOMPOO* (si chumpoo) | Pink |
| *SEE DAENG* (si dang) | Red |
| *SEE DUM* (si dam) | Black |
| *SEE KAO* (si khao) | White |
| *SEE KEO* (si kieo, si khieu) | Green |
| *SEE LEUNG* (si lerng) | Yellow |
| *SEE NAM TAN* (si nam taan) | Brown |
| *SEN MEE* (sen mi) | Rice vermicelli, rice stick noodle |
| *SOD SAI* (sawd sai) | Stuffed |
| *SOM* | Orange |
| *SOM OR* (som o) | Pomelo, shaddock, Thai grapefruit |
| *SUAN* (suwan) | Garden |
| *SUNGKAYA* (sankhaya) | Baked custard |
| *SUPPAROT* (sapparote) | Pineapple |
| *TAENG KWA* (tengkwa) | Cucumber |
| *TAKAW* (takor) | Sweets made from coconut milk and rice flour |
| *TAKRAI* | Lemon grass |
| *TALAT* (thalaat) | Market |
| *TAMADA* (tamadaa) | Plain, ordinary |
| *TAN* (taan) | Palmyra palm (source) |
| *TONG* (thong) | Gold |
| *TON HOM* | Green onions |
| *TOOA* (thua) | Peas, beans or peanuts |
| *TOO YEN* (tu yen) | Refrigerator |
| *TORD* (thort, taut) | To fry, fried |
| *UON* (oowan) | Fat, plump |

| THAI | ENGLISH |
| --- | --- |
| *WAI* (why) | Thai greeting with palms of hands placed together before the face; a mark of deference |
| *WOON SEN* (wun sen) | Bean thread or cellophane noodles |
| *YAI* | Large, big |
| *YAM* (yum) | Salad |
| *YARNG* (yaang) | Roasted |
| *YEN* | Cold |

# GLOSSARY

กล้วย

Banana *(Musa x paradisiaca,* et al.) KLUAY

There are 28 varieties in Thailand of which *Musa x paradisiaca,* the common banana, is the best known. The cooking plantain, *Musa Fehi,* a small, plump orange-/pink-skinned variety is used in vegetable dishes and fried and salted for the popular banana chips. The larger, green plantain is also used for chips. The sweet, dwarf banana, *Musa acuminata,* is found in most markets in Thailand. *Musa x paradisiaca* 'Champa', known as lady's fingers, is also common, but appears to have originated in Cambodia and Western Vietnam. Some banana trees are considered holy and are found in the grounds of Buddhist monasteries. Banana leaves are widely utilized in Thai cooking; fashioned into receptacles for steamed dishes, sweets and snacks and as wrapping for raw foods.

สาเก

Breadfruit *(Artocarpus altilis [communis])* SAKAY

A large yellow- (green before ripening) skinned fruit, the size of a baby's head. The skin is thin and uneven. The flesh is white and of the consistency of new bread—it can be cooked into a paste resembling the Hawaiian poi. The seeds are also eaten. It is closely related to jackfruit.

ลูกกระวาน

Cardamom *(Amomum cardamomum)* LUK GRAWAN

Both the whole and ground seeds are used in some dishes of Indian origin. Cardamom has been known in Thailand for some time: the plant has been found growing in the ruins of ancient Khmer trading posts circa A.D. 1000. The leaves, *bai grawan,* are often added to the curry *gaeng mussaman* or the beef dish *panaeng neua.*

คึ่นไฉ่

Celery *(Apium graveolens)* CEUN CHAI

The Thai variety looks like a cross between parsley and celery. Compared to ours, their variety is greener, thinner stemmed and more leafy with a stronger celery flavor. This same family of Thai *Umbelliferae* is widely known in Europe, and I do not understand why the delicate variety has not been transplanted in the United States. It is mainly used in Thai soups and stir-fried dishes. The young leaves from the center of our variety can be successfully substituted.

พริก

Chilli Peppers *(Capsicum)* PRIK

There are numerous varieties growing in Thailand, hence their popularity and indispensability in Thai cuisine. It is believed they were brought to Thailand by the Portuguese in the sixteenth century. The large red chilli, *prik chee fa (C. annuum* 'Longum'), is used for making chilli powder, cayenne, paprika and medicinal capsicum. It can be compared to a mature Mexican chile pablano. The tiny chillies are called *prik e noo* (*C. annuum conoides,* 'Red Chile' variety, syn. *frutescens)* and are used in curries as well as pickles and sauces. They are fiery, enormously hot and should be approached with particular caution. Serrano chillies can be substituted and, in fact, used in most dishes calling for chillies. Serranos are now grown in Thailand and called *prik e noo kaset. Prik yuak (C. annuum* 'Grossum') are mid-size, light green or red chillies. They are our common "Green bell pepper" or "Sweet red pepper" and are a source of pimento. In Thailand they are often stuffed and steamed or fried. The Thai yellow chillies, sometimes known as *prik leung,* are a variety of *(C. annuum* 'Longum'). In Thailand, chilli leaves are sometimes fried for vegetables. Both red and green chillies of all sizes are cut into flower shapes for decoration. For chilli handling, see Chapter 3, Fundamentals.

ซอสพริก หรือ น้ำจิ้มพริก

Chilli Sauce SAUS PRIK

Usually a smooth mixture of the following ingredients: chillies, water, vinegar, salt, sugar. There are many bottled Thai varieties. One of the best known and widely sold brands in Thailand and overseas is *Siracha* sauce. This was originally a chilli sauce made and sold locally in the little seaside town of Siracha. It was sold on the beachfront seafood stands to accompany the fish. Because of its regional popularity it was subsequently bottled and sold commercially throughout Thailand. *Siracha* is available here in Thai stores and some supermarkets. It comes in both red and yellow colorings and mild, medium and hot flavorings. Some other Thai chilli sauces are sweeter and have whole seeds and chilli fragments. To make your own, and it is usually superior, see Chapter 14, Sauces.

อบเชย

Cinnamon *(Cinnamomum zeylanicum)* OB CHEUY

The dried bark of the cinnamon tree. It is rare in Thai cooking and only used in those dishes with an Indian influence.

ก้านพู

Cloves *(Syzygium aromaticum)* GRAM PLOO

Rarely found in Thai cuisine, cloves are a component of curries with Indian origins, e.g., *gaeng mussaman.*

มะพร้าว

Coconut *(Cocos nucifera)* MAPRAO

An integral part of Thai culture and cuisine. The flesh of mature coconuts is grated for coconut milk. When fresh coconut is not available, dried (desiccated), grated coconut is reconstituted with water or milk. The flesh is then squeezed to extract the liquid *(nam katee).* The immature, green coconut is also used for many desserts and sweets including a baked custard dish called *sungkaya*—a smooth coconut custard baked in its shell. To make coconut milk, see Chapter 3, Fundamentals.

ผักชี

Coriander, Cilantro, Chinese Parsley *(Coriandrum sativum)* PAK CHEE

It has been used for thousands of years in Asia, the Middle East (previously mentioned in the twenty-first dynasty in Egypt), Europe and Central and South America; later and more explicit Biblical references. Essentially three parts of the coriander plant are used in Thai cooking: leaves, roots, seeds. Each has a unique flavor, character and use. The leaves are commonly used for decoration and in sauces and curries. The Thai seem to be the only people who use the roots in their cuisine. They are an equal part of an interesting marinade of garlic and black pepper, which coats fried chicken for *gai tord.* This coriander-root/garlic/black-pepper mixture is also used for fried meat balls *(tord man neua)* and in a pork/shrimp paste spread on bread and deep-fried *(kanom pan nar moo).* The seeds, *mellet pak chee,* bear no resemblance in flavor to the parent plant; usually only found in curry pastes, *krung gaeng.* Some people find the flavor of fresh coriander strange, but it is essential to Thai cuisine. If it is unavailable, parsley, mint or basil leaves may be substituted as garnish. For preparation, see Chapter 3, Fundamentals.

เมล็ดยี่หร่า

Cumin *(Cuminum cyminum)* MELLET YIRA

A native of Western Asia, cumin is cultivated in the Middle East, India and China. Only the seeds are used, dried and ground. In Thai curry pastes, *krung gaeng,* its ratio to ground coriander seeds is 1 to 2. In Thai, cumin, caraway and fennel have the interchangeable name *yira* and the seeds thereof are called *mellet.*

ใบกระหรี่

Curry Leaves *(Murraya koenigii)* BAI KAREE

Used more frequently in India, Malaysia and Indonesia than in Thailand, these leaves, resembling bay laurel *(Laurus nobilis),* are added to curries which have an Indian influence. Cassia Leaves *(Cinnamomum cassia),* called *bai kravan,* are also used for the same purpose but are smaller and thinner. Both varieties are sold by the Muslim vegetable sellers in the larger markets in Thailand. They are available (dried) here in Indian and Southeast Asian food-specialty shops.

น้อยหน่า

Custard Apple *(Annona squamosa)* NOI NAR

Also known as the sugar apple or sweet sop. The fruit is the size of a large apple having a peculiar, soft, scale-like, segmented rind—light green in color. When ripe, the segments break away separately, exposing the white, granular, sweet, custard-like pulp. It is possible the Thai name is an approximation of the Latin *annona.* The custard apple is native to other countries in Asia, but is not grown commercially in the United States at this time.

เห็ดหอม

Dried Chinese Mushrooms *(Lentinus edodes)* HED HOM

These fungi have a pronounced, different flavor from our varieties. They are always soaked in warm water before using. The stems are seldom eaten, being very tough. The use of *hed hom* shows the Chinese origins of Thai culture and cuisine. Their use is most common in Chinese-style clear soups and some stir-fry dishes. In spite of the resemblance, our mushrooms cannot be substituted. Dried Chinese mushrooms may be purchased from Oriental food stores.

ทุเรียน

Durian *(Durio zibethinus)* DURIAN

Native also to Indonesia and the Philippines, it is widely cultivated and much prized in Thailand. The fruit is the size of a man's head, varying in shape from round to ovoid, and greenish-yellow when ripe. The rind is thick and covered with sharp-pointed prickles about ½″ long and, when mature, it possesses a very strong, offensive odor

The taste of the creamy-white flesh surrounding the seed is considered sublime by durian *aficionados.* The seeds are sometimes roasted and eaten like chestnuts.

น้ำปลา

Fish Sauce NAM PLA

A thin, translucent brown sauce made from fish or shrimp. The fish is salted and fermented in jars, after which the liquid is extracted and bottled. Because of its saltiness and widespread use, little salt is called for in Thai recipes. *Nam pla* is rich in B vitamins and protein. It is to Thai cooking what soy sauce is to the Chinese and Japanese. *Nam pla* is the base of most Thai sauces, except bottled chilli sauces, and is used in most Thai dishes.

ข่า

Galangal, Laos (Indonesian) *(Alpinia galanga)* KA

Also known as Siamese Ginger because it is a member of the ginger family. This strange-looking rhizome is a light yellow root with pink sprouts and knobs. In Indonesia it is called Laos and this is thought by the Thai to be the correct foreign name. Because there is no common, current English name, Laos is frequently used in terminology and labeling. Galangal was generally used in England and Europe in the Middle Ages. It was known as Galingale. Galingale was regarded as an aphrodisiac, but its use mysteriously died out, thus the confusion about an English equivalent. It is now grown and used in Southeast Asia and Iran. The Thai consider *ka* a digestive stimulant apart from its common use as a spice. They mix the grated root with lime juice as a remedy for stomachaches. The dried root is sold whole or powdered in Oriental specialty shops in the United States. Some recipes call for the use of the whole root, sliced. A few recipes reconstitute the whole root with hot water and slice or pound it. If using powdered for whole; ¼″ slice equals 1 teaspoon ground.

กระเทียม

Garlic *(Allium sativum)* KRATIEM

Used in large quantities in most savory dishes, the Thai garlic pod is comprised of smaller cloves than the Western varieties. The Thai cloves are covered with a delicate, thin, pinkish skin and are not peeled before use. Garlic pods, pickled in vinegar, are a delicacy in Thailand. Garlic is rich in vitamins B, C and D. As a natural carminative, it has few equals. It is also rich in trace elements: zinc, copper, aluminum, manganese, sulphur, iron. It contains crotonic aldehyde, a powerful antiseptic. It is believed to have cholesterol-reducing properties, as a recent medical survey has confirmed.

ขิง

Ginger *(Zingiber officinale)* KING

In Thailand there are many varieties of ornamental and edible gingers, the latter's roots are used both medicinally and to flavor food. Common ginger, *king,* is plentiful during the rainy season. The freshly picked roots of "new ginger" are plump, pale yellow and pink. In this state the Thai pickle and crystalize them. They are also used to flavor drinks. The art of carving "pink ginger" is highly regarded, although its artisans are almost extinct. The roots are skillfully carved into fishes, flowers and other shapes, then pickled in pink-tinted vinegar and canned in jars. Young, fresh roots are also pounded into marinades for meat. During the remainder of the year, after the rainy season, the "old ginger" is used and keeps well. This is the ginger which we find in the produce sections of supermarkets in the United States, called "green ginger." Powdered ginger should not be substituted unless fresh is absolutely not available.

กระชาย

Ginger, Lesser *(Kaempferia pandurata)* KRACHAI

Largely unknown to the Occidental world, *krachai* is another rhizome related to ginger. It is milder and different in flavor to *ka* (q.v.). The tubers, brown on the outside and yellow inside, look like a bunch of fingers growing downward from the main body. They are the only part of the plant used. Lesser Ginger grows in South China, in addition to the Indochina Subcontinent. The Chinese do not cook with it, reserving it only for medicine. The whole, fresh tuber is eaten as a vegetable in Thailand and added to certain curried dishes. The recipes in this book call for the use of dried, powdered *krachai* or its dried, slivered roots. The former is sold in Thai stores here under the title "Powdered Rhizome," the latter as merely "Rhizome."

ต้นหอม

Green Onions *(Allium fistulosom)* TON HOM

Also called scallions or spring onions, these are the same long, green mild-flavored onions that are available in our markets. Used in stir-fried dishes, salads and as garnish. The Thai often cut green onions into tassels for decoration. See Chapter 3, Fundamentals.

ขนุน

Jackfruit *(Artocarpus heterophyllus)* KANOON

Related to the breadfruit (q.v.) and resembling the durian (q.v.), this fruit is enormous in size. One fruit can weigh up to 100 pounds. The rind is green and covered with prickles. The flesh is yellow and juicy with many seeds and an inimitable aromatic flavor. Chunks of fruit are sold by street vendors in Thailand as snacks. It is available in cans from Thai stores in the United States.

Ka *See* Galangal

มะกรูด

Kaffir Lime *(Citrus hystrix)* MAKRUT

A little known member of the citrus family, Kaffir Lime has a bumpy, dark green rind with a concentration of aromatic oils, the aroma of lemon geranium or lemon verbena. Historically the Malay and Singalese used the juice in ointments and the peel in tonic medications. The Malay superstition was that it drove away evil spirits. The Thai formerly incorporated the juice in a hair shampoo. Today in Thai cuisine, only the rind and leaves are used: the grated zest in curry pastes and dishes where a strong lemon aroma is needed; the leaves, *bai makrut,* are incorporated in gravies. The Kaffir lime is not commercially available in the United States although it has been grown experimentally in California for fifty years. Fresh citrus leaves can be substituted for *bai makrut,* as the grated zest of our fresh limes can replace the grated Kaffir lime zest. The dried, powdered or whole K. lime rind, called *pew makrut,* is available in Thai stores. One-quarter to one-half teaspoon should be added to dishes during cooking when a pronounced lemon flavor is desired and you have used local lime rind (Lime: *Citrus aurantifolia,* q.v.) or leaves.

Laos *See* Galangal

ตะไคร้

Lemon Grass *(Cymbopogon citratus)* TAKRAI

One of the most common herbs in Thai food—one of the half-dozen that give Thai cuisine its unique character. The plant has long, gray-green, spear-like leaves and has the appearance of Freesia before the flower stems have grown. The leaves and stem are fibrous and the lower part of the stem has a white, slightly bulbous, juicy base. Lemon

Grass, a sedge, and related to citronella, is also grown commercially in India, Australia, Africa, South America and the United States (in Florida). It is available freshly cut, dried in small lengths or powdered from Oriental markets. It gives a lemony flavor to curry pastes, such as *krung gaeng ped,* salads and soups. For preparation, use and information about how to grow your own, see Chapter 3, Fundamentals.

ลิ้นจี่

Lichee *(Litchi chinensis)* LEENCHEE

Also referred to as the litchi nut, this fruit originated in Southern China. They have a red, bumpy skin and grow in clusters. The white, juicy flesh grows around a central brown, shiny nut. Lichees are available in cans and are frequently used in Chinese and Thai desserts.

มะนาว

Lime *(Citrus aurantifolia)* MANAO

The Thai limes are smaller than ours and have very dark green skins. They are sweet, aromatic and juicy and are used mainly for garnish. The juice is used in cooking and for making lime cordials and limeade. The Thai prefer their lime drinks with salt rather than sugar. The use of *C. aurantifolia* in Thai cuisine is not to be confused with the use of the rind and leaves of the knobbly Kaffir lime, *C. hystrix* (q.v.). Because the latter is not commercially available in the United States, the leaves and rind of *C. aurantifolia* may be used.

มะม่วง

Mango *(Mangifera indica)* MAMUANG

There are several different varieties in Thailand, each with a different native name. The trees bear large clusters of greenish-white flowers and the fruit "sets" after the "mango showers" break into the hot season. The fruit is a flattened oval with a slight beak at the bottom end. It has a tough, thin skin, dark green when unripe; ripening to yellow or a reddish-orange and green. The unripe flesh is as crisp and tart as a cooking apple and is eaten raw with a dipping mixture of sugar, salt and ground chilli flakes. The ripe flesh varies in color from yellow to orange and is juicy, aromatic and luscious. In inferior varieties, the ripe flesh can be resinous and fibrous with a turpentine flavor. Ripe mangoes are often eaten with a sweetened glutinous rice cooked in coconut milk. Mangoes are available canned in the United States, and fresh, in season, from markets in the southwest. When buying fresh mangoes, check the stem end for an aromatic mango odor. If it is present, the mango has been properly ripened. If there is no odor, the fruit has been picked green and force-ripened; the flavor will be inferior.

มังคุด

Mangosteen *(Garcinia mangostana)* MUNGKUT

An apple-sized fruit with a purplish-brown smooth skin. The rind is thick and reddish-purple on the inside, containing tannic acid and a dye. The flesh is composed of segments of delicate, juicy white pulp, each surrounding a seed. The flavor is a cross between a peach and a grape. The *mungkut* is only in season in March in Thailand.

หมี่

Noodles MEE

Listed below are the four most common varieties used in Thai cooking.

วุ้นเส้น

Cellophane Noodles WOON SEN

These are also called bean-thread noodles and are made from mung beans. They are bought in long hanks and are tough and semitransparent when uncooked. After soaking in warm water, they have the appearance of fine jelly fish tentacles. Always soak before using. *Woon sen* are used in Thai soups and some stir-fried dishes.

เส้นหมี่

Rice Vermicelli, Rice Sticks SEN MEE

A thin, brittle, semitranslucent noodle sold in bundles. It is used directly from the packet, crisp-fried for *mee krob*. For all other dishes it is presoaked.

บะหมี่

Egg Noodles BA MEE

Thin egg and wheat-flour noodles; sometimes sold fresh in the markets in Thailand. Used in soups, stir-fried dishes and on their own with sauces.

ก๋วยเตี๋ยว

Rice Noodles, Fresh GWAYTIO (SEN YAI)

The only noodles packaged wet. Initially the noodle is rolled into one large disk of uniform thickness. The edges are folded to the center several times at the four cardinal points to form a thick rectangle. Used in soups and stir-fried dishes. Remove the wrapper and, without unfolding, slice into the desired widths. All of these varieties are available in Oriental food stores and some supermarkets in the United States. For preparation see Chapter 15, Noodles.

น้ำตาลปีบ

Palm Sugar NAM TAN PEEP

A coarse, brown, sticky sugar with a caramel flavor, palm

sugar is obtained from the Palmyra Palm *(Borassus flabellifer)*. The sap from the palm is boiled until it crystalizes, and is canned or sold in cakes. It is less cloyingly sweet than cane sugar. It is available here, canned, in Thai food stores. Refined or raw brown sugar half and half with molasses makes a good substitute in equal portions for palm sugar.

มะละกอ

Papaya *(Carica papaya)* MALAKOR

There are several varieties in Thailand, the fruit ranging in size and shape from about six to ten inches long, ovoid to oblong. The skin is smooth, thin and green and the flesh is firm, juicy and yellow. The unripe (green) fruit is cooked as a vegetable. The ripe fruit is commonly eaten raw, sometimes with sugar and a squeeze of lime juice, or with salt and ground chilli peppers. The sap of the plant contains a large quantity of pepsin, a digestive enzyme that tenderizes meat. Commercial tenderizers contain large quantities of dried, powdered papaya (papain). In their native habitat the sap and leaves from unripe fruit were (and are) used to tenderize meat long before Western technology discovered its properties. Fresh papaya is available in produce sections of better supermarkets during its season. The juice is generally available canned, sometimes frozen.

มะเขือพวง

Pea Eggplant *(Solanum torvum)* MAKEUA PUONG

*Solanum torvum* is a tiny member of the eggplant family. Many sizes and kinds of eggplant are grown and used in Thailand. The smaller, mature varieties vary in color among white, green, purple and yellow. The sizes range downward from that of a large lemon to that of the dark green, pea-size *makeua puong*. All, including *S. torvum*, are used unripe; raw as a part of chilli sauces (see *nam prik*, Chapter 14, Sauces). The pea eggplants are also used in curries mainly for decoration and add a fresh, slightly bitter taste. When unavailable, green peas are substituted. Unobtainable until recently, *makeua puong* can now be purchased at some Thai stores. Most Thai stores carry packets of seeds, including *makeua puong*, so cooks with gardening skills, in search of authenticity, can grow their own.

พริกไทย

Pepper, Black *(Piper nigrum)* PRIK THAI

Used in various forms (whole, cracked, pounded, ground), *prik thai* is an essential part of marinades, pastes, condiments and refers to the whole, dried, unripe pepper berry. Some say *prik thai* is indigenous to Thailand, hence the name. Others, with more authority, aver that the word *thai* means spread-out or free. It is known that black peppers were used in sauces for their "hot qualities" until chillies were introduced to Thailand around the sixteenth century.

สัปปะรด

Pineapple *(Ananas comosus)* SUPPAROT

The Thai variety is both sweet and flavorful, analogous to others. In some respects it is superior to the Hawaiian pineapple, although not so suitable for canning. In recent years a pineapple-canning industry has been started in Thailand, but mostly for local consumption.

ส้มโอ

Pomelo *(Citrus maxima)* SOM OR

Sometimes referred to as the shaddock, the pomelo is indigenous to Thailand, Indochina and Malaysia. It was taken to the West Indies by the master of a sailing ship, a captain named Shaddock, hence the second name. The fruit, of which there are several varieties, resembles a grapefruit both in size and flavor but the juicy segments of flesh separate much more easily. The rind is very thick, and the flesh often pinkish-yellow. The variety most popular in Thailand is seedless.

เงาะ
Rambutan *(Nephelium lappaceum)* NGOR

This very colorful fruit, resembling a chestnut with husk, both in size and shape, is indigenous to Thailand, Indochina and Malaysia. The skin is orange-red and covered with long, green, curly tendrils. It has a central stone and the white, juicy flesh has a delicate, scented flavor, similar to the lichee (q.v.).

ชมพู่
Rose Apple *(Syzygium malaccense)* CHOMPOO

There are three different varieties of this fruit in Thailand and Malaysia. The fruits grow in clusters and are rose pink and white, pear-shaped and about three inches long. They are close in flavor to our apples, but are full of seeds and rather woolly in texture. The Thai word for the color pink *(see chompoo* in Appendixes, Vocabulary) may derive from the color of the fruit.

ละมุดสีดา
Sapodilla *(Manilkara zapota)* LAMUT

Indigenous to South America where it is known by the Aztec name "chikl" or, at present, "chicle," it is the source for chicle gum. The Spaniards carried it across to the Philippines. In Thailand the tree is only known for its edible fruit, which is the size of a small apple and round or ovoid. It has a golden-brown, thin skin and the flesh resembles a pear in color, flavor and texture, but is a little sweeter.

ใบเตยหอม

Screw Pine *(Pandanus odoratissimus)* BAI TOEY HOM

Only the dried Pandanus leaf is sold in the United States, in packets. It is used for flavoring, e.g., coconut rice. It also flavors and colors sweets. In Thailand, both the fresh leaves and flowers are used. Difficult to describe, its flavor can be said to be somewhat nut-like.

กะปิ

Shrimp paste KAPEE

Rich in vitamin B, *kapee* and *nam pla* are the main sources of protein in most Southeast Asian diets. This very pungent ingredient, readily available in the United States, comes in two forms, fresh and dried. The fresh is rose pink and the dried varies in shades of beige/gray to pink. Both are made by pounding decomposed, salted shrimp. The dried, more pungent, is left in the sun for evaporation and concentration. It is then either compressed into slabs and packaged, or put into jars. The fresh paste is only available in jars, usually imported from Malaysia and must be refrigerated. The dried does not need refrigeration and the finest brands come from Rayong in South Thailand. Both have an overripe odor that disappears when cooked with other ingredients. Before you open either, be prepared to measure and cook quickly, because if the jar is left open, the pervasive aroma will soon dominate the kitchen. If using one for the other, approximately two portions of fresh equal one dried. Anchovy paste may be substituted, reducing the required amount of dried by one-half.

โป๊ยกั๊ก

Star Anise *(Illicium verum)* POY KAK BUA

The Star anise of the Magnoliacae family differs in flavor only slightly from the European anise seed, Umbelliferae *(Myrrhis odorata)* with its light licorice taste. Star anise is sold in dried whole flowerets or powdered in Oriental food stores. It is an essential component of the Chinese "Five Spice Powder." The Thai use *poy kak bua* to flavor pork dishes with a Chinese influence.

มะเฟือง

Star Apple *(Averrhoa carambola)* MAFUENG

Found all over Asia, it is also known as carambola, from the Latin. The fruit is about three to four inches long and has five prominent angles, producing a star shape when cut. The thin skin is green and turns yellow when ripening. The flesh is soft and juicy. It is used in pickles and preserves.

ใบหัวระพา

Sweet Basil *(Ocimum basilicum)* BAI HORAPA,

ใบแมงลัก ใบกระเพา

*(Ocimum canum)* BAI MANGLUK, *(Ocimum sanctum)* BAI GRAPAO

There are three popular varieties of sweet basil grown in Thailand—each with a slightly different appearance, flavor and use. *Horapa* is the well-known European and American basil. In Thailand it is used as a vegetable and as flavoring in curries. The leaves of the *mangluk* are slightly hairy and paler in color than those of *horapa. Mangluk* is sometimes referred to as lemon basil and looks rather like the Italian "dwarf basil." The Thai use it in soups and sprinkled over salad. *Grapao* is sometimes called and labeled "holy basil" because of an early Biblical reference. Its leaves are narrower than those of the *horapa* and are slightly reddish-purple in color. It is never eaten raw but cooked in fish dishes, beef and chicken curries and sautéed with frogs' legs. Our locally purchased sweet basil will substitute for all three varieties but, for those who would like to experiment, the seed packets can sometimes be found in Thai stores. The basils are easy to grow. In warm, sunny climates they will flourish happily out-of-doors in pots or beds. In more temperate climes, basils can be grown in pots indoors on sunny windowsills.

ส้มมะขาม

Tamarind *(Tamarindus indica)* MAK KAM

Tamarind is the popular name of the pods of the feathery tamarind tree. Literally translated from the Arabic, it means "Indian date." The pods are originally green and turn a rich, dark brown when ripe. Unripe fruit from the pods is eaten by the Thai, flavored with sugar, salt and dried chilli flakes. The pulp of the ripe tamarind fruit is separated from the fiber and squeezed repeatedly through water. The resultant liquid is used as a souring agent for curries, other dishes and beverages. The Thai roast the seeds and use them to flavor compotes of young coconut or palm. In Thai stores here, tamarind is sold moist in packets. Before using, the fibers and seeds must be separated from the flesh—this can be a tedious task. The concentrated pulp, without fibers and seeds, can be obtained in jars from Indian stores (there is widespread use of tamarind in Indian cuisine). This concentrate will then be diluted with water before use. For whole and concentrate preparation see Fundamentals, Chapter 3. As a crude substitute for "tamarind liquid," use equal portions of a sugar/vinegar mixture (six parts vinegar, one part sugar). Frozen orange-juice concentrate also makes a reasonable substitute in taste but not in color.

แดงน้อย มันสัมปะหลัง

Tapioca *(Manihot esculenta)* DANG NOI *or* MAN SUM PALUNG

Known as cassava, it is native to South America but began to be cultivated in the Far East in the 1800's. Tapioca is made from the root or tuber of this plant. The root, when raw, contains toxic portions of hydrocyanic or prussic acid but, after the juice is pressed out and the tuber pounded into a paste and cooked, it is edible. The cereal, tapioca, is made by rolling the paste into small balls and drying them. Tapioca flour is also produced from the paste.

เผือก

Taro *(Colocasia esculenta)* PUAK

In Thailand and all Indochina this root grows wild along the banks of streams. The swollen tuber is full of starch and is eaten in the same manner as potatoes. It is prevalent in Northern Thailand. The young leaves are also eaten.

ขมิ้นเหลือง

Turmeric *(Curcuma domestica)* KAMIN

A close relative of the ginger and arrowroot families, this tuberous rhizome is bright orange/yellow inside. Until the recent advent of colorfast dyestuffs, turmeric was used to color the robes of Buddhist monks. Its use in Thai cuisine is further evidence of the Indian influence. Sold in the markets by Muslim vendors, in Thailand it can be purchased either fresh or dried and powdered. Turmeric sold in the United States in Oriental and Indian food stores is always powdered and exactly the same as our local, commerical brands. It is used in curries and to color rice.

เห็ดหูหนู

Wood Fungus *(Auricalaria polytricha)* HED HUNU

This dried variety of fungus looks like pieces of burnt paper but, when soaked in water, turns a delicate brown and becomes jelly-like. Its use reflects the Chinese origins of many Thai dishes. It is a component of many stir-fried wok dishes.

# SOURCES AND SUPPLIERS

The following list should give some indication of the widespread availability of Thai foodstuffs. Those listed with addresses are either (a) personally familiar to me because I have traded with them or (b) responded to my inquiries (both in writing and by telephone) favorably, and/or (c) recommended by respected cooks. Please use the code below.

**W** = Wholesale
**R** = Retail
**D** = Direct Sales (walk-in)
**M** = Mail Order

The Bangkok Market, Inc.
4804-6 Melrose Ave.
Los Angeles, CA 90029
(213) 662–7990
**RD**
3718 E. 26th St.
Vernon, CA 90023
(213) 264–4898
**WM**
All Thai foods

Bezjian's Grocery, Inc.
4725 Santa Monica Blvd.
Los Angeles, CA 90029
(213) 662–1503
**RDM**
Indian and Middle Eastern, but stocks tamarind concentrate, rice, mung beans, dried coconut, rosewater, peanut oil, etc.

Yee Sing Chong Company
966 North Hill St.
Los Angeles, CA 90012
(213) 626-9619
**RD**
All Thai and Oriental foods, meat market, utensils

Mart's Oriental Market
8236 Coldwater Canyon
North Hollywood, CA 91605
(213) 989-9417
**RD**
All Thai foods

Thai & Oriental Market
25795 E. Highland Ave.
San Bernardino, CA 92404
(714) 864–1280
**RDM**
All Thai foods

Montana Mercantile
1324 Montana Ave.
Santa Monica, CA 90403
(213) 451-1418
**RDM**
Most Thai foods, international cookbooks, utensils, will lo cate unusual items

## ILLINOIS

Conte DiSavoila
555 W. Roosevelt Rd.
Jeffro Plaza-Store #7
Chicago, IL 60607
(312) 666–3471
**RDM**
Tamarind paste, rosewater, rice, mung beans, fish sauce, soy sauce, noodles, etc.

## NEW YORK

House of Spices
76-17 Broadway
Jackson Heights, Queens, NY 11373
(212) 476–1577
**RM**
Mostly Indian but stocks canned jackfruit, tamarind, mung beans, rice, dried coconut, etc.

Aphrodisia Products, Inc.
282 Bleeker St.
New York, NY 10014
(212) 989-6440
**RDWM**
Dried Chinese mushrooms, dried whole and powdered lemon grass, Laos powder,etc.

Chinese-American Trading Co.
91 Mulberry St.
New York, NY 10013
(212) 267–5224
**RD**
Chinese and some Thai foods, utensils

Duang
75-17 37th Ave.
Jackson Heights, Queens, NY 11372
(212) 672–2082
**RD**
All Thai foods

Siam Grocery
2745 Broadway
New York, NY 10025
(212) 864-3640
**RD**
All Thai foods

Taksin Grocery
857 9th Ave.
New York, NY 10019
(212) 247–1319
**RD**
All Thai foods

Thai Market
157a E. 170th St.
Bronx, NY 10452
(212) 681–1200
**RD**
All Thai foods

## OREGON

Anzen Japanese Foods and Imports
736 Northeast Union Ave.
Portland, OR 97232
(503) 233–5111
**RDM**

Despite the name, stocks some Thai foods and baby corn, chilli flakes, noodles, rice, coconut milk, rice flour, will locate unusual items

## TEXAS

Asian Grocery
9191 Forest Ln. #3
Dallas, TX 75243
(214) 235–3038
**RD**
All Thai foods

## WASHINGTON

Uwajimaya
519 6th Ave. S.
Seattle, WA 98104
(206) 624–6248
**RDM**

Dried whole and powdered chillies, Thai chilli sauce, coconut milk, fish sauce, dried Chinese mushrooms, lemon grass, noodles, palm sugar, shrimp paste, etc.

In addition, at this writing, there are retail Thai markets and additional food sources in the following cities:

## CALIFORNIA

Burbank
Concord
Glendale
Hollywood
Lawndale
Long Beach
Lynwood
Southgate
Vernon
Westminster

## COLORADO

Denver

## FLORIDA

Ft. Waldon Beach
Tampa

## MARYLAND

Baltimore
Rockville
Silver Spring
Wheaton

## MICHIGAN

Detroit

## NEBRASKA

Nellville

## NEVADA

Las Vegas

## PENNSYLVANIA

Bangor

## TEXAS

Houston

## VIRGINIA

Arlington
Falls Church

## WASHINGTON

Mercer Island

# Table of Recipes

## Fish and Seafood · (PLA LAE AHARN TA LAY)



## Salads · (YAM)

## Sauces · (NAM PRIK, LON)



## Noodles · (MEE)



## Accompaniments · (KREUNG KIEM, PAD PAK)



## Desserts and Sweets · (KONG WAN)

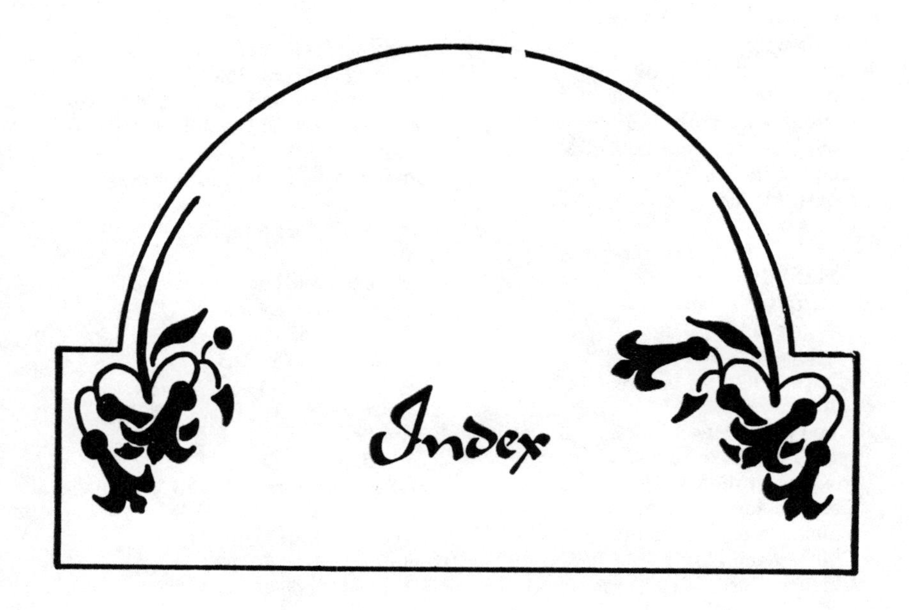
Index